ALL IN A DAY'S WORK

At Pasadena Crematorium it was standard operating procedure to examine the incoming bodies for gold. Normally David did the job himself. As the bodies came in, he would take a screwdriver and pry open the mouths, searching for a gleaming molar.

Sometimes the other workers would screen the bodies before David came in. When they discovered a body with dental gold, they would call it to David's attention by drawing a happy face on the cardboard sheet all bodies destined for cremation were wrapped in, along with the letters AU—the scientific symbol for gold.

Far from keeping this all a secret, David frequently joked about it. He could often be seen whistling while leaving the cold room, another extraction completed. One time, as a co-worker recalled, David's mother Laurieanne looked up from her paperwork and smiled at David's good humor.

"How much AU did you get today, honey?" she asked sweetly.

David grinned and showed her the cup he was carrying. It was half full of teeth. . . .

St. Martin's Paperbacks titles are available at quantity discounts for sales promotions, premiums or fund raising. Special books or book excerpts can also be created to fit specific needs.

For information write to special sales manager, St. Martin's Press, 175 Fifth Avenue, New York, N.Y. 10010.

A FAMILY BUSINESS

KEN ENGLADE

ST. MARTIN'S PAPERBACKS

A FAMILY BUSINESS

Copyright © 1992 by Ken Englade.
Excerpt from *Unanswered Cries* copyright © 1991 by Thomas French.

Building photo on cover courtesy of Sara Englade.
Photo of David, Jerry and Laurieanne Sconce courtesy of Stacey Gore.

ISBN: 0-312-92820-3

Printed in the United States of America

St. Martin's Paperbacks edition/January 1992

10 9 8 7 6 5 4 3 2 1

AUTHOR'S NOTE

Some of the dialogue represented in this book was reconstructed while other dialogue was drawn from courtroom testimony.

K.E.

For Charlie and Phyllis, God bless 'em

ACKNOWLEDGMENTS

This book is far and away the most complicated I have ever been involved with. More than any other story I have tried to tell, the saga of the Sconces has required explanations of extremely complex legal concepts and events. When I was wading through tall stacks of transcripts and enigmatic documents, there were times I was certain that I was truly and irretrievably lost in the wilderness. If it had not been for four particular men, I don't think I would ever have found my way home. Two of them were prosecutors at various stages of the case: Deputy District Attorneys Harvey Giss and Jim Rogan, who is now Judge Rogan. Another was Roger Diamond, who was David Sconce's attorney during some of the more crucial phases described herein. The fourth man has asked to remain anonymous. This is too bad because his input was among the most valuable of any I received during my research. They all gave graciously of their time and expertise, frequently taking me by the hand and leading me through what amounted to a crash course in advanced criminal law. I am grateful, for without them I undoubtedly would still be wandering.

There are two others who helped immeasurably, possibly more than they realized. One was Investigator Dennis

Acknowledgments

Diaz, whose aid came at a time when I had been searching fruitlessly for just the type of insight he provided. The other was Dr. Larry Podolsky, who provided invaluable assistance in helping me decipher the medical details that are such an important part of this story. I profusely thank them, as well as others who helped in less dramatic but nevertheless important ways.

I hope that I learned well from my guides, and that I have done justice to the tale.

K.E.

DRAMATIS PERSONAE

The family:

David Sconce—Founder and owner of Coastal Cremation Inc. and the Coastal International Eye & Tissue Bank; the older son of Jerry and Laurieanne Sconce.

Jerry "Coach" Sconce—David's father and co-operator of Lamb Funeral Home, the parent organization for Coastal Cremation and the CIE&TB.

Laurieanne "Mom" Sconce—Jerry's wife; David's mother; daughter of Lawrence and Lucille Lamb; former owner and operator of Lamb Funeral Home.

Lawrence and *Lucille Lamb*—Laurieanne's parents; David's grandparents; owners of Lamb Funeral home until they sold the business to their daughter.

Brad Sallard—Brother of David's wife, *Barbara,* and son of *Oscar Sallard,* who gave his name to Oscar's Ceramics.

The victims, possible, potential, and actual:

Timothy Waters—Owner of a Burbank cremation service, the Alpha Society, whose apparently natural death may turn out to be a murder.

Ron Hast and *Stephen Nimz*—The co-owner of a Los Angeles area mortuary and his housemate.

Elie Estephan—Former son-in-law of Frank Strunk; owner of Cremation Society of California, a business said to be coveted by David Sconce.

Frank Strunk—Father of Steve Strunk; former father-in-law of Elie Estephan, and former owner of the Cremation Society of California.

Walter Lewis—A deputy district attorney in Pasadena who prosecuted David Sconce on charges dealing with the operation of Coastal Cremation and the CIE&TB.

The aggressors:

Daniel Galambos and *Dave Edwards*—Beefy ex-football players hired by David Sconce to assault his enemies.

Andre Augustine—Cohort of Dan Galambos and Dave Edwards, who took part in attack on Ron Hast and Stephen Nimz.

Bob Garcia—Former David Sconce employee allegedly approached by his boss about killing Elie Estephan.

The inmates:

David Gearhardt, Rogelio Rojas, Steve Warren, and *Jack Dubois*—Men who testified that David Sconce either offered to hire them as murderers or sought references for a hit man.

The witnesses:

James Dame, Steve Strunk, John Hallinan, Joyji "George" Bristol, John Pollerana, Lisa Karlan—All former employees of the Sconces.

Richard Gray—Tim Waters's former best friend.

Dr. Frederic Rieders—Toxicologist who contended that Tim Waters was murdered by poisoning with oleander.

Dr. John Holloway—Former pathologist in Ventura County who ruled Tim Waters died a natural death, a position he continued to maintain.

Dennis Diaz—Pasadena detective who helped build the

case against David Sconce in relation to activities at the crematoriums and the tissue bank.

Robert Hopkins—An investigator from Simi Valley who worked on the Waters murder case.

Mary Lou Waters—Tim Waters's mother.

Scott Sorrentino—Tim Waters's boyhood friend; one of the last people to see Tim alive.

Dr. Jack Henion—A Cornell University toxicologist whose sophisticated tests were unable to find traces of oleander in Tim Waters's remains.

The legal contingent:

Elvira R. Mitchell—The Pasadena municipal court judge who enthusiastically agreed to a $500,000 bail for David Sconce.

Victor Person—Municipal court judge in Pasadena who conducted the preliminary hearing against David, Jerry, and Laurieanne Sconce on charges stemming from the crematorium and tissue bank operations.

Terry Smerling—The superior court judge in Pasadena who dealt with the case against the Sconces after it left Victor Person's court.

John Hunter—The Ventura municipal court judge who conducted the preliminary hearing in the Tim Waters murder case.

Frederick Jones—The Ventura County superior court judge who presided at the preliminaries for what would have been David Sconce's trial for the murder of Tim Waters. He would have presided at the trial had the charges not been dismissed at the last moment.

Harvey Giss—The Los Angeles County deputy district attorney scheduled to prosecute David Sconce for the murder of Tim Waters.

James Rogan—The deputy district attorney who took over the Los Angeles County prosecution of the Sconces after Walt Lewis was forced to withdraw. He also had to withdraw later when he was appointed a judge.

Eliott al Hadeff—The DDA who replaced Rogan as Jerry and Laurieanne's prosecutor in Los Angeles County.

Kevin De Noce—A young DDA in Ventura County who was named co-prosecutor, replacing Rogan, in the case alleging that David murdered Tim Waters.

Roger Diamond—The main attorney for David Sconce; represented him at the preliminary hearing in Pasadena and at the proceedings in Ventura.

Guy O'Brien—David Sconce's attorney in the proceedings before Judge Terry Smerling.

Thomas Nishi—Attorney for Jerry Sconce.

Edward A. Rucker—Attorney for Laurieanne Sconce.

Others:

Randy Welty—An adult bookstore owner who David said was the money man behind the Sconce tissue bank.

Mike Engwald—Long-time friend of David and Jerry Sconce who owned a company that dealt in gold; allegedly the buyer of dental gold collected by David.

Ron Jordan—Former David Sconce employee, and brother-in-law of another employee, Steve Strunk, found hanged in his closet. His death has been ruled a suicide.

The businesses:

Lamb Funeral Home—A well-respected Pasadena mortuary founded by David Sconce's great-grandfather, Charles Lamb. It was later renamed the Pasadena Funeral Home.

Pasadena Crematorium—The Lamb-owned facility that did the cremations for the Lamb Funeral Home. Despite its name, it was located in nearby Altadena rather than in Pasadena.

Coastal International Eye & Tissue Bank—The facility

founded by David Sconce, allegedly with financial backing from Randy Welty, to sell human organs.

Coastal Cremation Inc.—Formerly the Pasadena Crematorium; renamed and reorganized by David Sconce when he leased the facility from his mother.

Oscar's Ceramics—An illegal crematorium started by David Sconce in the high-desert community of Hesperia.

PART ONE

Oscar's Ceramics

1

David Sconce was in love.

The object of the thirty-year-old's affection was not a woman. He already had a woman. It was a town. And a most unlikely one at that.

It would have been perfectly understandable if David had fallen in love with any number of towns in Southern California, which, after all, is considered to be paradise by just about everyone. Verily, places like San Juan Capistrano, San Clemente, Ventura, and Santa Barbara are eminently lovable, bearing little resemblance to the ice-bound bedroom communities of the Midwest or the Northeast, the rain-soaked towns of the Northwest, or the humidity-draped communities of the Deep South. But, just as all wine is grape juice but not all grape juice is wine, all of Southern California is not Santa Barbara. Take Hesperia for instance, which hardly anyone wants to do.

Definitely not your basic slice of Southern California Eden, Hesperia might as well be in the Persian Gulf. Unlike its more glamorous and infinitely more attractive neighbors, Hesperia is not on any tourist's must-see agenda. It has no beautiful harbor or gently curving beach to recommend it. Nor does it have a zoo, a eucalyptus grove, a lake, or a hillside carpeted with bright flowers. It doesn't have a skyscraper, an adobe-walled mission, a film studio, or a Frank Lloyd Wright–designed building. It doesn't even boast a cloistered public garden. What it *does* have, situated as it is on the floor of the southwestern Mojave Desert, dozens of miles from nowhere, are thousands of weirdly shaped Joshua trees, a string of ugly power pylons, mounds of dirt generously referred to as the foothills of the San Bernardino Mountains, and a lot of cloudless, blazing sky.

Hesperia's principal and virtually singular attributes are sunshine, open space, and isolation, which are not unsubstantial qualities if those are the ones being sought. For many, however, they are not.

But Hesperia was exactly what David Sconce had been looking for. Where others saw brown, featureless desert, David saw green, the green of crisp currency. A century and three decades earlier, the Forty-niners and their cousins shunned the area because it yielded no gold. But David found an abundance of gold there, piles of fingernail-sized nuggets of the bright yellow material he drolly referred to by its chemical symbol, AU. The unimaginative saw Hesperia as a dead end; David saw it as a gateway to considerable and attainable riches, a place of virtually unlimited potential.

From the beginning, David was delighted with the town. He clasped it to his bosom with the enthusiasm of a handsome young husband embracing his homely but very rich wife. Unfortunately, it was a marriage that both the bride and the groom would come to regret. But that was later.

When David Sconce, with his wide, easy smile, blond, curly hair, Paul Newman–blue eyes, and broad, solid shoulders—weightlifter's shoulders with the arms and chest to go along—appeared in Hesperia in the sizzling summer of 1986, he was considered a remarkable catch for the community.

Always a fast-talker, he told anyone who would listen that he was a young businessman trying to make his fortune by investing in the future. And he was universally believed. After all, he was a personable guy. David could turn on the charm and appear as genuine as a newly-mined diamond. He had a line of patter that most salesmen would envy, and an active sense of humor, one that his friends called "quick" and his detractors "twisted." But everybody has a few enemies. At the time, David had no detractors in Hesperia.

David told Hesperians that he had been searching throughout Southern California for a location for a small manufacturing plant he planned to build. He was, he said, a manufacturer of heat-resistant tiles for the space shuttles, those little rectangles of ceramic material that cover the spacecraft like scales on a fish. After a lot of looking, he had decided that Hesperia was the place where he wanted to locate his production facility. Specifically, he had his eye on a site on Darwin Road in the community's industrial area, an isolated spot on an unpaved track in a neighborhood of auto and truck repair shops and salvage yards.

In October 1986 he secured a building permit from the city and erected a plain-looking oversized metal shed—his basic facility—which he surrounded with a tall chain-link fence topped with barbed wire. The only way to enter the site was through a gate secured by a sturdy padlock. The building itself was empty except for David's custom-made equipment: two industrial-sized kilns, which David said he needed to bake the space shuttle tiles. He christened the new business Oscar's Ceramics, naming it after his father-in-law.

That autumn Oscar's Ceramics went into production. But it wasn't making ceramic tiles.

⬦ ⬦ ⬦

At first no one suspected that David was anything but what he portrayed himself to be: a handsome, pleasant, bright and ambitious young entrepreneur, a Los Angeles yuppie who was intelligent enough to recognize Hesperia's potential.

He was reclusive, but in those reaches of Southern California, very few people find fault with a desire for privacy. And he may have seemed a bit of an oddball, as evidenced by the license plate on his white 1982 Corvette, the one which read I BRN 4U, the meaning of which escaped most people. But then California is the nation's capital for eccentrics and abstruse vanity plates.

David kept to himself, causing no trouble, attracting no unnecessary attention. There were a few workers who came and went as quietly as the owner, usually in station wagons or vans, which everyone believed were carrying cargo designed to support the tile manufacturing business. The fact that most of the manufacturing seemed to be done at night did not seem unusual; at least, it was not extraordinary enough to cause concern.

But there *was* one thing that was odd, and that was the smell. On occasion the odor that drifted down from Oscar's Ceramics was incredibly foul. At times a nauseating, black smoke belched from the company's chimney and settled over that section of the community like a cloud from hell. The smell was downright repulsive; sometimes it seemed strong enough to shrivel a yucca. When asked about this stench, David would shrug, flash his lopsided grin and apologize, explaining that he found it offensive, too, but it was one of the unfavorable by-products of his manufacturing process. "Nothing I can do about it," he'd say. "Sorry."

Almost all of those who operated businesses in the area grudgingly accepted David's explanation. They weren't happy with it—no one had told them that ceramics manufacturing was such a noisome process—but there appeared to be nothing they could do.

However, there was one neighbor who didn't buy David's story. To him, the smell portrayed something far more sinister. When he had been a young soldier in World War Two, his unit had been part of the American army spearhead into Germany. As a result, he had been among the first to arrive in some of Hitler's death camps. In some cases the ovens that had been used to incinerate the Jews were still burning, and that made a terrifying, lasting impression upon the young soldier. Seeing the emaciated bodies of the survivors and the stacks of corpses had struck him to his soul, but the thing he remembered most vividly about that experience was the smell. It was something he never forgot.

It came back to him years later, the first time he got a deep whiff of the smoke billowing from Oscar's Ceramics. David Sconce could say what he wanted, but the veteran was certain that the odor he smelled was not that of ceramics being produced; it was the stink of corpses being cremated.

Angrily, he began a search for someone who would believe he knew what he was talking about.

Actually, he was not alone. Others, although lacking the veteran's certainty, were nevertheless highly suspicious.

One of those with deep reservations about what was going on at Oscar's Ceramics was Wilbur W. Wentworth, Hesperia's fire marshal and assistant fire chief. A veteran of a different sort—a man with twenty years experience fighting and investigating fires—Wentworth was not unfamiliar with Oscar's Ceramics.

Since part of his job was to inspect new facilities, Wentworth had toured the facility in October 1986, soon after it was completed. In addition to the building permit, David also had to apply for a certificate to operate the kilns, and it was Wentworth's job to certify that the equipment met the community's fire safety standards.

At the time of his initial inspection, Wentworth found nothing to make him suspicious. But less than a month later he was back after one of the neighbors complained about the smoke belching from the small smokestack. As fire marshal, Wentworth had the authority to demand to inspect the facility, but both times he had been there he had not found it necessary to use pressure since David invited him inside and generally seemed anxious to cooperate. Other times when he went in response to complaints about the odor it had dissipated or the flames had died down by the time he arrived.

In December 1986, however, two days before Christmas, Wentworth made still another visit to Oscar's Ceramics—an unannounced one. Unlike the others, this one occurred in the middle of the night. It came about after a neighbor complained about flames leaping from the chimney.

Wentworth and three firemen answered the alarm, but when they arrived there was no one to let them in. Undeterred, they used a pair of bolt cutters on the padlock, forced their way into the building and doused the flames, which were pouring out of the kilns as well as the chimney. After the fire was extinguished, the firemen shut off the fuel supply to the ovens and prepared to leave. But as he was walking out the door, Wentworth detoured briefly to a corner of the room and peeked into one of several large metal barrels stacked there. The drum was filled with coarse ash and what appeared to be pieces of bone.

Curious, Wentworth pocketed some of the material. The next day, he took it to the sheriff's office and asked if they could have someone identify it. A few days later a deputy called him and told him not to worry: the bones were animal, not human. Wentworth was not convinced, but what could he do? The experts had spoken and he was in no position to contradict them.

However, his suspicions were aroused again a few weeks later. On January 20, 1987, less than a month after the fire, a man named Richard Wales telephoned. Identifying himself as an air quality engineer with the San Bernardino County Air Pollution Control District, Wales told Wentworth he would like to meet with him.

"What about?" Wentworth asked affably.

"About Oscar's Ceramics," Wales replied.

Not long before, a man had called Wales and told the engineer that he thought Oscar's Ceramics was being used as a crematorium.

Wales, caught totally off guard, was not sure how to respond.

"I don't believe so," he had stammered.

But the man refused to accept that answer.

"Don't tell me I don't know what burning bodies smell like," the caller had shouted. "I was at the ovens at Auschwitz and I *know* that smell."

Wales wrote him off as a crank, but he decided to keep an eye on Oscar's.

The engineer, in fact, had been receiving complaints about Oscar's Ceramics since mid-October, which was shortly after David set up his equipment. Soon after that first complaint, David let him onto the premises and, although Wales found no evidence of air pollution violations, he noticed a decidedly unpleasant odor. In his notebook he later wrote that the building smelled like "decaying material." He did not know how close he was to the truth.

Despite his visit and similar ones from Wentworth, David continued to operate as though he were above the law. Twice Wales cited David for operating a source of pollution without a permit. After the second citation, David grudgingly applied for a license. He was issued a temporary permit but it was scheduled to expire the day after the irate resident telephoned Wales.

There was, however, a more pressing reason than the expiration of David's permit that prompted Wales to get in touch with Wentworth: a third person had entered the equation, and what he had to say gave substance to Wales's and Wentworth's suspicions.

"It's not just me," Wales told the fire marshal. "There's someone else who has an interesting story to tell, someone I think you'd be interested in talking to."

Meeting in Wentworth's cramped office, Wales introduced himself and the two men who accompanied him. One was Joseph Westall, an investigator for the state Cemetery Board, and the other was an official from the state Funeral Board named John Gallagher. Westall did most of the talking, and what he had to say greatly troubled the fire marshal.

According to Westall, David Sconce, before he came to Hesperia, had been operating a licensed crematorium in Altadena, near Pasadena, in suburban Los Angeles about seventy miles from Hesperia. The previous autumn, about the time David began building Oscar's Ceramics, Westall had become skeptical about the Altadena operation because of the extraordinary number of cremations that David was reporting he performed there. Westall was sure something was fishy because his records showed the Altadena crematorium had only two ovens, and with only two ovens David could not possibly be performing as many cremations as he said he was, at least not legally.

Determined to get to the bottom of it, Westall paid an unannounced visit to the Altadena facility and asked to be allowed inside so he could inspect the operation. Since Westall had no legal authority to demand such an inspection, David turned him away. Frustrated, Westall went back to his office to ponder his next move.

Less than a month later, however, before Westall could take further action, a fire destroyed the Altadena facility. In one respect the news cheered Westall. If the Altadena crematorium was out of business, it meant a probable end to any possible illegal activity. The fact that Westall probably would never know exactly what had been occurring there was of little consequence. At least whatever had been happening would stop. Except it did not.

Not long after the fire at Altadena—beyond the point at which Westall would have expected to stop receiving cremation reports from David—he got another summary indicating that David was cremating just as many bodies as he had been before the fire. To Westall that meant only one thing: David had opened an illegal crematorium. Of that he had no doubt; David's own reports substantiated it. The big question was *where*. Although David continued to report cremations, he had not applied to the state for a permit to construct a new facility, and his reports did not indicate where he was operating from. Instinctively Westall knew that David was still in Southern California. Still, that was a big area and finding him would not be easy. But Westall resolved to try.

From another state agency he secured a list of all the air pollution control districts in that part of California. Methodically, one by one, he began calling them, asking each if a man named David Sconce had applied for a permit to operate *any* kind of facility in their area. When he got an affirmative answer from San Bernardino, he swung into action.

2

Early in January, Westall drove to Hesperia to see for himself what Oscar's Ceramics looked like. Parking across the road and far enough away to prevent arousing David's suspicion, Westall studied the facility. What he saw was an unremarkable metal building some forty feet wide and fifty feet long, painted a light green. There were no windows and only one door, which was closed, so Westall had no clue of what the interior might contain. He had no hope of getting a closer look because of the tall chain-link fence surrounding the building, a fence with only one gate, which was secured with a formidable-looking padlock.

What particularly interested him, however, was the chimney. There were no large smokestacks such as would be necessary for a proper crematorium. Under ordinary circumstances large smokestacks would be essential in controlling emissions. Instead, Oscar's was equipped with only one small pipe. That was curious, Westall told himself, since if the chimney he could see was the only exhaust, it meant that either David was not using the facility as a crematorium or, if he was, the smell would be horrendous because the smoke would not be properly filtered.

On the first day he was there, there were no cars

parked inside the fence and no smoke coming from the chimney, which told Westall that he had not picked a time when cremations were in progress. He came back several times after that, always in the daytime, and each time he was there, Oscar's Ceramics appeared deserted. Yet David's reports of cremations kept coming in.

Certain in his own mind that he had found David's secret crematorium, Westall considered his next move. Having learned from his experience at Altadena that all David had to say was no to keep him out, Westall determined that this time he would seek the help of someone whom David could not refuse, someone who had the authority to enter the building despite David's likely unwillingness to cooperate.

Westall decided late in January to take his suspicions to Richard Wales. Intrigued by his tale, Wales had brought him to Will Wentworth. Wentworth had the authority to get into Oscar's.

As Westall explained how his search for David's elusive, illegal crematorium had brought him to Hesperia, Wentworth grew increasingly anxious. The lack of smokestacks appropriate for a crematorium would explain why he had been receiving complaints about a foul smell, Wentworth figured, and the fact that David had to keep the existence of a crematorium secret would explain why he was so standoffish and why so much work seemed to be done at night. The more he listened to Westall, the more certain he became that the Cemetery Board official was correct.

"Let's go take a look at Oscar's," he said when Westall had finished his tale. "Let's go see if we can find out just what's going on."

Piling into Wentworth's four-wheel-drive vehicle for the short trip, the men decided that Wentworth would do the talking since he alone among the four had the law behind him. He was the only one who could insist on being allowed inside. When they got there, however, Oscar's was deserted. As Westall had experienced on previous trips, there were no cars within the enclosure and no one came to the gate when they called out. Disappointed, they climbed back into Wentworth's vehicle for the trip back to his office. En route they agreed they would try again another day.

While Wentworth and Wales went back to their respective offices, Westall and Gallagher decided to grab a quick lunch before returning to Los Angeles. After their sandwiches, however, instead of going straight back to the city, they agreed to make one more pass by Oscar's to see if they might be able to detect something they had not spotted earlier.

This time, unlike on their visit ninety minutes previously, there was a car parked inside the fence. What excited the two men even more, however, was that there was evidence of activity inside the building. On the earlier trip a bare wisp of smoke had been issuing from the chimney but it was not in sufficient quantity to indicate that the kilns were in full use. This time, however, both flames and clouds of heavy black smoke were gushing out of the small pipe, proof to Westall that the ovens were wholly fired.

Westall rushed to a pay phone and dialed Wentworth's number. "You have to come back," Westall told the fire marshal breathlessly, "things are happening."

When Wentworth screeched to a stop in front of the locked gate, he was slightly taken aback to see that the man who got out of the car and approached them was not David Sconce but one of his workers, a man whose name Wentworth later learned was John Pollerana. Every time Wentworth had been there before, David had been present.

Identifying himself as an assistant fire chief and fire

marshal, Wentworth told Pollerana he had the right to inspect the facility and asked to be admitted.

"I can't do that," Pollerana said, "not without checking with my boss."

Wentworth looked down; the gate was chained and padlocked. "Do you have some way of getting in touch with him?" he asked.

"Yeah," Pollerana replied sullenly. "Wait here a minute."

Turning on his heels, he returned to his car. For the first time, Wentworth noticed there was a desk telephone sitting on the car's dashboard with a long cord running to the telephone connection box on the side of the building. Apparently, the man had rigged an outside extension.

As he watched, Pollerana lifted the receiver and dialed a number. He was too far away, however, for Wentworth and the others to hear the conversation.

When David came on the line, he was totally calm, unlike Pollerana, who obviously was quite agitated.

"Be cool," he told Pollerana after his employee excitedly explained the situation.

"What do you mean, 'be cool'?" Pollerana asked edgily. "Something's wrong. Otherwise the man from the Cemetery Board wouldn't be here."

"Are you burning?" David asked calmly.

"Yeah."

"How far along?"

Pollerana paused to consider. "About four and a half hours," he replied.

David was silent for several moments, contemplating his options. If Pollerana had been running the kilns for as long as he said, the process was almost complete. If he could stall them just a little longer he might—just might —be able to reach the point where they would not be able to prove their suspicions. In the end, though, he knew he had only one choice. If it had been the police banging on the gate, David could tell them to go away until they produced a search warrant. But a fire marshal didn't need a warrant; he had the authority to insist on being allowed to make a fire inspection at any time during normal working hours, provided he had permission. And David had no grounds to deny him that permission.

"Go inside," David instructed Pollerana carefully, "and get things straightened out as much as you can. And then let them in."

Pollerana hung up and, without a glance at the men standing outside the fence, he strode across the open ground and into the building.

The men at the gate stared at each other in amazement. Pollerana had disappeared without a word of explanation. Now they were stranded outside without anyone to talk to or any way to summon Pollerana. There was no bell at the gate, and even if they yelled, they could not be certain that the man inside the building, a good fifty feet away, would be able to hear them. They could not telephone because Pollerana had left the instrument sitting on the car's dash.

What made it worse was the weather. A cold front had swept through earlier in the day and, although the brisk north wind had died down, the air was still frigid. In an attempt to keep warm, the four men bounced from foot to foot, angrily discussing what they could do.

"I'm going to call for some help," Wentworth finally announced. Returning to his vehicle, he picked up the microphone on his fire department radio and asked the dispatcher to send a couple of deputies to Oscar's Ceramics.

When they arrived, Wentworth explained that he wanted to make an inspection of the facility but the only man who could let them in had disappeared and they had no way to get his attention.

"That's no problem," one of the deputies said. Striding to the patrol car, he opened the door, reached inside and flipped a switch. The unexpected blast of the siren almost knocked Wentworth off his feet.

The noise also startled Pollerana, who had been working so hard trying to conceal evidence of the operation that he had lost track of time. It had been thirty minutes since he talked to David.

The first thing he had done when he walked inside, ignoring the men standing at the gate, was scoop up several pieces of blackened metal, which he tossed into an empty ice chest, slamming the lid closed.

Scattered around the room, particularly near the kilns, were several large drums which Pollerana wrestled into a corner and covered with a tarp in a vain attempt to make them inconspicuous. He was gathering up some discarded clothing and stuffing it into a bag when the siren went off. When he heard that, he knew his time was up.

Crossing quickly to the door, he peeked outside. It took only a glance to confirm that the cavalry had arrived. That's it, Pollerana told himself, the stall's over. From now on it's David's problem.

Resignedly, he walked across the open space and unlocked the gate. As Westall, Gallagher, and the two deputies started for the building, Pollerana stopped Wentworth and Wales.

"My boss wants to talk to you," he told the fire marshal, leading him and Wales to the extension phone. Silently, he dialed David's number a second time and handed over the receiver.

"Why are you there?" David asked Wentworth.

"I want to make a fire inspection," Wentworth replied.

"Go ahead," David said without hesitation.

Wales tapped Wentworth on the shoulder. "I want to talk to him," he said.

Wentworth passed the receiver to the air pollution control official and walked away, heading straight for the building, which was so filled with foul smoke that Wentworth was afraid he might retch.

Despite Pollerana's efforts to clean up the place, Wentworth found the interior in considerable disarray. On the concrete floor was a huge pool of dark, smelly liquid that analysis later determined was a mixture of diesel fuel and amino acids, which are fluids emitted from a body when it is incinerated. Flames were spurting from around the metal doors of the two homemade kilns, which were nothing more than simple rectangular boxes constructed of angle iron and firebrick. Wentworth kept a wary eye on the flames, fearful they might ignite the fuel on the floor.

Picking his way through the clutter, Wentworth was joined by Wales, who had finished his conversation with David. Together they searched the large room, and what they found seemed to bolster their suspicions.

Lifting the tarp that Pollerana had thrown over the metal drums, Wales spotted the remains of a garment that once had been either a pajama top or a hospital gown. The drums themselves contained ashes and pieces of a substance that Wentworth, for the second time, suspected was human bone. They found the ice chest and tentatively identified the pieces of charred metal inside as the remains of human prostheses. Impatiently, they waited for the kilns to cool enough for them to open the doors. But when the point had been reached, Wentworth was sorry that it had.

Grasping one of the handles and giving it a heavy tug, he swung open the door. As it creaked open, a burning object plopped out and fell virtually between Wentworth's once highly polished shoes. It was the very recognizable remains of a human foot.

* * *

Pollerana, who had been standing silently by during the search, asked quietly if he could leave. He knew what he had been doing was illegal, and he could hardly wait to escape before he was cuffed and led away. Wentworth, still numbed by the sight of the burning, detached foot, nodded his consent. Instead of returning home, however, the terrified Pollerana drove to a friend's house in Pasadena, where he holed up for three weeks. When they went to his home looking for him later, investigators were not able to find him. David, however, proved much easier to track down.

PART TWO

The Family . . .
the Business

3

When news of what had been found at Oscar's Ceramics was splashed on the front page of the Pasadena newspaper two days later under the headline CREMATORIUM OWNER INVESTIGATED, it had about the same effect on its readers as if the weatherman had forecast rain for the Rose Bowl parade: surprise ard incredulity.

The newspaper was quick to underscore the involvement of Pasadena's David Sconce, whose family was well-known. For four generations his family had been associated with one of the city's more respected businesses: Lamb Funeral Home. Indeed, the East Orange Grove Boulevard address that David had given to officials in Hesperia when he applied for the assorted permits was that of the Spanish-style mortuary.

In its first report the Pasadena *Star-News* seemed as interested in the family connection as it was in what had transpired in Hesperia. The initial dispatch listed several names, besides David's, that were considered significant. For example, Laurieanne Lamb Sconce was named. That was David's mother and owner of Lamb Funeral Home. Her husband and David's father, Jerry Sconce, also was mentioned. But the name that long-time city residents had no trouble at all recognizing was that of Lawrence

Lamb, Laurieanne's father and David's maternal grandfather, who was a distinguished, well-known figure in Pasadena.

The full implications of the search at Oscar's—the web of criminal activity and deceit to which it ultimately would lead—would not be known for quite some time. But at the moment it was sufficient that at least one prominent resident seemed to be involved, although he would later prove not to be, in a highly suspect operation. Up until then the Lambs and Sconces had not been viewed in any way except as pillars of the community. And thus it had been for sixty-five years.

In 1921, the year the University of California trounced Ohio State 28–0 in what later would become known as the Rose Bowl Football Classic, a fifty-four-year-old midwesterner named Charles F. Lamb first visited Pasadena. Following their thrashing, the Buckeyes went home suitably impressed with the city. For different reasons, so did Charles Lamb.

When he visited California, Lamb was living in Ottawa, Kansas, where he was the owner and operator of an establishment named the Lamb Funeral Home. His fortune and family were in Kansas and, until he saw Pasadena, which was then a sleepy, flower-bedecked haven outside smog-ridden Los Angeles, he never intended to leave. But the trip to Southern California left him smitten with the region. Anxious perhaps to escape Kansas' bitter winters and scorching summers, Lamb made a difficult decision: he turned the Kansas business over to his eldest son, Harold, then packed up his wife and six other children and headed west.

Soon after he arrived in Pasadena, Lamb bought two already-established businesses, the Reynolds and Van Nuys Funeral Homes, and merged them into a single organization which he called the C. F. Lamb Funeral

Home. In a separate deal, he also bought the Pasadena Crematorium, a small, double-oven facility which dated to 1895 and was mildly famous as the oldest crematorium west of the Mississippi River. It, too, was absorbed into the new operation, although the whitewashed, chapel-like building in which it was housed was located on a leased plot of land in the middle of Mountain View Cemetery several miles away in the town of Altadena.

In Kansas, Lamb had been active in civic affairs, serving as treasurer of the town of Ottawa for several years and as treasurer of Ottawa University for eight years. He also won local recognition for reorganizing one of the city's main financial institutions, the Bank of Ottawa. As a reward, he was appointed a vice-president of the bank, and held the post for five years before moving to California. Other pet projects of his ranged from the First Baptist Church to fraternal organizations, including the Knights of Pythias and Knights of the Roundtable.

After moving to Pasadena, he continued his interest in civic affairs, although on a reduced basis. Five years after he relocated, he was elected president of the Southern California Funeral Directors Association, and the year after that he was chosen president of the state association. He and his family lived in style in an elegant mansion less than a block from the Tournament of Roses House, and they dined frequently at the University Club, hobnobbing with the city's rich and powerful.

Satisfied that he had made the right decision in leaving Kansas, Lamb elected to enjoy his new surroundings. As soon as his Pasadena businesses were established, he retired. He gave up the modest empire he had built to spend his time cultivating roses, playing golf, and whiling away sunny Southern California afternoons on lawn bowling.

Since his oldest son was still running the funeral home in Kansas, Lamb turned the Pasadena business over to two other sons, Lawrence and John. Not many years later, John retired and the business fell to Lawrence, a handsome, strong-jawed, strong-willed man, who had inherited not only his father's business sense but his desire to serve.

In 1949, when he was forty-three years old, Lawrence Lamb was elected to the first of two consecutive terms as president of the Pasadena School Board. According to newspaper clippings of the day, he also was president of the Pasadena Hi Twelve Club International, chairman of the building committee at Tremont Baptist Church, a member of the Tournament of Roses Association, and a fellow of the Baptist University of Redlands. Lawrence and his wife, the former Lucille Jeffries, had four children, two sons and two daughters.

Although the Lamb Funeral Home was then going into its third generation in Pasadena, both of Lawrence's sons sought careers elsewhere. That left Lawrence in a dilemma. With his two sons gone, who would keep the family business going? Of his two daughters, Laurieanne and Linda Elaine, only Laurieanne, the elder by two years, seemed interested.

As her brothers had done, Linda went off on her own. She helped create a successful public relations firm where she worked for a decade, building a reputation as a shrewd and clever businesswoman. By then, for all practical purposes, Pasadena had been engulfed by Los Angeles, with all its attendant environmental problems, and Linda left the city. She moved to Watsonville, a small town in central California, where she bought an apple orchard and became a determined environmental activist as well as a leader in the fight against drug and alcohol abuse. Then tragedy struck. In 1977, in the middle of a long overdue vacation, the thirty-nine-year-old Linda was killed in the collision of two jumbo jets in the Canary Islands, an accident that claimed 575 other lives. That ended forever any chance that Linda would return to Pasadena and take an active part in the operation of Lamb Funeral Home.

But by then, even if Linda had lived and had decided to come back, she would have been out in the cold. By 1977, Laurieanne, at age forty-one, had become indispensable to her father and his business. Lawrence, then seventy-one, was anxious to retire, and the death of his younger daughter propelled him further in that direction. If the business was going to continue, he thought, it would be up to Laurieanne. And why not?

In her youth Laurieanne had been a vivacious, handsome woman, comely enough to be described later by one breathless admirer as a potential beauty queen. But her interests lay in other, less worldly, directions. Along with her good looks she also had a soft, soothing voice and a rare way with people. No matter how distraught survivors might be over the death of a loved one, it was always Laurieanne who could calm them down, whispering words of encouragement and hope that never failed to provide the strength to help them get through the desperate days between death and burial. Some of those she helped claimed to regard her as a living angel, and it was not a description with which Laurieanne herself would find fault. Many years later she told a reporter that one of the happiest times of her life had been when she was involved in day-to-day work at the funeral home, the days when her favorite task had been preparing women's bodies for prefuneral display. "I would do the cosmetics and hair," she said nostalgically. "I had a God-given talent. I had so many people say, 'She never looked so good.'"

In an era before it was fashionable to be Born Again, Laurieanne was a very assertive Christian, liberally sprinkling her conversations with quotes from the bible and exclamations like "Sweet Jesus" while proclaiming the depth of her faith and her desire to convert others. The mortuary was not her workplace, she said. It was her "ministry." She spent much of her spare time writing hymns, and she played the organ at the Loraine Avenue Baptist Church as well as at the funeral home. She even founded a gospel trio called the Chapelbelles, which achieved considerable local fame.

After she graduated from high school, Laurieanne enrolled in Pasadena City College, where she matriculated for two years before switching to the University of the Redlands, a Baptist school where her father had served as a Fellow. However, she left Redlands after one year, shy of her degree, to marry a dashing young man named Jerry Sconce, whom she had met at Sunday school.

Jerry, a native of Oregon, had come south to attend the University of California at Santa Barbara. A striking-looking six-foot 200-pounder with blond wavy hair and blue eyes (physical traits that he would pass on to his older son), Jerry swept Laurieanne off her feet. An irrepressible extrovert, Jerry never met a stranger or a man he wouldn't try to charm. Brash, boisterous, unrestrainable, Jerry had a slap-'em-on-the-back, hand-crunching, glad-to-meet-you personality that completely overwhelmed the shy daughter of the Pasadena funeral home owner.

The two married almost as soon as Jerry was graduated from UCSB. At the time, Laurieanne was still in her teens. Even when their first child, David, was born in 1956, Jerry was only twenty-two and Laurieanne was three weeks shy of twenty. A couple of years later they had a second child, another son, whom they named Gary.

As they grew older, they promoted an All-American family image. Laurieanne was known as "Mom" by her children's friends, and the convivial Jerry was widely called "Coach," because that's what he did for a living for more than two decades. Their home was a gathering spot for neighborhood children, and Laurieanne's kitchen was always open. They were so successful at promoting their clean-cut personas that one day, when the boys were young, the four of them posed for a magazine ad for Maytag. In the foreground of the portrait the four of them huddled over a washing machine, while in the background Jerry's team's jerseys flapped in the California breeze.

Despite her innate reticence, Laurieanne realized early on that if the family business was going to continue, it would be up to her. Her brother Bruce, despite being a licensed embalmer, had abandoned the business in 1961, when Laurieanne was twenty-five, for a career in the Marine Corps. Eleven years later Laurieanne's other brother, Kirk, quit the funeral home to be a real estate broker. A year after that, when it looked as though Laurieanne, at thirty-seven, was going to inherit the business by default if for no other reason, she and her parents incorporated and Laurieanne was named secretary-treasurer.

After Laurieanne's sister Linda was killed, Lawrence began talking more often about retiring. Gradually, in preparation for that day, he gave Laurieanne more responsibility. This, however, did not sit well with Bruce and Kirk, even though they had forfeited their positions at the funeral home for careers of their own. As the brothers watched from a distance, Jerry and David, who had turned into a handsome teenage copy of his father, became more involved in the business. That made the Lamb brothers increasingly uneasy because they feared the business would slip out of the family hands into those of Jerry and David. As time went by, those fears moved closer toward reality.

In 1985, when she was forty-nine and already older by several years than her father had been when he took over the business, Laurieanne formed her own company, which she called Little Black Sheep Inc. The intention was to formally take over Lamb Funeral Home. With

$65,000 down and a promise to pay an additional $100,000 over the next fifteen years—at nine percent interest—Laurieanne agreed to buy the business from her father.

Not surprisingly, considering their fears, Bruce and Kirk opposed the sale. The reason they gave was concern for Laurieanne's welfare. They said their father already was breathing heavily down Laurieanne's neck and it was making her very nervous. If she bought the funeral home, the parental pressure would only grow worse and they were worried about her health—whether she could continue under the stress not only of running the business, but of keeping Lawrence out of the office. Perhaps the real reason they opposed the sale, however, was because Bruce and Kirk feared that the business, once sold, would slip completely away from Lamb control. It would become a Sconce business, not a Lamb business.

Despite his sons' objections, Lawrence went through with the sale.

In retrospect, it was a fateful decision on Lawrence's part. But at age seventy-nine and anxious to step out the door, it may have seemed like the only reasonable step he could take. Turning the family business over to someone who was still a Lamb, even if non-Lambs were wielding considerable power, may have appeared a more desirable option than selling it to a total stranger and watching his life's work disappear entirely.

But judging by what was to happen later, and what had already happened that he did not know about, Lawrence had, by passing the reins to his daughter, simply ensured that his last days would be spent in apparent pain and turmoil. Not even in his worst nightmares could he have imagined the strife that was to test his family's strength.

But even if Lawrence had recognized the danger, it was already too late by the time he and Laurieanne consummated the sale agreement. The problems that began to surface with the incident at Oscar's Ceramics early in 1987 actually had their origin some five years earlier. With benefit of hindsight, it can easily be seen that the troubles which befell the Sconces started in 1982. And they started with David.

4

The year 1982 held special significance for David. It was the year that he felt his life was over; that his situation was about as bad as it could get. He was twenty-six years old, an age when many of his peers were beginning to make their career mark; but David had no job, no marketable skills, no experience to speak of, and no prospects. He felt as though he were traveling backward.

Perhaps worse, his personal life had gone to hell as well. His wife, to whom he had been married for a year—an attractive, vivacious woman he had met at a football game and wed after a whirlwind romance—had left him. That had taught him what a devastating event divorce could be. It had not taken him long to recognize that being on the rebound was no fun; that freedom had its downside.

When everything came crashing down, David went into an uncharacteristic funk. Usually a buoyant optimist, like his father, he went into a deep depression. Life, he decided, was unfair. How did I get into this mess? he asked himself again and again. And how am I going to get out? But an answer continued to elude him. He was confused, unfocused, and unhappy.

To someone who didn't know him well, David appeared to be both a charmed and a charming person. A physically handsome man with a trim, athletic physique, blue eyes that sloped slightly downward, and an infectious, ready grin, he could have graced a poster hyping the California Good Life.

A true Golden Boy, he was born in the Los Angeles suburbs, grew up there, and had planned to always stay there. He went to high school in Glendora, not far from Pasadena, the same school where his father coached football. Not surprisingly, since he was the son of a coach, David grew up with athletics as the center of his life. Sports represented the core of his universe, and he was lucky enough to have some talent as well. At Glendora High he ran track and he played defensive back on the football team. An extrovert who would try to strike up a conversation with a telephone pole, David made friends easily and was well-liked by his teammates. As in most schools around the country, from junior high through college, the jocks have their own clique, and David quickly became one of the more prominent members in the local group. In his senior year he was elected president of the Letterman's Club.

After graduation in 1974, David enrolled at Azusa Pacific College, a small Christian school not far from his home. There were two reasons for choosing that particular college. One was his mother, whose devoutness had not diminished. All his life David had been particularly attached to his mother, and he realized that his selection of a college like Azusa Pacific would be especially comforting to her. His other and more practical reason was that his father had taken over as head football coach at the school, having made the transition in 1972, when David was a sophomore at Glendora High. David was motivated, therefore, by a desire to please both his parents: his mother, by choosing a Christian school; his father, by showing he trusted him enough to place his future directly in his hands.

David's not-so-secret ambition was to play professional football, preferably for a relatively new and struggling West Coast team, the Seattle Seahawks. He thought the best way to attain that goal was to develop his talents through his father's tutelage, to let Jerry shape him and guide him until he was ready to make his mark in big-time athletics. Unfortunately, things did not work out entirely as planned. Under Jerry, Azusa Pacific fielded only a mediocre team; under his tenure, the Cougars' won-loss record was a less than glorious 25–30. The fact that the teams lost more than they won undoubtedly influenced Jerry's departure; when he left the college in 1977, he opened a sporting goods store. It also undoubtedly affected David's plans for a career as a pro. Players from small teams like Azusa Pacific, particularly teams with losing records, are not as attractive to professional scouts, especially if the players are not significantly outstanding. David was not. One of the hard facts that he had to learn early in his college career was that his athletic talents were limited. He might make a career as a coach, as his father had, but he was not destined to play pro football.

When David had enrolled at Azusa Pacific, he announced an intention to major in business. But that declaration was for the clerks in the front office; his real interest was athletics, not accounting. When he realized that Azusa Pacific was not going to put him on a fast track to the Seahawks, he lost interest in college. Well before he had enough credits to graduate, he quit.

On the surface, David had always been a confident, cheerful, happy-go-lucky, eager, Eagle Scout kind of youth, a young man who took things in stride and never let adversity get him down. If Plan A fell apart, he always had a Plan B. In that context, dropping out of college was no big deal. He still had his quick mind, his conviviality, and a gift for sounding absolutely, totally sincere. Superficially, David was living up to the Golden Boy image. But there was a darker side to his personality as well.

It is a requisite part of many athlete-composed subcultures—the jock set—to engage in wild and sometimes destructive pranks. Such activities are virtually de rigueur in certain brotherhoods. It certainly was in parts of David's crowd. Members of the group to which David belonged were not only together on the athletic fields, they hung out together, partied together, and raised hell together. And whenever they gathered, David was always there, especially when they joined to raise hell.

One of David's favorite capers, according to one co-worker, involved loading up a car with raw eggs and cruising the Los Angeles suburbs looking for likely targets. When he found a hapless victim, they pelted him with eggs, laughing uproariously as the yolk and mucouslike white seeped into his clothing. After all, egg-throwing was a time-honored youthful escapade and it was all in good fun, except, of course, for the victim. The problem was, not all of his activities were as temperate as egg-throwing. According to another co-worker, David made the half hour drive to L.A.'s skid row, where he would beat up drunks, and then joke about it afterward.

In November 1974, when he was eighteen years old and a freshman at Azusa Pacific, David was faced with a not uncommon situation: his girlfriend decided to break off their relationship.

This presented more serious problems to him than it might to other teenagers. David lived in a macho world, surrounded by jock, macho friends. They lived by a macho code, one that had little tolerance for rejection, especially female rejection. The brush-off was a threat to his group status as well as a blow to his considerable ego. So David did what he thought was the macho thing: he tried to get even.

While the girl and her parents were out one night, he burgled their home. Although he escaped undetected, his satisfaction was short-lived. Even though he had been successful, the act somehow failed to vindicate the indignity he had suffered; it didn't erase the shame.

This was an early indicator of David's exceptional ability to hold a grudge, a characteristic that would be more apparent in an even more serious vein several years later. But in David's teenage mind, the insult he had suffered extended much beyond the hurt he had actually felt by the dissolution of the affair. His craving for revenge proved totally disproportionate to the injury endured. And the thirst to inflict further harm was not yet sated.

Thirteen months after the initial break-in, on Christmas Eve 1975, while his former girlfriend and her parents were attending midnight church services, David burgled their home a second time, walking off with some $2500 worth of stereo equipment. Still, that did not satisfy his determination to seek retribution. He had to make his act more personal, to let his victim know, even if in a very subtle way, that he was a person not to be trifled with. The way he chose to articulate this was very strange. It also was very telling. After hiding his loot, David went to the church where the girl and her family were worshiping and squeezed into the pew with his victims, joining them when they raised their voices in song proclaiming peace on earth and goodwill to men.

Soon afterward, motivated by the realization that his name had been given to authorities as a suspect, David went to the police and tearfully confessed. He had committed the burglaries, he sobbed, as part of a misguided attempt to make the girl suffer for jilting him. Turning on the charm, he simulated contrition. It was a dumb thing to do, he admitted, but he was young, and his testosterone was flowing, and it seemed like a good idea at the time.

The policeman nodded. In a way, the officer said, he could understand that. He could see how a teenager might be so upset by being brushed off by his girlfriend that he would do something stupid. David bobbed his head in agreement. But the breakup had occurred more than a year earlier, the officer pointed out. Why wait a year to get even?

Eventually, David pleaded guilty to misdemeanor charges stemming from the incidents and lightened his responsibility still further by helping police recover the stolen merchandise. As a reward for his cooperation, his one-year sentence was suspended, allowing him to escape without pulling jail time. He did, however, serve two years on probation and was ordered to pay a fine of $500, plus $125 in restitution.

Actually, he was very lucky. Not long afterward the law was changed to make *every* residential burglary a felony, completely eliminating the misdemeanor provision. If David were accused today of the same violations, he almost certainly would face a stiff jail sentence.

In 1982, seven years after the break-ins, David was desperate for a job. After dropping out of college, he went to work for his father in his sporting goods store, but that venture failed fairly rapidly, either because of Jerry's lack of talent in running a small business or, as David would later contend, because his father was cheated by another entrepreneur. Whether he was right or wrong, David vowed revenge against the man he thought was responsible for his father's store closing. It was still another example of his inability to forget a slight, either real or imagined.

After the store closed, Jerry took a much more active

role in the operation of the funeral home, while David made a stab at a few other jobs. He worked for a short while as a card dealer in a gambling casino, and he ushered at hockey games. He even applied for a job as a deputy with the Los Angeles County Sheriff's Office. Surprisingly, considering what would occur later, he almost made it. He survived the preliminary weeding-out process for deputy trainees, but he ran into trouble on the physical. When he took the vision test, he discovered he was color-blind, and that automatically disqualified him.

When the possibility of a deputy's job fell through, David became even more depressed. By then he had become infected with the yuppie disease: he wanted to make *big* money; he just didn't know how.

Upset because his son seemed to be wandering without direction, Jerry had a suggestion: Why didn't he go back to school? Become a licensed embalmer, he suggested, and join the funeral home as a skilled contributor. All his life David had been doing odd jobs around the mortuary, but his function was little more than that of a hired hand. As an embalmer, however, he could play a valuable role.

David was lukewarm about the idea. His dream of personal fortune extended beyond pumping preservatives into dead bodies. But since he didn't have anything better to do, he went along. However, as he had already proved at Azusa Pacific, the disciplined life of a student did not fit his personality. It wasn't long before he became restless and decided to quit. His decision was greeted with a decided lack of enthusiasm by his parents, who were hoping that he would become interested in the profession and accept his place in the generational succession. But David brushed off their fears. Don't worry, he told them eagerly, I have a much better idea.

5

While struggling to keep up with his class in embalming school, David worked part-time for his parents at the funeral home, performing unskilled jobs such as picking up bodies at hospitals or nursing homes and transporting them either to the funeral home or to the crematorium. It was the first time in several years that he had taken any active, sustained part in the funeral home's operation, and he was struck immediately by the changes that had taken place. For one thing, he noticed that more people were being cremated than had been the case in the past; so many, in fact, that the demand was putting a strain on the area's existing cremation facilities. But that was only part of the industry's metamorphosis. From top to bottom it was undergoing a quiet revolt, and David was working out a plan so he could employ this to his and his family's financial advantage.

Until the early eighties a funeral home, for several reasons, had proved to be a good, solid investment for its owners. For one thing, the number of customers a funeral home could count on receiving in any given year was remarkably predictable since, over the long haul, the death rate did not fluctuate by very much. For another, owners of mortuaries, unlike those of other service-oriented businesses, did not have to spend a lot of money on advertising, since funeral homes tended to draw their clients by word of mouth or tradition, a twist on the definition of brand loyalty. For still another reason, studies had revealed that potential customers did not engage in much comparison shopping. When someone died, the grief-stricken loved ones tended to go to a particular funeral home and arrange the services without telephoning around to see if a competitor might offer better rates. Most people apparently regard shopping for a funeral as demeaning to the dead. Finally, and very importantly, a funeral home's profit margin was relatively high. Funeral homes bought their supplies at reasonable costs, then sometimes charged fees that bordered on the extortive when the customers were billed for the service. In the industry, a thirty-percent profit was not unusual.

That is not a statistic to be sneered at, not when other studies have shown that a funeral is a person's third most expensive purchase, topped only by a home and an auto. In the mid-eighties the average cost of a funeral was $1950, which did not include the cost of a plot, a vault, or a marker. That easily added another $1200 to the cost, bringing the total to more than $3000.

Since it took time to build up a clientele, the funeral industry tended to be both stable and comparatively exclusive; not too many new funeral homes were being added, and not too many of the old ones were folding.

However, beginning in the late sixties, change began to sweep through the industry. One of the major factors precipitating this transformation was inflation. Although prices had been steadily rising all along, they took a big jump in the mid-seventies. Between 1975 and 1985 the cost of a funeral rose 95 percent.

Naturally, the escalating costs upset a number of potential customers. Sooner or later everyone *has* to use a funeral home, and as cost-conscious consumers became more interested in the financial dynamics of the industry, a new idea was born: the pay-in-advance funeral, the ultimate layaway plan. The principle had already proved successful in the retail industry, so why not transfer it to the funeral home industry?

Basically it worked like this: An individual worried that his death was going to place a major financial burden upon his survivors could subscribe to a plan whereby he or she could put something down and pay so much a month over a period of time until the whole service had been paid for in advance. This allowed that person to ease his or her conscience by not leaving loved ones with a large debt. Additionally, if that person were money conscious as well, it opened the way for a bargain. No telling what the cost of a funeral would rise to by the time the person actually died, so by paying at the then-current rates, the planner would be guarding against inflation.

This idea, which in application was called a prepaid or preneed funeral, sounded good to the funeral home owners as well. It allowed them to lock in a prospective customer, plus it provided them with a predictable amount of income. Although the money for the prepaid funeral went into a special account that could not be touched by the funeral home until the person died, there was the interest on the preneed accounts, which could, in the aggregate, be considerable.

In California the law mandated that interest on preneed accounts be totaled separately. That money, with one exception, also was sacrosanct. Recognizing that mortuaries needed to make *some* money on such transactions, the state allowed the funeral home to withdraw a fixed percentage of the accumulated interest to help defray administrative costs involved in setting up and maintaining the account. Much later this would be an important issue to Jerry and Laurieanne.

While the preneed concept seemed to be beneficial

both to the consumer and the funeral home, it was relatively slow getting started. It did not hit the public with an exceptional impact until a company called Service Corporation International, or SCI, came along. The Houston-based company had made its early mark by developing the notion that funeral homes could be run like K marts. SCI's plan was to buy small and struggling funeral homes and turn them around by using techniques developed in the retail discount-house industry. For example, supplies such as caskets and embalming fluids could be purchased more economically in bulk. SCI could make even more money if it manufactured the products itself, which it did in some cases. But SCI's plan did not limit the company's offerings to supplies. It also opened florist shops, since flowers are a big-demand item at funerals, and it offered consolidated services.

The nature of the death business demands that a funeral home have someone on duty twenty-four hours a day. Whenever a call comes in to go pick up a body, someone has to be there to answer it. Similarly, someone had to be available to perform the embalming and see to the routine tasks such as collecting death certificates. SCI said it could provide a central agency to take care of these tasks for several funeral homes, thus freeing the homes from individual financial obligations.

Another major expense for funeral homes was vehicles. Each funeral home had to have a fleet of vans or station wagons to pick up bodies, for example, and another fleet of fancy vehicles—hearses and limousines—to use at funerals. This was an expensive operation. What SCI proposed was a central vehicle pool whereby it could provide vehicles to several funeral homes.

In the end SCI offered a broad menu of services, ranging from low-cost caskets and centralized transportation to economical burial in SCI-owned cemeteries. But the real genius of the SCI plan lay in its buy-out offer. Realizing that a good reputation was worth its weight in gold, SCI did *not* propose to open its own funeral homes or put an SCI sign on the doors of the homes it bought. Rather, it retained the name of the original owner in order to take advantage of the goodwill that had been built up over the years, sometimes for generations. As far as the public was concerned, the home had not changed hands. Many times, the previous owner was kept on as manager.

SCI also proved very aggressive in promoting its concepts. While it began by buying funeral homes one at a time—specializing in businesses out of the big cities, targeting instead homes in smaller cities, particularly in the Sun Belt—it made a major leap forward in 1971 when it purchased a network of twenty-six funeral homes owned by a company called Kinney Systems. It made a larger jump in 1981 when it purchased IFS Industries, its only major competitor, for $48 million. In return, SCI got ninety-one more homes and twenty-two cemeteries.

It did not take SCI long to tumble onto the preneed possibilities as well. Since selling preneed plans by individual funeral homes was a slow process, SCI decided to form its own insurance company, which it called Memorial Guardian, which would handle preneed accounts on a national basis. A purchaser of a Memorial Guardian preneed account could take his choice among SCI-owned funeral homes and would not be restricted to one specific funeral home, as dictated by the ordinary preneed account. This idea proved wildly popular; at one time SCI's preneed accounts totaled nearly $1 billion dollars.

Although several years later it decided to strip itself of many of its enterprises, electing to sell off its supply division, its insurance business, and its florist shops, it continued to hold on to its funeral homes and its cemeteries. By 1990, SCI owned 551 funeral homes and 122 cemeteries in the United States and Canada. Although the total number of funeral homes owned by SCI were only a fraction of the 22,000 homes around the country, the *concept* it promoted ensured that the industry would never be the same again.

The significance of these changes in the industry had not been lost on Jerry Sconce. After his sporting goods store closed and he went to work full-time for Laurieanne, he took over the handling of the preneed accounts, which Lamb Funeral Home had started selling when they saw the possibilities the plans offered. Since Jerry was a born salesman anyway, the transition from coaching and owning a small business to peddling prepaid funerals proved fortuitous. He not only enjoyed it, but he was good at it. Jerry sold a lot of preneed accounts.

Ever receptive to innovation, Jerry also became fascinated with another important development affecting the funeral home industry: the increased demand for cremation.

While this phenomenon may not have begun in California, the state was one of the major areas affected, a fact that probably had much to do with the background and disposition of Californians. A large number of them had come west, as had Charles Lamb, from other areas of the country. When they died, their survivors became increasingly hesitant about spending large sums of money to send their bodies back east, or in using funds for expensive funerals in California when most of the people who might visit the graves were in the nation's midland or on the opposite coast.

The increased interest in cremation also may have had something to do with the state's skyrocketing land prices. To many it seemed a waste of valuable land to take over a large parcel for a cemetery. Rather than burying someone in the land and using a sizable plot, it seemed much more practical, from an environmentalist's point of view, to simply burn the body and keep the remains, which were called "cremains," or spread them in some scenic area.

David and his father discussed this public swerve toward cremation. David was just as fascinated by the trend as Jerry, mainly because he had the opportunity to observe the results firsthand. While making his rounds to retrieve bodies for Lamb Funeral Home, David found that more and more often the bodies he had been sent to collect were tagged for the ovens rather than the embalmer.

What David and Jerry were learning from personal observation was abundantly backed up by statistics. According to industry figures, up until 1968 only 4.1 percent of the roughly two million people who died every year were cremated. But the ratio had changed rapidly, especially in California. And it would change even more. By the mid-eighties some 34 percent of all deaths in California would result in cremations, roughly 71,000 per year. Only three states—Hawaii, Nevada, and Washington—had a higher percentage. But since California was the country's most populous state, what happened there was significant.

Jerry locked in on this trend. Cremation, he predicted, was about to become a big business indeed. And who in Southern California, he asked David, was more ideally positioned to cash in on it than Lamb Funeral Home? David grinned. "Nobody," he replied.

At some point early in 1982, David sat down with his parents for a serious discussion about his future. Look, he explained, he was only minimally interested in finishing embalming school. Even if he plodded ahead and got his license, he would be just another laborer, just another guy drawing hourly wages for a limited salary. That was not the route to big bucks, not for him and not for his parents.

Jerry nodded his enthusiastic agreement. He knew that David was not very happy in embalming school and he felt his talents could be put to use in a more creative way. Why didn't he, Jerry asked David, consider starting a cremation service?

David's eyes lit up. "Exactly!" he said.

However, what Jerry and David were proposing went considerably beyond the services that Lamb Funeral Home was then offering. Although it was one of the relatively few funeral homes that did its own cremations— thanks to the purchase of the Pasadena Crematorium some six decades previously by Charles Lamb—it had not, up to that point, aggressively sought cremation business from other funeral homes. If a customer came in to see Laurieanne and said he or she wanted a loved one cremated, Lamb's was willing to handle it. But that was about as far as it went. What father and son were proposing was that Lamb's actively seek bodies for cremation; go around to funeral homes that did not have their own crematoriums and offer to incinerate their bodies for them.

David suggested that this would be a great enterprise for him since he had made a number of valuable contacts in the months he had been driving hither and yon picking up bodies. He could use those contacts to build a base for the new service.

This thought greatly excited the family. It fed David's entrepreneurial ambitions and it helped Jerry and Laurieanne put their older son on a career track. If done correctly, David reasoned, he and his parents could extend the business beyond the immediate geographical area. In his imagination, they could even corner the cremation business in Southern California.

A few days after Jerry made the suggestion to his son, David came back with a plan. How much, they had asked, would he suggest charging for the service? David had an answer: $55, he said, which would include picking up the bodies and returning the remains.

They shook their heads. The few others who were doing similar work, they pointed out, were charging twice that amount, which was still a good deal for the funeral homes who were engaging the services since they could, in turn, charge the customer as much as $1000. But at $55 they figured they would be losing money. Their facility, Pasadena Crematorium, had only two ovens. Since, depending on the efficiency of the oven, it took about two hours to cremate a single body—about one hour burntime then another hour for the oven to cool down enough to remove the remains—they could process, at best, twenty-four bodies per day. That would bring in an absolute maximum, without allowing for down-time, of $1320 per day. But if they were running twenty-four hours a day then they would have to hire additional workers and that would eat into the earnings. To Jerry and Laurieanne, David's fee proposal did not seem like a money-making proposition.

David took issue with their assessment. Who was talking about cremating just one body in each oven? he asked. What if he cremated more than that? What if he jammed the ovens and could do maybe five or six in each oven at one time? That would work out, at $55 per body, to about $660 per load, using both ovens.

Of course, what David was suggesting was both illegal and unethical. When next of kin asked a funeral home to cremate a body, they had a right to expect that the remains they received were actually those of the loved one. But if several were to be cremated at one time, there would be no way to separate the remains, no way to assure the customers that the remains they received were indeed those of the loved one. How about that? Laurieanne asked.

How about it! David replied. "How can you tell if the remains are mixed? Anyway, what difference does it make. They're dead."

6

Over the next few months, David began putting the plan into operation. The first thing he had to do, he reasoned, was gather around him a group of young men who were not too particular about what they did or, like him, did not care. This had to be a totally separate crew than the one working for Laurieanne. Although he could use Lamb Funeral Home as a base, the bulk of the work would be done in the crematorium, which was several miles away in Altadena. It was, nevertheless, imperative that his workers know better than to go around shooting off their mouths about what was going on inside the small building in Mountain View Cemetery.

One of the first people he hired was John Pollerana, who, at twenty-three, was only three years younger than David. Pollerana showed up at the crematorium just before Christmas in 1982 looking for work. But his education did not really begin until he started drawing a paycheck from Pasadena Crematorium.

Pollerana found it confusing at first to understand what David was talking about; most of the time it seemed as if his new boss was speaking a foreign language. However, he quickly determined that "cases" were cadavers collected for cremation; that the "cold room" was the refrigerated compartment where cadavers were kept pending disposition; that "take-backs" were remains that had to be returned, sometimes as "twenty-four-hour turnarounds"; that the "ash palace" was the room behind the mortuary where remains were processed; that a "single-burn"—a rare event at Pasadena Crematorium—was the cremation of a single individual; and that the containers in which "cases" were cremated were not ovens, but "retorts."

Pollerana's first job was taking care of the retorts. He quickly discovered that even though remains were often referred to as "ashes," there actually was very little ash in the residue from a cremation. When a body is incinerated at 1600 degrees Fahrenheit, all of the soft tissue—the fat, muscles, and tendons—dissipates as a gas. What is left are primarily chunks of bone that have to be pulverized until they are reduced to a consistency somewhat finer than rock salt. At Pasadena Crematorium they did the job with a small cement mixer and two shot puts. Sometimes white powder was added to the take-backs to make the mixture "more attractive" in case anyone wanted to examine what was in the "take-back" container.

The crematorium routine was amazingly easy to learn. David had one commandment: cram as many bodies as possible into the retorts, each of which was only three and a half feet tall, four feet wide, and eight feet long—about the size of the interior of an American sedan. The workers, carefully picked by David, made a game of it, holding a running contest to see who could jam in the most. Normally, Pollerana learned, it was only about nine bodies per retort, but much depended on the sizes of the cadavers. Once, with effort, he got fifteen bodies inside one of the ovens.

When bodies first came in, they were held in the cold room until there were enough to fill the retorts. Then they were stacked one atop another, like dishes on a shelf, until the retort could hold no more. When space started getting tight, a worker would go to the opposite end of the retort, which also could be opened, and use a pole with a large hook on the end, similar to a fisherman's gaff, to snag the cadavers and pull them inside. Usually the workers were not particular about where the hook went. Sometimes it went through the cheek, sometimes through the neck, and sometimes through the shoulder. When space really got tight, a worker used a two-by-four as a pusher, usually inserting the end of the board in the armpit or groin. After a while, like soldiers in a war, the bodies ceased being bodies and became merely large, heavy mounds of material to be treated with the same sensitivity they would use if they were loading bags of cement or sacks of grain.

Pollerana worked for David from December 1982 until the raid on Oscar's Ceramics in January 1987. During that time, he could recall performing a single-burn only one time. In that instance, the mother of a local lawyer had died and the attorney insisted on being present for the cremation. Every other cremation he witnessed or participated in, he said, involved at least two cadavers.

About two hours after the retorts were fired up, they were cleaned out. The process then was to rake out the remains and put them in large drums for storage or until they were cool enough for sifting. This involved spreading them across a large table and separating large bones and pieces of prosthetic devices from the smaller residue. Often, the sifters would find pieces of metal, such as pins that had been surgically inserted. One thing all of David's workers had been warned to be careful about was removing pacemakers before the body was cremated: they could explode in the heat. Sifters threw the bits of metal into the trash and put the larger pieces of bone into the pulverizer. Once they were ground up, they too went into the drums.

When they had to return remains to the next of kin,

Pollerana or one of the other workers used an empty coffee can to scoop an appropriate amount of residue out of the barrels. The rule of thumb was three and a half pounds if the remains were to represent those of a woman, and five to seven pounds for a man.

Not surprisingly, there were occasions when things got confused. Once, Pollerana accidentally cremated a body that was supposed to have been buried instead. When he told David about the mistake, David said not to worry. He replaced the incinerated cadaver with another that had been scheduled for the retort. The coffin was sealed. On another occasion, when there had been a rush order to have remains returned, ashes were packaged and taken to the funeral home before the body had actually been cremated.

David's cremation methods were profitable. Although he did not take over operation of the crematorium until 1982 was more than half over, the number of cremations he performed that year went up almost 1000 percent. In 1981, Lamb Funeral Home had cremated only 194 bodies; in 1982, David recorded 1675 cremations. And that was only the beginning. In 1983 the number doubled, then doubled again in 1984. In 1985, David cremated 8173 bodies, over a 4000 percent increase from the day he took over the operation. In 1986 he reported another 8000-plus cremations. It amounted to more than twenty-two cadavers a day, day in and day out, Sundays and holidays included, for 1985 and 1986—almost all in the two small retorts in the Altadena cemetery.

To keep up with the backlog, David kept the retorts running sixteen to eighteen hours a day, three full shifts for four workers. But it was worth it. At $55 a body, his gross income from cremations alone in 1985 and 1986 would be roughly $1 million.

Business was so good, in fact, that David had to struggle to keep up. He bought a fleet of vehicles and hired drivers to make calls all along the Southern California coast, picking up bodies. By 1985 he was servicing more than 100 mortuaries, retirement homes, hospitals, and cremation services. Eventually his empire stretched from Santa Barbara on the north to the Mexican border on the south and inland to the foothills, an area of roughly 14,000 square miles of heavily populated country. With only two retorts, he was cremating considerably more bodies than any other facility in the state. He could justifiably be crowned the Cremation King of California.

Although his college and high school jock days were far behind him, David still moved in the macho world of athletics as extensively as he could. One of his favorite pastimes in that period was attending the games of the Los Angeles Kings, the local ice hockey team. Hardly a more macho sport could be found, and David revelled in it. In fact, he even worked as an usher at the Forum, the Kings' home arena, for a period when he was floundering about looking for direction.

He had season tickets to the Kings games, and he and several other regulars formed an exceptionally vocal cheering squad in their own section of the arena. One of the group was a hulking weightlifter and former football player named Daniel Galambos. It was only natural that Galambos and David would strike up a friendship.

At one of the hockey games, Galambos introduced David to his friend, David Edwards. Galambos and Edwards had played football together, first at Pierce College in Los Angeles and later at the University of the Pacific in Stockton. Over the years, they continued to be friends, frequently partying and playing together.

Edwards was introduced to David in 1981, well before David was involved in the crematorium. From the beginning, it was clear that Edwards was exactly the kind of guy David would seek out as a friend. When they met, Edwards was twenty-four and David was one year older. Edwards was six feet tall, weighed more than 200 pounds, and had been a minor star in football. He had been captain of the football team in his second year at Pierce and was voted the MVP. That year, as a running back, he had amassed 750 yards on the ground and another 114 in receptions. Before that, during his senior year at Culver City High School, he had rushed for 1000 yards and scored nine touchdowns, although injuries limited him to only six and a half games. As a high schooler, Edwards had been named to the first team All-Ocean League allstars.

Throughout the 1981 and part of the 1982 Kings season, Edwards and David cemented their friendship. Early in 1983, when Edwards mentioned to David that he was looking for work, David quickly offered him a job.

"What would I do?" he asked.

"Not much," David replied. "Just drive a van for me, picking up bodies."

Since he needed the money, Edwards agreed. But, like Pollerana, he quickly got an education in the inside operations of a funeral home and crematorium, Sconce-style.

Perhaps more than Pollerana, Edwards was shocked when he learned that multiple burns were the rule at Pasadena Crematorium. But since his job kept him on the road, he did not have to spend much time either at the crematorium at Altadena or the Lamb Funeral Home in Pasadena. Usually he was there only to unload bodies and get pickup orders for the next run. That was sufficient for him, since he had seen enough.

If Edwards had to rank his degree of revulsion to the events he witnessed, the multiple cremations would have come in second. In first place would have been David's other primary moneymaking scheme: yanking gold teeth. As Pollerana and others had already learned, and still others would learn later, when David talked about "making the pliers sing," "popping chops," or "going to the mine," he meant extracting gold-filled teeth from cadavers.

At Pasadena Crematorium it was standard operating procedure to examine the incoming bodies for gold. Normally David did the job himself. As the bodies came in, he would take a screwdriver and pry open the mouths, searching for a gleaming molar. If he spotted the precious metal, he whipped out a pair of pliers and extracted the tooth or teeth, placing them in any handy container. A styrofoam cup or an empty soda can would do, although he sometimes used an empty coffee can or just a paper napkin.

Occasionally the cadaver's jaws would be locked shut so tightly that it would require a real effort to get inside. Edwards watched in horror one day as David, frustrated in being unable to force a cadaver's mouth open with a screwdriver, cursed and went for a crowbar. Apparently that was the right tool; it worked. Edwards said he could hear the dead man's jaws crack all the way across the room.

Sometimes the other workers would screen the bodies before David came in. When they discovered a body with dental gold, they would call it to David's attention by drawing a happy face on the cardboard sheet all bodies destined for cremation were wrapped in, along with the letters AU. The symbol for gold on the Periodic Table of Elements used almost exclusively by scientists was the way David preferred to refer to the precious metal.

The fact that David was extracting the teeth was far from secret around the funeral home and crematorium. He frequently joked about it. On more than one occasion he was seen whistling while leaving the cold room, shaking a cup or can containing gold-filled teeth. On time, as worker Steve Strunk recalled, Laurieanne looked up from her paperwork and smiled at David's good humor.

"How much AU did you get today, honey?" she asked sweetly.

David grinned and showed her the cup he was carrying. It was half full of teeth.

Exactly how much money David made off the teeth probably never will be precisely determined. As the number of bodies he handled went up, so did the number of teeth he extracted, but investigators were never able to get a firm handle on exactly what the volume was. It must have been considerable, though, at least well into tens of thousands of dollars. David himself bragged that in 1985 and 1986 he was making five to six thousand a month from the enterprise. It was so productive that the employees at the Burbank gold exchange company he usually dealt with called him "Digger."

Although David later tried to claim that dental gold was valueless because it contained so many other metals, that statement was patently false. Dental gold, rather than being *less* pure, is actually *more* pure than that used in everyday objects such as rings, bracelets, and necklaces. Usually, dentists use 18k gold, compared to 14k used in most jewelry. It is not unusual for a man, particularly, to wear more gold in his mouth than he does on his fingers. A typical gold crown weighs two pennyweight, one-tenth of an ounce. With gold selling at upwards of $350 an ounce, a single crown would contain $35 worth of the precious metal, not a lot on its own, but in volume the value could be substantial. Very few people who have gold crowns limit themselves to one. Also, more elderly people have crowns than younger people, and David was cremating a lot of elderly people.

If half of the bodies David cremated in 1985 and 1986 contained just one gold crown, he could have reaped as much as $280,000 from his extraction program. Although no one probably will ever know, the figure could have been much higher because David was relentless in seeing that the gold was collected. It was a rare body that went into one of his retorts with the gold-filled teeth still in place. And even if some occasionally did slip by him and his workers, the sifters were under standing instructions to be particularly watchful for chunks of gold among the remains.

7

Ever on the lookout for a way to make a buck, David hit upon another idea in the summer of 1985—a scheme that was ambitious, but one that would, in the end, be a major contributor to his downfall. Just as he had astutely noted the increasing demand for cremations three years earlier, and had moved quickly to capitalize on the development, he soon picked up on another trend as well: the quiet proliferation of facilities known as tissue banks.

At the time, sophisticated tissue banking was a comparatively recent phenomenon in California, although some banks had been around for years. In fact, tissue transplantation, in one form or another, dated to the Middle Ages. But up until the seventies, it had been a hit-or-miss kind of business. There were eye banks, which of course provided eyes, and there were joint banks, which specialized in supplying parts like hip joints, and there were bone banks. But until techniques and drugs were developed to make transplantation of tissue and organs a relatively risk-free procedure, there had been little demand for large-volume providers.

David wanted to be large-volume. And why not? After all, he had access to the tissues and organs from thousands of bodies, bodies that were going to be incinerated anyway. He figured that he might as well take what he could from them before he shoved them into the retorts, since after that they were of no financial benefit to anyone. David's plan was to strip the bodies brought to him to be cremated for usable parts—"harvesting" them, as it were, much as a California junk car dealer might strip a wrecked vehicle of its usable parts. However, he was soon to discover that harvesting body parts was a little more delicate than removing auto parts.

To be transplantable, tissue and organs have to be fresh. Very fresh. This crossed off a lot of David's bodies immediately, because by the time he was called to pick up a cadaver, the person's organs had usually begun deteriorating. Although he could shelve bodies in the cold room to keep them from decaying too rapidly, that was far from adequate as a place to store tissue that might be suitable for transplantation.

But that did not mean the idea was a write-off. Eyes were fairly durable, and if a few simple precautions were taken immediately—such as keeping them moist with wet cloths—they could be salvaged hours after death. And just because organs were not suitable for transplantation did not mean they were not valuable. Medical schools across the country were screaming for organs they could use in their research labs or in the classrooms. But it did not necessarily follow that the operation would be profitable. There is a federal law prohibiting organs from being bought or sold, which is why up until then the tissue banks that did exist tended to be nonprofit organizations.

However, as with most laws, there was a loophole. While an organization might be prohibited from charging for an actual organ, say a heart, there was nothing to prohibit the provider from charging a fee to recoup his costs in collecting the organ. Since these fees were fairly standard, David could predict what his rate of return would be. Besides, whatever money came in would be gravy; the raw material was not only free, it was already revenue-producing. So if he could make a little more money off the same product, it was a good plan.

That was the basic idea. In theory it was simple enough, but in practice it proved considerably more complicated. For one thing, David discovered that he would need a certain amount of specialized equipment. He also would need someone who knew what he was doing. Although, technically speaking, stripping organs from a cadaver is not a particularly delicate procedure—surgery it is not—it does nevertheless require a certain amount of expertise. Most nonmedical people don't realize it, but human organs are not difficult to remove. If someone wants to take out a heart, for instance, all that is required is snipping the connectors. The organ doesn't even have to be lifted out, it literally falls into the hand. But getting to the heart is another matter. Opening the chest is not an effortless procedure, certainly not without the proper equipment. Then removing the organ without damaging it, and knowing which connectors to snip while retaining the organ's usefulness to a potential buyer, requires some basic knowledge of human anatomy that neither David nor his co-workers at the funeral home/crematorium possessed.

Plus there was the legal process to consider. Yanking gold-filled teeth from the mouths of about-to-be-cremated cadavers was one thing, yanking hearts and brains was another. The odds were very great that no one was going to miss a cremated cadaver's gold teeth. But the sale of organs was a much more regulated procedure; for organs, there had to be a paper trail. The buyer, who was a legitimate supplier, wanted to know where the material came from and be assured that it had been removed with permission. A major reason for this was a very practical one: Organs could spread disease. At the time David launched his business, AIDS was not the issue it would become later, but there were still risks from disease in organ transplants, and buyers were very aware of these hazards. Hepatitis was always a worry, for example, as were some of the rarer illnesses, such as Creutzfeldt-Jakob disease, a fatal, degenerative, neurological ailment spread through corneal transplants. As a result, those in the organ industry were very concerned about the history of the organs for sale.

To comply with state regulations in the normal operation of his business, David already had to produce a certain amount of paperwork. Every time he cremated a body, for instance, someone had to sign a document called an Authority to Cremate, or ATC, form. In its most common incarnation, the form was a simple legal instrument that transferred authority to the crematorium to incinerate that particular cadaver. The form being used at the time by David was only two paragraphs long. What it did was set down the ground rules for the crematorium to follow in performing its service. It specified that prostheses—such as artificial hip joints, surgical pins, and artificial limbs—would be discarded. Also to be tossed out, at least according to the form, was whatever remained of gold inlays and fillings that survived the incineration. (Lamb Funeral Home employees were instructed to tell anyone who asked that the heat in the retort was so intense that the gold was either vaporized or so affected by the process that it was unrecoverable or unusable.) Additionally, the form promised that the "bulk" of the ashes would be returned. It also—and this would be the crucial part—gave David authorization "to remove tissues, remove pacemakers . . ." If anyone asked about this phrase, Jerry had coached the workers to respond that it was virtually impossible to remove a pacemaker without removing a small amount of tissue as well, and that the phrase had been inserted to keep the lawyers happy. Later, the Sconces would claim that this phrasing gave them permission to remove "tissue" such as hearts, lungs, and brains.

✗ After David got into the tissue bank business, his crematorium's ATC form underwent several subtle revisions, most notably in the section that referred to the removal of tissue. On one version of the form the phrase was capitalized so it would draw a casual reader's attention. In a later one it was not, perhaps on the theory that he did not *want* the reader to notice the wording. And in one of the early forms, tissue removal was not mentioned at all. Furthermore, the phraseology and typography used in the forms would prove to be a very contentious point among the people David brought in to help in the tissue bank operation; they had more scruples than David or the laborers who jammed the retorts and extracted gold teeth. Eventually the forms would play a major role in David's undoing. But in the beginning he was blind to potential problems; he saw nothing but dollar signs.

The more David studied the possibility of creating a tissue bank, the better the idea looked. If a serious harvester went to work on a human body, it was possible to collect organs and tissue—parts ranging from bone and ligaments to valves and the organs themselves—worth a considerable amount of money. According to a fee list used by the University of California at San Diego, organs, bone, skin, corneas, and other parts could easily bring in $25,000 per body. That included $2600 for a knee joint and $750 for a set of three tiny bones from the ear. A single heart valve, according to the list, was worth $2300.

But David did not envision an operation as sophisticated as would be required to thoroughly mine the cadavers that passed through his crematorium. Even if he could not reap the really big bucks, like those paid for transplantable organs, he could nevertheless realize a quite tidy profit just by stripping bodies of the more obvious and easiest to obtain organs and selling them for research purposes. At the time, a brain that could be used by a tissue supply house would bring $80. A heart fetched $95; a pair of lungs $60. Corneas started at about $525, and whole eyes—called "globes" in the industry—could be sold separately at fluctuating prices depending on the market. This was not *big* money, but it could add up. David confided to one co-worker that he hoped to make as much as $500,000 a year from just one supply house. If he was processing 8000 or more bodies a year and he could salvage one usable body part—a brain, heart, lung, cornea, globe, or spinal column—from each cadaver, plus an average of one gold crown, he could easily double the fee he was getting for a cremation. If he were cremating a minimum of 8000 bodies a year, he could, even figuring conservatively, increase his gross annual income to more than $1.25 million, plus an unknown amount, maybe as much as $75,000 a year, from the surreptitious sale of dental gold. And this was exclusive of any fees being brought in by Jerry and Laurieanne through the Lamb Funeral Home.

Again moving swiftly, like any businessman seeking advice in a field outside his own area of expertise, David zeroed in on someone who could help him turn his tissue bank idea into cash. The person he picked was a Japanese exchange student barely out of his teens, a shy youth named Joyji Bristol, nicknamed "George."

On the surface there was nothing exceptional about Bristol. He was about twenty years old, of average height and build, with dark hair and dark eyes, and a fairly poor working knowledge of the English language. In short, he could have disappeared without a trace in Southern California's large Asian community. But there was one thing about him that attracted David, one quality in particular that prompted David to court him as avidly as a sought-after lover: Bristol *knew* about tissue banks; not only how to remove organs, but how to maneuver through the laborious record-keeping and inspection processes. He was, in fact, knowledgeable enough about such operations for David to begin what proved to be a successful campaign to lure him away from his then current employer, the Medical Eye Bank of Orange County. It was a change that Bristol would later come to regret in the worst possible way.

In June 1985, David invited Bristol to lunch. Over hamburgers he explained that he was interested in setting up a tissue bank and he wanted Bristol to help him. The bait for Bristol was the promise of a fifty-fifty partnership in the operation.

As David laid it out, the new business, which he was going to call the Coastal International Eye and Tissue Bank (CIE&TB) would operate temporarily out of Lamb Funeral Home. But after revenue started flowing in, David would be able to build a separate facility. David told Bristol he would take care of raising money for the start-up. What he needed from Bristol, he said, was his knowledge of the industry, including his contacts with potential buyers, and his expertise, both in removing tissue and in taking care of the paperwork. Even though tissue banks were comparatively new, they still fell under state regulation, albeit rather ineffective. Bristol would be responsible, David told him, for applying for the proper licenses, for supervising the removal of tissue and organs, and for helping to find sources for sale of the material. On the papers of incorporation, David promised, Bristol would be listed as a director.

Naturally, David had not mentioned the multiple cremations or the stealing of gold teeth. To Bristol, David appeared to be an enterprising young businessman, and his offer sounded like too good a deal to pass up. Late that summer, Bristol quit his job with the Orange County firm and joined David in Pasadena. He did not know—in fact he did not *need* to know—about some of the other internal changes that were going on at the funeral home at roughly the same time.

For more than a year David had been operating what had previously been called the Pasadena Crematorium under a new name: Coastal Cremation Inc. For all intents and purposes, Pasadena Crematorium was defunct, although that was not generally known. Also, even though Laurieanne had been operating Lamb Funeral Home for quite some time, she did not technically own it. On September 30, not long after Bristol came aboard, she took care of that detail by formally buying the operation from her father. She apparently did not feel it was necessary to explain to Lawrence the full extent of what was going on at the East Orange Grove Boulevard parlor, because in the purchase agreement she claimed that Pasadena Crematorium was performing only a small number of cremations every year. Evidently she did not want to tell her father that David was performing *thousands* of cremations, and that most of the customers thought they were dealing all the while with Lamb Funeral Home's Pasadena Crematorium, an organization whose good reputation Lawrence Lamb had worked hard to build.

By this time the entire operation had undergone a major reorganization. Where before there had been two entities, Lamb Funeral Home and Pasadena Crematorium, there became three: Lamb Funeral Home, Coastal Cremation, and CIE&TB. All of the entities operated out of the funeral home location, and to most of their customers and the public they were indistinguishable *from* the funeral home. What was happening internally was not for public consumption. The Sconces were perfectly content to let their customers believe that they were dealing with the venerable institution with an unsmirchable reputation.

Another reason for secrecy was that Laurieanne, Jerry, and David feared that they would lose business if it became widely known that they were operating a tissue bank. Their clients—other funeral homes or cremation services, likely would quit sending cadavers for cremation if they thought those bodies were first being stripped for tissues and organs, even if authorized by the ATC form. Many of *their* customers were justifiably sensitive about having organs removed from the bodies of their loved ones. Also, the Sconces' clients felt that before they could recommend organ and tissue donation, special counseling with the customers would be necessary, and the Sconces shrewdly judged that many of these clients would be unwilling to take on the added responsibility—*if they knew about it.* They wanted to make sure they did not. Possible reaction from their clients was presumably another major reason that the ATC form was written in vague terms, that and the obvious reason that the Sconces figured they could harvest more body parts if no one outside the operation knew exactly what was going on.

While the Sconces felt that a certain amount of concealment was paramount, they also realized they could not keep their plans entirely under wraps. They had to raise enough money to get CIE&TB started, and to do that they had to reveal a minimum number of details. Actually, the Sconces were in a precarious position, one that required some very delicate handling. Realizing this, it was no surprise that Laurieanne was selected to make the initial fund-raising contacts, since she had such a winning way with people. No doubt about it, her demure, soft-sell approach was more useful in this context than Jerry's hard-sell or David's flippant attitude. Additionally, there was one other advantage in having her as the front person: She was a Lamb, and the moneyed people of Pasadena respected the Lambs.

In the end, raising the money did not prove to be an extremely difficult task. While the exact amount of cash Laurieanne brought in is unclear, it is known that her fund-raising efforts were so successful that she actually turned down some people who wanted to invest, telling them they had already raised all that was needed. What would prove significant about Laurieanne's efforts, especially in light of later developments, was the personal role she took in the fundraising for the tissue bank. In an attempt to make a criminal case against all three Sconces, prosecutors later would point to Laurieanne's alleged complicity in setting up the tissue bank as one of the major indicators that she was indeed involved in its operation.

Sometimes, when talking with friends or potential investors, Laurieanne referred to the tissue bank as something the family had been thinking about for years, ever since her sister Linda had died in the plane crash in the Canary Islands. Many of those aboard the two planes had been burned, and when doctors tried to help survivors, they discovered there was a shortage of skin tissue that could be used for grafting. That brought the issue home to her, Laurieanne said, explaining that her desire to open a tissue bank was one way of memorializing her sister.

And then there was the letter. In making his case for Laurieanne's complicity, one prosecutor would refer specifically to a letter from Laurieanne to a woman who eventually invested $15,000 in the tissue bank project. On October 1, 1985, Laurieanne wrote the woman telling her how wise her investment decision had been. In the letter, Laurieanne claimed that the tissue bank's operating room already had a long list of physicians anxious to use the facility, and that the prep room was going to be functional within two weeks. What was notable about the letter, in the prosecutor's opinion, was Laurieanne's frequent use of the plural possessive: She liberally laced the document with references to "we" and "our."

8

Laurieanne's possessiveness was not lost on George Bristol. While he had agreed to go into the operation believing that he would be a fifty-percent partner, David soon disabused him of that notion. Even before Bristol could get settled in, David explained that there had been a change in the way the proceeds would be split. Instead of getting half of the profit, as had been promised, Bristol would get only one-third. David would get another third, and the remaining third would go to Jerry and Laurieanne.

In addition, Bristol also was supposed to draw a weekly salary of $200. But that turned out to be an illusion as well. Often the checks were for less, and sometimes they didn't come at all. Finally, at Bristol's insistence, David drafted a contract specifying that Bristol would get $30,000 a year from the CIE&TB. At least Bristol had something on paper, but it was a far cry from the quarter of a million dollars he envisioned receiving when he quit his Orange County job.

Not surprisingly, Bristol felt as though he had been cheated. And as time went on, he became increasingly disillusioned about working with David. It had not taken him long to realize that he'd become entangled with some very strange people. But David was more than strange. Bristol also felt he might be dangerous. And he had reason for this opinion. One day he and David had gotten into an argument over Bristol's handling of the CIE&TB affairs, and it built to the point where David started screaming at him.

"If you're really unhappy with me," Bristol screamed back, "I'll quit."

That really set David off. Bounding across the room, he wrapped his hands around Bristol's throat and slammed him against the wall.

"If you try to quit," David growled, "I'll kill you."

After that, Bristol began carrying a .45-caliber pistol in the nylon knapsack he took with him everywhere.

The odd thing was, Bristol's weapon was only one of several floating around Lamb Funeral Home at any given time. David almost always carried a gun. Sometimes it was a small pistol and sometimes it was a huge .380-caliber handgun that had been given to him as a Christmas gift from the man to whom he sold the dental gold. The man had also given Jerry a matching weapon, which he occasionally toted, although Jerry preferred a smaller pistol, one he could fit into the shoulder or ankle holster he habitually sported.

Father and son also had an affinity for shotguns, and they invariably carried one in the van when they were out on a job. At times Lamb's resembled an armed camp more than a funeral home, a situation that even Laurieanne did not find unsettling or unusual. In a letter to an auditor with the Board of Funeral Directors and Embalmers, she casually mentioned that the neighborhood in which the funeral home was located had gotten so rough that employees were "forced" to carry guns even on the job.

◦ ◦ ◦

There were other reasons, too, that Bristol began feeling increasingly uncomfortable around David. One day he came to work and found David in a particularly dark mood. Solicitously, Bristol asked what the problem was.

"It's the competition in the cremation business," David replied. "It's driving me crazy."

When Bristol replied there was not much he could do about the competition, David got a strange look in his eye.

"You know what I'd like to do," he said, phrasing it as a statement not as a question. Knowing that David was going to tell him anyway, Bristol waited in silence.

"I'd like to get some plastic explosive and stick it in one of these cases," he said, referring to a cadaver waiting for cremation.

"*What?*" Bristol asked, astounded.

"Then I'd send it to one of my competitors," David said, "and when they stuck it in the retort, it would explode. *That* would get rid of the competition."

Disturbing to Bristol, too, were the frequent disputes he witnessed between David and Lisa Karlan, another tissue bank specialist David had sweet-talked into coming to work for CIE&TB. As it turned out, Karlan's career with CIE&TB was both tumultuous and short-lived. While she was still there, she and David argued constantly, usually about the wording in the ATC forms. Their discussions often ended in shouting matches that would leave David fuming for hours.

Jim Dame, another worker, witnessed one such quarrel. After the two wore themselves out yelling at each other and stalked off to separate corners, David had turned to Dame and said: "That girl has gone too far. One of these days she's going to wind up dead."

Karlan's term of employment at CIE&TB was measured in weeks, but even after she left, her disagreements with David did not cease. They continued to argue over money. Their telephone calls invariably ended the same way their face-to-face disputes had: David would remain in a ferocious mood, snapping at anyone who crossed his path. Bristol was passing David's desk one afternoon while David was having a telephone argument with Karlan. He intended to go on by, but David's tone of voice made him stop. When he did, he heard David say: "For five hundred dollars I can have you shot. For a thousand I can have you killed, and then I'll burn up the parts so no one will know what happened to you." As Bristol stood there staring, David slammed down the receiver. Turning to Bristol, he said: "I'll kill anyone who threatens me or my family." Bristol walked away.

Bristol tried to justify David's tantrums as mere manifestations of a bad temper, but then he had a conversation with David that made him rethink his position. After that, he began to believe that David was far more menacing than he had originally thought.

The incident occurred just before Christmas 1985, less than four months after he had joined CIE&TB. Bristol was on his way to work one morning when David stopped him in the carport outside the building. Apropos of nothing they had discussed before, David began telling Bristol how much he hated his grandparents, Lawrence and Lucille Lamb.

"My grandfather keeps interfering with things," David told him, "and my grandmother told me once that she would see to it that I was never part of the business."

Although Bristol had thought that David could do little to astonish him any longer, he nevertheless was shocked.

"Why are you telling me this?" he asked.

"You have good contacts," David replied "and I need your help."

Bristol was suspicious. "What kind of help?" he asked softly.

"I need a poison," David said. "An untraceable poison, one that can simulate a heart attack."

"What do you want to do with the poison?" Bristol asked, fearing he already knew the answer.

"I want to use it on my grandparents," David replied.

By now Bristol was totally intimidated by David, and he feared if he turned down the request for help, David would fly off the handle.

"What you need to do," Bristol told him, "is talk to one of the assistant coroners in L.A. One of them ought to be able to help you."

The response seemed to mollify David, and he let the subject drop for the time being. He did not, however, forget about it.

Practically every time David saw him after that, he asked about the poison. However, Bristol managed to avoid a direct answer. Finally, David let his exasperation show.

"Goddamn it," he exploded, "I need the shit. I'm ready to go to their house," he added, referring to the Lambs' retirement house on the Colorado River.

Bristol didn't know what to say, so he said nothing.

David's eccentricities and unpredictable moods were balanced in part by attempts at generosity. To keep his business going at the volume it was, David had accumulated a large fleet of vehicles. When he was feeling philanthropic, he parceled these out among his workers and some of his customers. One of the beneficiaries of David's largesse was a man named Richard Gray, who operated a small cremation service and brought his business to David. Once when Gray's station wagon had broken down and repairs promised to take a long time, David flipped him the keys to one of the vans and told him to keep it as long as he needed.

On another day he did the same for George Bristol.

Knowing that Bristol had long envied his white Corvette, David surprised him with an almost identical car. "Take it," David had said. "Keep it as long as you like."

Bristol was only mildly astonished when he learned soon afterward that the vehicle had been stolen, boldly driven off a local dealer's lot by another of David's employees. Oddly, even though he knew it was hot, Bristol continued to drive it almost up to the time he quit.

PART THREE

The Victims

9

George Bristol had discovered that working for David was a strange, uncomfortable experience. And Dave Edwards, like Bristol, also was developing mixed feelings about his employer.

Initially, Edwards had been astonished by some of the things he saw taking place at Pasadena Crematorium, but he was not overly concerned because he was not directly involved. Although David sometimes asked him to hold the flashlight while he searched a cadaver's mouth for gold-filled teeth, and David occasionally called upon him to help stack bodies in the retorts, those were not tasks Edwards was required to perform on an everyday basis. Most of the time, in fact, he was on his own, working just about when he wanted, with no one looking over his shoulder. Besides, as Bristol also had learned, David was a benevolent employer. He regularly bought the crew lunch and took them along to sit in his box at the Kings games.

But there was another demonstration of employer loyalty that deeply impressed the ex-football player: Not long after Edwards began working at Pasadena Crematorium, David demonstrated allegiance to his employee in a very unusual way. Edwards had been out partying one night and was stabbed in the side. The wound was serious enough to keep Edwards in bed for several weeks. During that time, David continued to pay him his salary, and even arranged for Edwards's roommate, another massive, black, ex-football player named Andre Augustine, to drive his van. That in itself was unusual, but the really strange part of the story had to do with David's attitude toward the stabbing. One day while Edwards still was recovering, David pulled Dan Galambos, their mutual friend, aside at a Kings game and asked him to take a message to Edwards. "Tell Dave," David told him, "that if he can find out who it was who stabbed him and he wants to get rid of him, I can burn the body and no one will ever know."

David seemed to take great pleasure in keeping Edwards and Augustine around, since they were both ex-jocks, members of the group that David felt most comfortable with. When talking about them to others—in their absence, of course—he frequently referred to them as "my niggers." Whether they were aware of what David was calling them is not clear. But as Edwards confessed later, they had their own nicknames for him. Sometimes he was "Captain Cremator," but usually he was known as "Little Hitler" because he liked to strut around barking orders, and because there was a definite, dark side to his personality.

Much of the time, David was easy to get along with, provided things were going his way. He joked with the workers a lot, but he was always bragging about one thing or another, particularly his athletic prowess. He told a lot of people that he had actually played for the Seahawks, even though most of them knew he had not, and he exaggerated his college football accomplishments. He was very vain about his physique and about how strong he was. Lifting dead bodies was hard work, and David prided himself on how well he could perform. Frequently, if an especially old or frail person came into the funeral home,

David would eye the individual up and down, then, be-hind his back, whisper: "That's a one-hander!" meaning he thought he could heft the elderly person with only one hand. Sometimes, if the person appeared ill as well as frail, David would comment, "There's fifty-five dollars!" meaning he appeared to be an immediate candidate for the retort.

Edwards had not been working for David for very long before he learned that his boss not only had a terrible temper, but that he held grudges for a long, long time. Sometimes, too, he was just mean.

One day, for instance, David came to work in a particu-larly foul mood, complaining about how a neighbor's tree was shading his swimming pool. It blocked the sun, he whined, and the leaves fell into the pool, which required that he clean it more often. On that day, he decided to do something about it.

"How would you and Danny like to get rid of that tree for me?" David asked Edwards.

Intrigued by the unusual request, Edwards agreed. The next day he and Galambos rented a chain saw, drove to David's neighborhood, went into the neighbor's yard and cut down the tree. Perhaps intimidated by the size of the two men—Edwards was six feet tall and weighed 200 pounds; Galambos was six-foot-three and weighed 245—no one said a word to them. Not right away anyway. But then they had a problem. When the tree fell, it knocked down a power pole and caused an electrical failure. When the power company crew showed up, Edwards and Galambos had a *lot* of explaining to do.

David got a good laugh when Edwards recounted the incident. Still chuckling, he pulled out his wallet and counted out $600, which he handed over with a job-well-done grin. Edwards pocketed $400 and gave the rest to Galambos.

* * *

Several months later, in August 1984, more than eighteen months after Edwards had begun working at the funeral home, David approached him with a second unusual request. There was another mortician, David said, who was giving him trouble. The man, Ron Hast, published an industry newsletter and he was threatening to expose David and his parents for performing multiple cremations. By then it was whispered within the funeral home community that David was cremating more than one body at a time. If anyone took the time to run the figures on a calculator, they could see it was the only way he could charge as little as $55 per body and still stay in business. That Hast was promising to make the rumors public was bad enough, but even worse than the threat of exposure, in David's eyes, was the fact that Hast had telephoned Laurieanne and told her what he planned to do. That upset his mother terribly, David said. And having his mother upset was something that David could not tolerate.

David pulled Edwards aside and explained the situation to him. If Hast carried through on his threat, David added, he and his parents would have to shut down their operation. Then they all would be out of work. Would Edwards be willing to help keep that from happening?

Edwards nodded. "What do I have to do?"

"I want you to beat him up," David replied. "Him and his friend, Stephen Nimz. If you do, I'll pay you eight hundred dollars."

David suggested that Edwards might want to get some help, probably from Andre Augustine. Edwards agreed and went off to recruit his roommate.

A couple of nights later, having gotten the Hast/Nimz address from David, Edwards and Augustine knocked on their door. When Nimz answered, they told him they were college students looking for odd jobs to help pay their way through school. Did he have anything they could do?

When Nimz said no, they thanked him politely and left.

The next day, Edwards went back to David and said he was going to need some more help. Did he have any objection if he brought Galambos into it as well? David said no.

So that night the three former football players, who together weighed almost half a ton, got ready for the unsuspecting Hast and Nimz.

Gathering at the apartment shared by Edwards and Augustine, they hatched a quick plan. Galambos would buy a badge at a toy store and they would pretend they were cops, as a ruse to draw Hast and Nimz out of the house. Once they got them outside, they could attack them and then make a hasty retreat.

They agreed it was a good idea and got ready to go. At the last minute Edwards ran back inside. From a drawer he extracted a squirt bottle that was made to resemble a flashlight. Then he dashed into the kitchen and started dumping liquids into the device. In went some ammonia. Then some vinegar. Then some jalapeno juice. Then he just started grabbing bottles at random, pouring whatever was handy down the spout. Finally they were ready. They jumped into Galambos's gray Toyota Celica for the trip across town to Hollywood Hills, where Hast and Nimz lived.

When they got there, Galambos and Edwards went to the door. According to the plan, Galambos would flash the badge and be the spokesman. Edwards would carry the fake flashlight, and Augustine would hide in the bushes along the drive, ready to jump out if the others needed help. They were confident the scheme would work; they certainly looked husky enough to be cops.

Hast answered the door. Calmly, Galambos produced the badge and told the mortician they were policemen investigating a hit and run. They thought Hast's car was involved and they would like to inspect the vehicle. Hast readily agreed. He called Nimz, and the two men led Galambos and Edwards into the garage. They had taken no more than two steps into the building when Edwards yelled, "Now!"

At the signal, Galambos slugged Hast on the chin. The mortician fell to the floor. Simultaneously, Edwards sprayed the vile liquid from the fake flashlight into Nimz's face. As Nimz's hands went to his eyes, Edwards punched him on the jaw. Nimz went down too. Pivoting, Edwards pointed the spray bottle at Hast, who was squirming on his back. But before he could squeeze it, Nimz bounced to his feet and started running down the driveway. When he saw Nimz coming, the 265-pound Augustine leaped out of the bushes and threw a perfect body block, just as he had practiced on countless football fields. Nimz grunted and went tumbling to the concrete. Augustine, Galambos, and Edwards, laughing wildly, ran to Galambos's car and drove hurriedly away.

An hour later Edwards telephoned David and told him everything had been taken care of. "Good," said David. "Did you do a good job?" Edwards assured him they had, embellishing the tale with an exaggerated account of the amount of physical punishment they had inflicted upon the pair. A couple of days later David gave Dave Edwards $1200 and told him to split it with the other two.

After that incident, Hast made no more threats about exposing David and his parents. But regardless of what Hast did or did not do, the rumor about the multiple burns at Pasadena Crematorium continued to spread. It proved so persistent, in fact, that Laurieanne felt compelled to try to eradicate it herself. On November 14, 1983, she wrote to the crematorium's clients. In her letters she did not acknowledge the existence of the rumor but described the

A FAMILY BUSINESS

Pasadena Crematorium's policy. All of their cremations, she wrote, were done one at a time. She also invited mortuary directors to inspect the facility as long as they called ahead. She signed the letters as the crematorium's secretary-treasurer and manager.

10

Unhappily for the Sconces, Ron Hast was not the only one in the local industry spreading the rumor about multiple cremations at Pasadena Crematorium. Hast's partner in the mortuary was a man named Alan Abbott, who also had another business—a limousine rental service that specialized in furnishing vehicles to the movie industry. His partner in *that* enterprise was a grossly overweight young man named Tim Waters. In addition to the limousine rental company, Waters also owned a cremation service called the Alpha Society.

While both Tim and David operated cremation services, their businesses differed in one major respect: Tim Waters did not have a crematorium of his own. Nor did he have a funeral home. He had a storefront in Burbank with a couple of desks and a telephone. His service was strictly that of a middleman. For a fee, he would collect bodies and deliver them to a crematorium, then return the remains to his clients. He had no cold room, no retort, and he did not prepare bodies for cremation.

Since Tim had to pay a crematorium and still make a profit, he could not come close to matching the fee David was charging for roughly the same service. David's advantage was that he did not have to deal with a middleman.

He performed the same services as Tim except he carried the process one step further: He actually cremated the cadavers. That and the fact that he was cremating a number of cadavers at one time, not one at a time as other crematoriums were doing, meant he could seriously undercut the fees of any of his competitors.

Tim's only way to fight David was to convince his clients that Pasadena Crematorium was acting illegally and hope that they would react by retracting their business from David and giving it to him. Although Tim evidently had no *proof* that David was performing multiple cremations, he was sharp enough to deduce that was the *only* way David could be offering the service for $55.

In some ways Tim and David were remarkably alike. For one thing, both were highly competitive and felt that anything was fair in business. At the time, one of Tim's best friends was Richard Gray, who was working as an embalmer. In the late spring of 1984, the shy, slight, deep-voiced mortician had confided to Tim that he was planning to give up embalming and start his own cremation service, which he was going to call the After-Care Funeral Society. Tim's first reaction was shock, then anger. Like David, he had a quick temper and was not above bullying someone to try to get his way. If Gray went ahead with his plan, he would be a competitor. And Tim was not enthused about that possibility.

At first Tim tried to verbally discourage Gray from opening the competing service. When that didn't work, he tried to dissuade his friend from using Pasadena Crematorium for his cremations, pointing out that he strongly suspected David was performing multiple burns. Perhaps he thought that would convince Gray that the business he was thinking about entering was a very cutthroat one indeed, and that might make him think twice about jumping in. But if that had been Tim's motive, it failed.

Although Gray had been shocked by what Tim had

said, his reaction was to go straight to Jerry and Laurie-anne and confront them with the accusation. They laughed. "That's ridiculous," said Jerry.

Not satisfied, Gray went to David.

"Where did you hear that?" David wanted to know.

Gray replied that it came from his friend, Tim Waters.

"Well, it isn't true," David said, adding: "I guess I'll have to go have a talk with your friend."

A few days later, when Gray was delivering several bodies to Lamb Funeral Home to be cremated, David told him that he and his father had gone to Tim's office but he had not been in. David said he had also tried to find Tim at the Holiday Inn in Burbank, where he lived, but he had not been there either.

Gray did not pursue the issue further; he was having troubles enough of his own. Just before he was scheduled to open his service, someone cut the telephone lines going into his office, and a few days later someone slashed the tires on his car. Although Gray did not know it for a fact, he strongly suspected that his friend Tim was behind both acts of sabotage, indulging in a misdirected effort to try to convince him not to open a competing service. The reason he suspected Tim was because Tim had been aware of both incidents almost as soon as they occurred.

"How did you know?" Gray asked when Tim telephoned to commiserate.

"A little bird told me," Tim replied.

Things came to a head early that summer for the two old friends. Tim called Gray one afternoon and suggested they have dinner together at a restaurant called Otto's Pink Pig in Van Nuys. Since he and Tim usually dined together at least once a week, Gray thought nothing about it.

That evening, Tim picked Gray up at his office and they drove to the restaurant in Tim's car. From Gray's point of view, it was a pleasant meal. Tim did not even mention business until after they had finished. While Gray was having coffee and Tim was sipping water, Tim reached in his pocket and pulled out a check. Slapping it on the table, Tim pointed out that it was blank. "I'll pay you what you've already invested in setting up your operation if you'll get out of the business," Tim proposed.

Shocked that his friend would even make such a suggestion, Gray refused.

Tim's reaction was not what his friend had expected. When Gray said no, Tim leaped to his feet. Slipping his hands underneath the table edge, he flipped it over, dumping dirty dishes, coffee, and glasses of water into Gray's lap. Then he stormed out the door, leaving Gray to find his way home.

That, Gray said later, marked the end of their friendship. Although he talked to Tim once or twice on the telephone after that, he never saw his former friend alive again. His next personal contact would be as a visitor at Tim's memorial service.

David, however, had no intention of letting Tim intimidate *him*. He had nothing but contempt for the 300-pound, quick-tempered cremation service operator, who he also suspected was gay. He could not afford to sit by while Tim continued to spread the rumor about multiple cremations. There was too much at stake.

By then, early in 1985, David had taken complete control of Pasadena Crematorium, making it official by signing a lease with his mother and renaming the business Coastal Cremation Inc. In the two-plus years he had been running the operation, the business had prospered beyond his wildest expectations, and with any luck at all, he could corner the cremation market in the entire state of California.

Already in his mind was a half-formed plan to expand

his operation northward into the Bay Area. Since cremation licenses were difficult to get and San Francisco had
reached the saturation point for such permits, David had
to come up with a way to get the business without having
to secure a license or building a crematorium in the area.
What he decided to do was buy a building within com-
muting distance of San Francisco—it was too expensive to
even contemplate buying one actually in the city—and
turn it into a giant cold room in which he could store
cadavers for short periods. Then he would build a crematorium near Bakersfield, in the central part of the state. A
couple of times a week he could pick up the bodies from
the Bay Area cold room, transport them to Bakersfield for
cremation, and then return the remains. That way he
could double his volume since he could continue his
southern operation by using the facility at Altadena.

It was a good plan provided he could get the necessary
permits to build the Bakersfield crematorium *and* provided no one like Tim Waters rocked his boat. If Tim
mentioned the rumors about multiple cremations to the
right people, it could bring investigators from the state
regulatory offices down on David's back and they could
close his entire operation. David was determined he
would not let that happen; Tim had to be discouraged
from talking too much. In David's mind there was only
one way that could be satisfactorily accomplished: reenter
Dave Edwards.

One day early in 1985, David pulled Edwards aside and
asked him if he was interested in "another job." Edwards
knew exactly what he meant. When Edwards asked David
who the victim was going to be that time, David said it
was a guy in Burbank who, like Hast and Nimz, was
threatening to make trouble. His name, he said, was Tim
Waters. If Edwards agreed to take care of him, he would
pay him $800. David added that Waters was a "real fat
guy" and Edwards would have no trouble handling him.

Edwards agreed. But first he planned to enlist Augustine again. As they had done before the attack on Hast and Nimz, the two decided to case Tim's place before committing themselves to an attack. When they went to the address furnished by David, however, Edwards and Augustine discovered an unanticipated problem.

Burbank is an almost exclusively white community, and black men—particularly large, ferocious-looking black men—are viewed with suspicion by the local police. The two were sitting outside the Alpha Society's offices waiting for Tim to appear when a patrol car passed by. They thought the officers gave them a suspicious look, although they did not stop. But a few minutes later a cop on a motorcycle came down the street. And not long after that a police helicopter flew over. By this time Augustine and Edwards definitely were getting paranoid.

Edwards turned to his friend.

"Hey, man," he said, "you notice something?"

Augustine looked around. "Yeah," he said slowly, "we're the only blacks here. Shit," he added, expanding on the thought, "we might be the *only* blacks in Burbank."

Edwards nodded. "Let's go," he said, shifting the car into gear.

They left without ever seeing Tim Waters. But that mattered little to the two. The next day, Edwards went to David and gave him a detailed but totally fictitious report about how they had beaten Tim, striking him again and again until "blood was squirting." Then, Edwards said, he and Augustine dropped Tim in a heap on the floor and left.

"Great!" David cheered. "That's just great!"

They had done a terrific job, he told Edwards. They had been so efficient, in fact, that he might want them to take care of another guy in Glendora, a man who David felt had swindled his father in a business deal several years earlier.

"Any time," Edwards said, holding out his hand. David counted out $800. That night, Edwards gave Augustine his half. Then, over a couple of beers, they got to laughing so hard about how they had been paid for beating up a guy they never even saw, they thought they'd piss their pants.

David has never said whether he found out that he had been taken. In any case, Tim kept telling others about what he thought was going on at Coastal Cremation. That prompted David to decide anew that he could not let it continue. This time David went to Danny Galambos.

As he had with Edwards, David asked his friend if he would be willing to rough up someone else, as he had done with Hast and Nimz.

"Sure," Galambos replied. "Can I get some help?"

"Yeah," David replied, "but don't take Edwards."

"Why not?" Galambos asked.

"Because he's already 'done' him once," David replied.

The target, David told Galambos, was an obese crematory service owner named Tim Waters.

"I want some bones broken," David told Galambos. "I want him hospitalized. Beat him up and make it look like a robbery."

"Okay," Galambos said agreeably.

"And don't worry about getting too rough," David added.

"How's that?" Galambos asked.

"If you accidentally kill him I can always get rid of the body. I'll just burn it."

As a partner for the job, Galambos picked a weightlifting buddy named Christopher Long, who was only six feet tall and 220 pounds, but he had such a fierce disposition that even Galambos, who was considerably taller and heavier, confessed to being afraid of him.

Galambos and Long drove to Burbank in Galambos's gray Toyota and parked outside, making themselves comfortable while waiting for Tim to appear. As they sat, Galambos consumed a sandwich and emptied a carton of milk. When he finished, he carelessly tossed the empty container out the window onto the sidewalk. Eventually, Galambos would pay an extraordinarily heavy fine for littering.

When Tim showed up a few minutes later, Galambos and Long sat quietly, watching him disappear into his office. As soon as he closed the door, they jumped out of the car and made for the building. They opened the door and saw Tim sitting at his desk, looking like a happy John Goodman before he lost his baby fat. Long crossed the room in two strides. Without saying a word, he punched Tim squarely in the face, breaking his nose and knocking him out of his chair.

Galambos had paused to quietly close the door. When he turned back into the room, Tim already was supine and Long was leaning over him. Galambos quickly covered the short distance and looked down. Blood was spurting from Tim's nose and he was whimpering, sounding like a puppy afraid of the thunder. Also without speaking, Galambos bent over and hit him twice. Tim's whimper gave way to a gurgle. As he lay there trying to catch his breath through the blood and the panic, Galambos began stripping off his jewelry: a gold chain Tim wore around his neck, a gold bracelet, and two rings. A few days later Galambos took the items to a fence and collected $400, which he pocketed without sharing with Long. He did, however, give his confederate $400 of the $1000 David forked over as the agreed-upon fee for the beating.

* * *

If David thought that a beating would be enough to convince Tim to keep his mouth shut, he miscalculated. Although it made Tim more cautious, he did not try to keep secret the fact that he believed he had been attacked as part of a scheme to discourage his aggressive approach to competition. Exactly what he said after the beating, and to whom, is not clear, but whatever it was, it may have been enough to provoke an even more violent reaction.

The beating took place on February 12, 1985. Less than two months later, on Easter weekend, an even more traumatic thing happened to Tim. He died.

11

Tim Waters was sick, as sick as he had ever been in his entire life. Even a sip of water taken to relieve his raging thirst sent him dashing for the bathroom. Tim had had intestinal flu before, bad cases of vomiting and diarrhea. But never had he experienced anything like this.

It had begun late on April 5, Good Friday, after he and his friend since grammar school, Scott Sorrentino, pigged out on Chinese food. It must have been the chicken with almonds, he told himself, although Scott had not complained about being sick. Whatever it was, it was certainly hanging in there. Nothing had passed his lips except water, but still he was sicker than he had been before.

At noon on Saturday, soon after Scott left to drive back to Los Angeles, Waters telephoned his mother, as he did virtually every day.

"Where are you?" Mary Lou Waters asked.

"In Malibu," he replied. "At Susan's," he added, referring to his older sister. "She went off for the weekend and I'm house-sitting."

They chatted for a few minutes and Tim hung up. He had not told his mother he was ill. No sense worrying her, he thought, convincing himself he was going to feel better in a few hours. But as the day went on, he felt worse rather than better. Late that afternoon, as he was sitting on the john for the umpteenth time, he looked into the toilet bowl and saw the water was stained with blood.

That evening he called his mother again.

"I don't feel very good," he confessed. "I've been sick all day."

Mary Lou Waters frowned. Tim seldom complained about his health. "Are you going to be all right?" she asked worriedly. "Do you want me to call a doctor?"

"You always want me to go to the doctor, Mother. I'll be all right."

"You're still coming tomorrow, aren't you?" she asked, suddenly faced with a potential new problem. "You haven't forgotten Easter dinner?"

How could he forget, Tim thought. Every year his parents made a huge production out of Easter dinner, inviting a couple of dozen guests as well as family members. "No, I haven't forgotten," he assured her. "I'll be there."

However, on Sunday morning he wished he had not made a promise he might not be able to keep. When the sun came up, the day promised to be bright and cheerful, as almost every day is in Southern California. Except Tim felt anything but bright and cheerful. He had been up most of the night, running to the toilet, passing more blood. He felt so weak he was not sure he could stand, much less get in his station wagon and drive somewhere.

Before mid-morning his mother telephoned and asked if he was coming over in time to go to mass with her. In the last few months Tim had formed the habit of attending mass every day, going alone and standing quietly in the rear of the church. But Easter was special. On Easter he always went with his mother. This year, though, he knew he was not going to be able to make it. That thought disturbed him greatly. *Everybody,* even the Catholics who never went to mass at any other time, went on Easter Sunday.

"I'm still not feeling too well," he said, trying, for his mother's benefit, to sound chipper.

"You don't have to go to church when you don't feel well, Tim." Mary Lou Waters said condescendingly, treating the twenty-four-year-old, as mothers are wont to do, as if he were still in the fifth grade. "I'll go to church and then I'll come by and pick you up."

Tim sighed. "Okay," he agreed, not feeling up to an argument.

They had barely hung up when Tim called her back, telling her not to drive to Malibu to get him. "I'll need my station wagon later anyway and I don't want to have to come back to Susan's to get it," he explained.

"That's fine," his mother said after a moment's hesitation. "I'll see you after mass."

By noon Tim was feeling a little better, but he was still incredibly weak. With effort, he dressed himself and prepared to leave. On the way out he was overcome with thirst. Taking a glass from the kitchen cabinet, he shuffled into the garage, where his sister kept her mineral water dispenser. But when he bent over to fill his glass, dizziness swept over him like a wave. The tumbler slipped from his hand, hit the floor and shattered. Tim cursed. He knew if he bent to clean it up he would be overcome with vertigo and would collapse. So he left the broken glass on the floor and slid behind the wheel of his black Ford station wagon, a vehicle that looked exactly like what it was—a miniature hearse, a vehicle he used to transport bodies from wherever they happened to be to a crematorium. On weekends, especially holiday weekends, Tim was on call. Since he never knew when he would be summoned to pick up a body, he had to have his station wagon handy. On such occasions, it did double duty as his personal vehicle.

As he pulled out of the driveway, Tim was confronted with a new worry. It was a forty-five-minute drive from Susan's house in Malibu to his parents' house in Camarillo, and he wasn't sure he could make it without having to find a gas station with a rest room. But there was nothing he could do about it, Tim told himself. If he didn't show up for Easter dinner, his mother would never let him forget it.

When he got there, miraculously without having to stop en route, his mother had not yet returned from church. After greeting his father, he went into the room that had been his as a child and stretched out on the bed.

A few minutes later Mary Lou Waters pulled into the driveway. When she saw Tim's station wagon outside, she felt more than slightly relieved. He had sounded so bad over the phone, she wasn't sure he'd be able to make it. After telling her husband she was back, Mary Lou walked down the corridor and opened the door to Tim's room. Immediately, the comfort she had felt on seeing his station wagon vanished. Taking one look at her son, she gasped. "You're deathly pale," she said, shocked at how drained he looked. He was not at all the bubbly young man she had seen only a few days earlier. All color was gone from his face, and his eyes were circled with deep shadows. When he tried to smile, it looked more like a grimace.

"I'm going to call a doctor," she said, turning on her heel.

"Wait," Tim called after her. "Don't do that. I'm going to be all right. I don't need a doctor. Just let me take a quick nap," he begged, "and after that I'll feel better. Then we can talk."

Reluctantly, she left the room. As she walked down the hall, Tim closed his eyes. His heart was thumping wildly and his head was spinning; he knew he was losing consciousness. It was like the time he was going under the anesthetic for an operation to remove a growth from his neck: He had no control over his body. This is it, he told himself. I'm going to die.

When he awoke after a short sleep, he felt somewhat better, at least good enough to drag himself out of bed and into the kitchen, where his mother was preparing an Easter feast for thirty people.

"There's something I want to tell you, Mother," he said.

Startled by his tone of voice, Mary Lou Waters stopped sticking cloves into the Easter ham. "What is it?" she asked uncertainly, noticing that Tim's appearance had not improved; he still looked like a refugee from the intensive care unit.

Unsteady on his feet, Tim pulled up a chair. As he made himself as comfortable as he could, he told her that after the two goons had come bursting into his office and attacked him, seemingly without reason, breaking his nose, he decided to make a will.

In the weeks since the attack, Tim had been reflecting on the incident. His intuition told him that the attack had been intentional. The reason behind it may not have been obvious at first, but the more he thought about it, the more he was convinced that it had to do with his business and the nature of the fiercely competitive mortuary industry in Southern California. He had stepped on one set of toes too many, Tim conceded, and he had to pay for it. But how much did he have to pay?

The possibility that his current illness might also be related to his business had flicked through his thoughts as well, but he had dismissed the idea. Thinking *that* way, he had decided, would really make him paranoid.

But as he mechanically ticked off the details of his simple will to a flabbergasted Mary Lou, Tim's thoughts drifted back over the events leading up to the holiday weekend. Maybe it wasn't so farfetched after all to suspect that he may have been poisoned. That's dumb, he told himself, again pushing the idea away. I must be going crazy. He told himself it was just too preposterous to believe.

"You and Dad get everything," he told his mother, and then explained where the document could be found in case anything should happen to him.

A discussion about death and wills and the possibility of losing her only son were things that Mary Lou definitely did not want to discuss on Easter Sunday. That kind of talk frightened her. Fleetingly she wondered if Tim was trying to make a joke. That would be in character for her fun-loving son. But when she saw how serious he was, she became very agitated. Tim had never acted like this before. He was usually cheerful and optimistic, even when he had the surgery on his neck a year and a half earlier, even when the biopsy report had come back saying that the growth had been malignant. "Cancer isn't going to get me," Tim had predicted. In that case he had been right. The doctors had kept a close watch, and there was never any indication that the disease had spread. But even then Tim had never talked about dying. So why should he feel that way now, she asked herself, when all he has is a bad case of intestinal flu?

"Don't talk like that, Tim," she admonished him, speaking more sharply than she intended. "You're not going to die. Everything is going to be fine."

Tim smiled weakly and went back to bed.

By the time the guests had arrived, Tim was feeling so much better that he decided to join them. Clad in a pair of dark pants and a white shirt, which made him look even more pale, Tim circulated among the family friends and tried feebly to join in the festivities. Pulling Susan into a corner, he apologized for leaving the broken glass on the floor of the garage. "Be careful when you drive in," he cautioned her.

When Mary Lou called everyone to dinner, Tim sat down as well. Others had wine or something stronger, but Tim stuck to 7-Up. He never drank alcohol anyway, and with his stomach rebelling the way it was, he had no intention of starting then. Sipping slowly from his glass of soda, Tim picked dejectedly at his food.

His mother glanced worriedly at him. Tim did not get to be almost 300 pounds by being a finicky eater. But he was just too sick to care. Every few minutes, he excused himself and hurried to the bathroom. Then, before the dishes could even be cleared away and the party could really get going, Tim kissed his mother good night. "I'll be back to normal by morning," he said, with little conviction.

When Mary Lou entered the living room on Monday morning, she brightened. Tim was sitting on the couch trying to make jokes with his cousin and her boyfriend, who had stayed over the night before. Her son was still incredibly pale, but Mary Lou noted happily that he must be feeling better; he was making an effort at humor. Then he shivered, shaking visibly.

"I'm so cold, Mother," he said. "Will you get me an afghan?"

"It isn't cold in here, Tim," she replied, examining him closely, "but I'll get one for you."

When she returned, Tim was on his feet. "I'd better . . . I'd better go lay back down," he said weakly. "I think I'll go in Dad's bed."

He started toward his parents' room and stopped. "I'll bet you've made it already," he said, almost in a whisper.

"That doesn't matter, Tim," Mary Lou replied. "We'll unmake it."

As his mother fussed with a blanket, Tim lay back and tried to smile. His gaze drifted upward until he was staring at the ceiling. His heart hammered in his chest. As Mary Lou Waters stood there, gazing anxiously at her son, his eyes rolled back in his head. "Stop it!" she screamed, thinking at first that he was teasing her. When she saw he wasn't, she screamed again.

The paramedics arrived minutes later. Bustling about with their equipment, they tried vigorously but unsuccessfully to get Tim breathing again. Handling his huge bulk as delicately as they could, they wrestled him onto a gurney and into the ambulance. They made good time getting to Pleasant Valley Hospital, where emergency room personnel tried to triumph where the paramedics had failed. They made an incision in his throat and jammed a tube down his windpipe. They attached various pieces of shiny equipment to sundry parts of Tim's enormous body. They did everything it was possible to do. But it wasn't good enough. After a while they gave up. Shaking his head, the attending physician picked up a pen and scribbled three initials on the form shoved into his hand: DOA.

12

In efforts to save his life, Tim had been pummeled, probed, and prodded, all to no avail. But even in death his indignities were not yet over. Before he could be laid to rest, there was one final humiliation to be imposed. Since he was not under the care of a physician at the time of his death, he had to undergo a postmortem as well. It was the law. In Tim's case, since he had been formally pronounced dead in a hospital in Camarillo, in Ventura County, the task fell to Dr. John E. Holloway, an assistant county medical examiner.

The process began at 10:35 A.M. on Tuesday, April 9, in the morgue in the basement of the Ventura County Medical Center. On the plus side, there was never any question about Tim having fallen into inexperienced hands: Holloway had been a practicing physician for more than thirty-one years. All of that time, except for three years as a researcher in nuclear medicine, had been spent as a pathologist. Holloway had autopsied thousands of bodies before Tim's, and there would be a lot more afterward.

A pathologist is, in essence, as much a specialist as a surgeon. But a pathologist is a medical investigator, a physician disciplined to look at the evidence left behind and come to a reasonable conclusion about what caused the death. In performing this task, the pathologist calls on training, experience, skill, and a wealth of modern technology.

To begin, a pathologist examines the entire body, from the crown of the cadaver's head to the soles of the feet, searching for clues. Sometimes the signals blink like a neon sign: maybe a bullet hole in the head. Sometimes they are not so obvious, such as a needle prick between the toes, under the tongue, or beneath the breast. And sometimes there are no external signs at all, as would prove to be the case with Tim, unless his severe obesity counted as a clue. As far as Holloway was concerned, it did.

Once the exterior of the body is examined, the pathologist looks inside. Plainly put, the body is cut open and the major organs removed, one by one. Each is examined for signs of disease, defect, or damage, called trauma in medical terminology. Such examinations, for example, typically turn up evidence of heart disease, strokes, or kidney failure. To help in this stage of the examination, the pathologist performs a microscopic inspection of tissue, which frequently reveals clues not apparent to the naked eye.

The third and sometimes most meaningful examination includes toxicological studies of bodily fluids: blood, urine, bile, and stomach contents, to name four. These studies are helpful in determining, for example, if the deceased was drunk or drugged at the time of death, and if the intoxication was sufficient to kill.

Not all three examinations are always performed. Sometimes a pathologist will become so convinced after completing the first two phases that the third is unnecessary. If a cadaver is brought in and examination of the heart reveals evidence of a massive coronary, so massive that death was both inevitable and quick, then the pathologist may not order toxicological studies, figuring that even if the deceased had been drunk or under the influence of drugs, neither of those conditions killed him. But regardless of whether the third phase is carried out in a competent autopsy, the first two, virtually without exception, are.

While donning his gown and gloves, Holloway, who had seen bodies of all shapes and sizes over the years, took one look at the sheet-covered mound that had been Tim Waters and thought, my God, he's a big one. Although there were no body scales in the morgue, Holloway, who was no flyweight himself, estimated Tim weighed a minimum of 300 pounds.

Sighing, he flicked on his tape recorder—a pathologist's notebook—and began dictating a visual report of Tim's condition.

Tim had been lying in the morgue for almost twenty-four hours when Holloway began his autopsy, and the pathologist noted the signs: *Breakable rigor is present . . . Lividity is dorsal and blanching . . . The fingernails reveal marked cyanosis of the beds . . . The pupils are equal and dilated . . .* Translation: Rigor mortis had obviously set in and, since the body had been supine, the blood had settled in the lower half, giving Tim's back a purplish cast. By the same token, his fingernails were a slatelike color because there was no blood circulating beneath them.

Having gotten on the record the fact that Tim was undeniably dead, Holloway noted evidence of Tim having undergone recent resuscitation attempts: *An endotracheal tube is present in the appropriate anatomic location. There are six monitor patches, including one at the left anterior deltoid region, two in the corresponding region on the right, and one each in the infraxyphoid and bilateral upper quadrants of the abdomen.* Tim had clearly received expert medical help either at the time of death or shortly afterward, a fact the pathologist already knew.

As he examined the body, Holloway remarked on the outward indications of normality, which was necessary to show that there were no readily apparent signs of what had killed him. *No scleral or conjunctival lesion is seen . . .* Translation: Tim's eyes were not damaged. *The external ears are free from hemorrhage . . . The nose is symmetrical and shows no hemorrhage . . . The lips, buccal mucosa, and tongue show no intrinsic lesion . . . The teeth are natural and in good repair . . . The scalp shows no evidence of trauma . . . All anatomic structures of the neck are intact . . . The bony framework is well-developed and well-retained . . .* Whatever had killed Tim, Holloway was saying, he had not been beaten to death. So far, as well as the pathologist could tell, there were no signs that Tim had met a violent death.

Then Holloway began the *real* work. With no more hesitation than a programmer would demonstrate in switching on his computer, or a mechanic in raising a car hood, Holloway picked up a scalpel and began the customary Y incision, effectively slitting Tim down the front from his shoulders to his groin. Methodically, he reported on what he found inside Tim's body, system by system, organ by organ.

Regarding the cardiovascular system, Holloway said: *The 440-gram heart is enlarged on the basis of left ventricular hypertrophy and dilation.* The fact that it was enlarged on the left side was a vital clue, one that pointed toward chronic strain on the organ. *The thickness of the left ventricle wall is 1.3 centimeters, and that of the right 0.4 centimeters.* He found it unnecessary to articulate in his notes that this also was unusual. *The valves show no lesion . . . The coronary arterial tree arises in the usual sites and distributes normally . . . The aorta has a uniform diameter of only 1.25 centimeters internally . . . small for the habitus.* Translation: Considering his size, the main artery in Tim's body was comparatively tiny. *Other blood vessels studied are generally of similar small scale, but not otherwise remarkable.* Conclusion: There were enough irregularities in Tim's heart—the organ itself was enlarged and the primary artery serving the organ was smaller than normal—to make the pathologist believe, in lieu of any more obvious finding, that these were, at the least, contributing factors in Tim's death.

The respiratory system: *The left lung weighs 590 grams, and the right 630 grams . . . There is marked congestion throughout. The bronchial rami are clear.* Conclusion: In themselves these factors were not alarming, but combined with his heart irregularities, they could have been fatal.

Holloway kept searching.

The heptobilary (liver and gall bladder) system: *The 3780-gram liver is enormously enlarged and has a smooth intact capsule and generous rounding of the edges.* Holloway paused to consider the implications of this discovery. A liver that size, more than seven pounds and roughly twice as large as could be expected in an adult male, was a serious matter. Not only was it hugely oversized, but the fact that the edges were generously rounded indicated more problems. In a normal liver the edges are sharp, but Tim's liver looked like a balloon on the verge of bursting.

The gastrointestinal system: *The stomach contains about 250 milliliters of hemorrhagic mucoid material in which no food particles are identified.* It takes the stomach two to three hours to empty, and since there was no food present, it meant that it had been at least that long since Tim had eaten. That and the presence of blood-flecked mucous pointed to a serious stomach upset just before death. *There is no evidence of pills, capsules, or other residual medication . . . The duodenum, small intestine, appendix, and colon show no gross abnormalities of mucosal or serosal elements or of content. The rectum is empty.*

° ° °

Based on what he could see with his naked eye, Holloway developed a three-pronged diagnosis, which he dutifully dictated into the recorder. In the first place, he said, Tim was extremely overweight. Second, he must have had trouble breathing because of his size and the congestion in his lungs. And third, Tim had a "markedly enlarged liver," a fact that Holloway considered particularly significant.

By this time the pathologist was well on his way toward forming a formal opinion about what had killed Tim Waters. Although he felt virtually certain that he was going to discover that Tim had died a natural death, one precipitated by his extreme obesity, Holloway wanted to reserve final judgment until he could perform the second phase of the autopsy—a microscopic study of tissue from Tim's organs. But that took time. To prepare for such a study, tissue first has to be dehydrated, then repleted with alcohol and other solvents. That product has to be left overnight, then embedded in paraffin. After that, it can be sectioned—sliced—with a special device that cuts it into incredibly thin, translucent segments. The final stage is the staining and mounting of the sections. Only then can the tissue be examined microscopically.

While waiting for this process to be completed, Holloway issued a preliminary report listing the cause of Tim's death as "pending."

Several weeks later Holloway pulled up a stool at a lab table and slipped a slide containing tissue from Tim's heart under the lens. What he saw confirmed his earlier suspicions: There were serious irregularities present. He dictated: *A section shows focally massive fragmentation of nominal hypoxic myocardial fibers.* Translation: He could detect evidence that Tim's heart had not been receiving sufficient oxygen.

Holloway also discovered a "marked thickening" on the inside of Tim's coronary artery, but he did not find that disturbing. He did not notice any unusual change in Tim's aorta, the body's main blood-carrying channel, which would have complicated the situation for Tim. He did, however, find evidence of additional problems while studying tissue from Tim's lungs. *A section shows massive edema and lesser degrees of alveolar hemorrhage and congestion.* Translation: There was a significant amount of fluid in Tim's lungs, particularly—and distressingly—blood.

Also, confirming what he had already predicted about Tim's liver, a microscopic examination of the organ tissue indicated big trouble. Although Tim's liver apparently had been trying to restore itself, the degree of degeneration was considerable. To the pathologist this, too, was a major clue as to what caused Tim's death.

Another area that troubled Holloway was Tim's esophagus, the tube that runs between the mouth and the stomach. When he cut into Tim's food and drink pipeline, he found what he identified as a *mass of inflammatory debris lodged in a wedgelike configuration into a cleft of otherwise unremarkable mucosa.* Clearly, it was material that was not supposed to be there.

Summing up his microscopic studies, Holloway noted that Tim had suffered from a long-standing inflammation of that section of the esophagus just above the stomach; a serious accumulation of fluid in his lungs, namely blood; massive enlargement of the liver, and a dangerous degeneration of that organ.

He was aware, Holloway noted, that Tim had been brutally beaten not long before his death. However, he felt that the attack had nothing to do with what happened. *There was no evidence from gross and microscopic findings of any residua of blunt trauma.* Rather, he opined,

Tim died from a combination of natural occurrences. Tim had been so overweight and his liver was so enlarged, Holloway concluded, that his diaphragm had been pushed upward. In the best of times, this would have made Tim significantly short-winded; there probably were times when he was fairly gasping for breath. Then, when Tim's lungs became congested, it put unexpected strain on his heart—an intolerable strain, it seemed. A fatal strain. Holloway determined that, taken all together, these conditions were more than Tim's body could stand. His heart simply stopped beating.

His official ruling, issued on May 20, reflected that conviction. In the space on the form for "Cause of Death," Holloway filled in: *Acute myocardial insufficiency with pulmonary edema.* The next line, the one that said "Due to," Holloway typed: *Massive fatty metamorphosis of [the] liver.* And in the third blank, the one set aside for "Other Conditions," the pathologist added: *Exogenous obesity.*

In Holloway's expert opinion, Tim's death was unfortunate but perfectly explainable, perfectly natural. The causes, in fact, were so apparent to the pathologist that he did not bother to order the toxicological tests that normally round out a complete autopsy. He had not seen anything to give him reason to believe that Tim had been intoxicated either by drugs or alcohol. Whether the possibility of poison crossed his mind is not known. Still, in keeping with policy dictated by his boss, Dr. F. Warren Lovell, the Ventura County coroner, Holloway collected samples of Tim's fluids: a vial of his blood; a small amount of bile from his liver; some fluid from his kidneys, and slices from his major organs. He filed these away in the morgue's huge refrigerator, where they routinely would be kept for five years. He had no way of knowing it at the time, but the fact that he had saved the material would, many months later, prove invaluable.

Satisfied that he had performed a thorough post-mortem, Holloway pushed Tim Waters out of his mind and concentrated on his worries about his own future. For some time he had been unhappy in his job. The workload kept getting heavier, and new demands for increased paperwork were coming down daily from Lovell's office. He had been in Ventura County for five years, Holloway reminded himself, but it was time he considered going somewhere else.

Less than four months later, he submitted his resignation. By August he had taken a job as a contract pathologist in Kern County, which abutted Ventura County on the north. Tim Waters quickly slipped into his past; it would be years before he would give him a second thought.

13

David apparently did not give much thought to Tim Waters, either, although he did mention him to several people at various times. Soon after Tim was beaten in February, Richard Gray was at Lamb Funeral Home to deliver several bodies for the retorts when he ran into David in the parking lot. He brought up the attack. To his surprise, David's response was unnecessarily abrupt. "It seems to me he got what he deserved," David said. "Maybe now he'll keep his mouth shut."

What David said about Tim to Dave Edwards, according to Edwards, was considerably more significant. And more chilling.

A number of weeks after Edwards and Augustine lied to David about beating Tim, Edwards was talking on the phone to his boss when David casually mentioned that the "fat guy" had died.

At first Edwards was not sure who David was talking about. "What do you mean?" he asked.

"He had a heart attack," David said, then added cryptically, "but he had a little help."

It clicked. Edwards realized David was talking about Tim Waters. Although he pressed for more details, David refused to say more about it. All he would add, Edwards recalled later, was that he—David—had gotten Tim away from "the table" and "slipped something" into his glass of water. He did not explain what table, why he was sharing it with Tim, or what he had "slipped" into his glass.

At the time, Edwards wrote it off as typical David braggadocio, not unusual for David, who liked to talk tough. Nevertheless, when he connected it with some other things David had said, it began to trouble him.

Earlier in the year, after the fictitious attack by Edwards and Augustine on Tim, and after David had mentioned to Edwards that he might like him to "take care" of a "guy in Glendora," David told Edwards that he was interested in having his grandfather, Lawrence Lamb, killed.

Edwards kept silent, not sure that David was serious. But when David brought up his grandfather again not long afterward, Edwards felt certain that he was not joking. The second time David raised the subject, he said he would like to find a poison he could use to get rid of him.

Still later he mentioned to Edwards that he was angry at another of his neighbors. This one, David explained, owned a dog that had attacked one of his cats. "I'd like to find a poison to get rid of that dog," he told Edwards. "Do you have any ideas?"

Edwards thought a minute. He didn't know anything about poisons, he said, but he had a book that might offer some insight. He said the book, *The Poor Man's James Bond*, contained information about a variety of subjects, such as how to make a silencer for a handgun and how to build a bomb. He was pretty sure it had a section on poisons as well.

In fact, it did. The book, authored by former Angelino Kurt Saxon, devoted several paragraphs to "Plant Poisons," specifically listing rhubarb, castor beans, oleander, poinsettia, yew, and laurel. "Plant poisons are very easy to administer and are hard to trace," Saxon wrote. "A few leaves in the salad aren't noticed, and the victim dies without knowing why."

Edwards promised David he would bring him the book. He kept his promise and delivered it to David. But he never got it back.

Although some of David's references to Edwards about various people he considered to be enemies were vague, he was more forthright in conversations with Danny Galambos.

Not long after Galambos and Chris Long had beaten Tim, David approached the weightlifter again, with a request to beat up a man named Frank Strunk. Strunk owned a business called the Cremation Society of California, another rival cremation service. Although he was the father of one of David's employees, Stephen Strunk, the elder Strunk evidently had worked his way onto David's hit list because he had refused to sell him his business. Apparently, by David's reasoning, that made him eligible to be "done."

Galambos and Andre Augustine went to Strunk's offices on three different occasions. Each time, they waited in their car outside the building, hoping for a chance to catch him alone and work him over. In each instance, however, there were too many other people around for them to attack him and escape undetected. Eventually they gave up and reported to David that it was an impossible job.

During the period between the attacks on Hast, Nimz, and Waters, and the planned assault on Strunk, David and Galambos continued to see each other at the Kings games, and David continued to bring Galambos up to date on his activities and plans.

One night when David was in a particularly bad mood, he complained bitterly about his grandfather, Lawrence Lamb. The old man was giving both him and his mother a lot of trouble, David confided, and he was thinking about getting rid of him. He decided to take a direct method: He planned to poison his grandparents' jug of mineral water. It was, in essence, the same scenario he outlined for George Bristol.

Galambos, who knew David fairly well by then, figured David was just shooting off his mouth again. Then David leaned closer. Getting very serious, he asked quietly: "Would you be willing to kill someone?"

Galambos stared at him for a long time. "No!" he said firmly.

After that, David did not mention his grandparents again to Galambos. But one night he had other news.

"Remember the guy you 'did'?" David asked. "The fat guy?"

"Sure," Galambos replied.

"Well, he died," David said.

"Oh, yeah," Galambos said, surprised.

"Yeah," David said. "It was a coronary."

"Oh," answered Galambos, not sure how to respond.

"But it wasn't really a coronary," David added.

Galambos waited.

"Actually, I poisoned him," David added. "I took him to a restaurant and I got him away from the table and I slipped some poison in his drink."

"Is that right?" Galambos said, not believing a word of what he was hearing.

"That's right," David said. Then he changed the subject.

David's separate conversations with Edwards and Galambos about his grandparents and Tim Waters occurred in the late spring or early summer of 1985. After that, David said no more to Galambos or Edwards, but he had similar conversations with others. There was, for in-

stance, George Bristol, to whom David confided early in
1986 about planning to kill his grandparents. Plus, there
were two other curious incidents at roughly the same
time.

One of them occurred in the summer of 1985, only a
few months after Tim Waters died, and it indirectly involved the Strunks.

Steve Strunk was already working for David when
David hired Steve's brother-in-law, Ron Jordan. After a
few months Jordan apparently decided he had no stomach
for the job at the crematorium. He was particularly disturbed by the multiple cremations, the mixing of remains,
the yanking of gold-filled teeth, so much so that he decided to quit. But more than that, he told his brother-in-
law that he was wrestling with his conscience about
whether he should report these obviously illegal activities
to the authorities. On one hand, he told Steve Strunk, he
knew he should. But on the other hand, he had great
qualms about becoming a stool pigeon. He told his
brother-in-law he was going to think about it some more.
Jordan had just finished fixing up an old boat and was
going to take it on a shakedown voyage down the coast. By
the time he got back, and had the time and solitude to
think the problem through, he expected to have made a
decision about reporting David's activities. Then he said
something very strange. If anything happens to me, he
said, "it will be David's fault."

Strunk shrugged off the comments. But just hours after
the conversation, Jordan was found dead in his apartment
in Newport Beach. He was on his knees and a rope ran
from his neck to a pull-up bar he had installed in a closet.
Orange County officials ruled the death a suicide. There
was no note, but authorities deduced that he died while
performing an autoerotic act. Allegedly, he had been mas-
turbating while cutting off his own air supply, a method
claimed by some to heighten the sexual experience. His

body was buried soon afterward without any toxicology tests being performed. Although Jordan's name would come up several times later, investigators were never able to develop any evidence of wrongdoing. It was, nevertheless, a peculiar circumstance which, for awhile, had investigators running down blind alleys trying unsuccessfully to find evidence of murder. But they could hardly afford not to, given the bad things that happened to other people who crossed David.

The second incident involved three other funeral home employees—John Pollerana, Bob Garcia, and Brad Sallard—and a man named Elie Estephan. Pollerana and Garcia were long-time employees of David's, and Sallard was the brother of David's second wife, Barbara, whom David had married in 1984 when she was twenty-six and David was twenty-eight. A shy, dark-haired woman, Barbara was working as the supervisor of the interior design department at a branch of a major West Coast department store when she and David met. David quickly established strong ties with the entire Sallard family, putting his brother-in-law on the payroll and naming the Hesperia operation after his father-in-law.

Estephan, an Arab-American gas station owner, became part of the narrative in a complicated and interesting way. He was married to Frank Strunk's daughter, Cindy. After rejecting David's offer to buy his business, Strunk sold the cremation service to Estephan. This, however, did not deter David from continuing to try to get hold of the operation. It led to the development of a convoluted plan which David hoped would get him the business and make his brother-in-law, Sallard, rich in the process.

After he took over the cremation service, Estephan and Cindy began having marital problems, so they separated.

Soon after that, David introduced Sallard to Cindy. They hit it off immediately and began dating.

In June 1985, Estephan and Cindy decided to divorce. Realizing that Cindy would need a lawyer, David offered the services of the attorney who handled routine matters for the funeral home. To help facilitate the new relationship, David accompanied Cindy to her first meeting, and sat in on the session. When the attorney asked Cindy what assets she and her husband had, Cindy mentioned a $250,000 policy on Estephan's life. She was listed as beneficiary.

Soon after that, David was in the Estephan cremation service office when Estephan and Cindy got into a loud argument. Screaming at her soon-to-be-divorced husband, Cindy tried to run from the room. Estephan grabbed her and pushed her down a short flight of stairs. She was angry but unhurt.

The next day, David pulled his worker, John Pollerana, aside. Pollerana had also been in Estephan's office when the argument broke out and had witnessed the incident in which Estephan pushed Cindy. "If I give you ten thousand dollars, will you get rid of Elie?" David asked him.

Pollerana shook his head.

Two weeks later Pollerana was chatting with another worker, Bob Garcia, when Garcia mentioned that David had offered *him* $10,000 to kill Estephan.

Pollerana was surprised. "David offered me the same thing," Pollerana said, "but I told him I wouldn't do it."

Garcia, however, was more amenable. Garcia told David that he would either find someone to do it or he would do it himself.

In the meantime, Cindy and Sallard had moved in together and gave every indication that the relationship was getting serious.

Remembering what Cindy had said about the life insurance policy on Estephan, David began formulating a two-pronged plan which revolved around Estephan being murdered.

Once Estephan had been killed, David planned to arrange for another of his employees, Jim Dame, to buy the Estephan nee Frank Strunk cremation service. Ostensibly, Dame would be the owner but the purchase money would come from David, who would call the shots. The advantage of having the service in Dame's name would be that David would then own *two* cremation services, while the fact that the second business was in someone else's name meant that he could also service clients who, for one reason or another, did not want to do business with the Sconces. He would, in effect, be working both sides of the street.

The second part of the plan had to do with the insurance money. When the company paid off on Estephan's death, the money would go to Cindy, who was living with Sallard, and she would presumably share her wealth with her lover.

Although Garcia had expressed a willingness to accept David's offer, he said he wanted to enlist some help. With David's blessing—and an updated promise of $15,000—Garcia approached an old acquaintance from his days on the street, an ex-convict named Herbert Dutton. Together they began plotting to kill Estephan. One way to do the job, Garcia suggested, was to blow him up in his car. Another was for Garcia and Dutton to ambush Estephan on the freeway and shoot him. In the end they settled on the car-bomb plan.

To make sure Garcia could identify Estephan and therefore kill the right man, David took Garcia to a fast-food restaurant across the street from Estephan's gas station, where they took turns watching the potential victim through a pair of binoculars. Frank Strunk, Estephan's soon-to-be-former father-in-law saw David and Garcia and confronted David.

"What are you looking at?" he demanded to know.

"Just the gas station," David replied.

For the next three weeks—almost daily, Garcia said— David would sidle up to him and ask him the same question: "Is he still walking?"

"Don't worry," Garcia always answered, "we'll take care of it."

However, word about the incident with the binoculars had gotten back to Cindy, who insisted that Sallard tell her what was going on. Not satisfied with his reply, Cindy told her lover that she feared for her life and was moving out. As she left, Sallard warned her not to tell anyone what she had heard because no one would believe her anyway. If she insisted and tried to repeat the tale, Sallard said, she had better "watch her back." Sallard did not want to see her endanger herself.

Disappointed with the abrupt end to Sallard's and Cindy's romance, and perhaps unhappy with Garcia's apparent procrastination, David withdrew his offer. "Forget about it," he told Garcia abruptly. "Disregard doing it."

Eventually David would be called to answer for the various incidents and alleged plots, but not for several years. In fact, it was not until mid-1987, two years after Tim Waters's death, that officials learned of David's alleged conversations with Edwards and Galambos about the dead cremation service owner. It would be another year after that before scientists could pinpoint what they thought was a poison in Tim's system, and six months after *that* before David would be charged with Tim's murder.

In the meantime everything seemed to be going David's way. The year 1985, in fact, proved to be an extremely good one for him. His cremation business boomed and he was deep into plans to move his operation statewide.

The next year, 1986, also started out well for David and his parents. That was the year they opened the tissue bank, and at first it looked as though it would be the moneymaker he had hoped.

One avenue that George Bristol had opened for David after he began working for the tissue bank was with a firm called Carolina Biological Supply. On one day alone, October 20, 1986, the CIE&TB shipped 24 brains, 24 hearts, and 20 lungs to the Burlington, North Carolina, company. Over a three-month period, CIE&TB sent the supply house a total of 136 brains, 145 hearts, 100 lungs, and one spinal column. In return, David received a check for $29,262.05. This did not include some two-dozen corneas David sold to various institutions for approximately $525 each.

But then things turned downhill. In the end, 1986 was not kind to David; his salad days were over. Despite the year's optimistic beginning, things quickly started to unravel. And once they began to go, they went fairly rapidly.

14

In making the decision to open the tissue bank, David's greed outstretched his ability to control. Up until then he had been able to keep the multiple cremations and the stealing of dental gold a moderately well-kept secret. Although an ATC form was required for every cadaver that he put in the retort, the document was treated routinely by just about everyone concerned. If anyone asked—and very few did—about the wording of the form, Laurieanne would glibly explain it away. But after he created the CIE&TB and started removing tissue and organs, the situation got dicier. At that point the forms David used for securing releases from next of kin began going through a marked evolution.

The forms basically consisted of two paragraphs of small print explaining what was involved when a cadaver was turned over to a crematorium for incineration. The important part of the form was the second paragraph, the one that dealt with tissue removal. (Organs were never mentioned, apparently because it was assumed that organs were composed of tissue, and if tissue removal was permitted, that applied to organs as well.)

In one of the soon-to-be-discarded versions of the form, there were several words in large type and in capital

letters. The document read: "The undersigned hereby requests & authorizes COASTAL CREMATION Inc. . . .
TO REMOVE TISSUE, REMOVE PACEMAKERS, cremate & to cause final disposition of the remains . . ."

In its next progression, the document used the same
wording, but the phrase about removing tissue and pacemakers was relegated to lowercase and assigned to the
same small type as the rest of the document.

In still another version, the wording was changed considerably. In that rendering, the phrases about removal of
tissue and pacemakers were separated and an entire sentence was devoted to tissue. It read: "The undersigned
does hereby make a donation of any or all of the usable
tissue [to] Coastal International Eye & Tissue Bank." The
operative word, of course, was "donation," which implied
that whoever signed the form was surrendering rights to
use of the tissue. It was a point that would prove extremely argumentative later when courts tried to determine whether there was any criminal liability.

While the wording of the form changed over the
months, the need for having *some kind* of form did not.
The forms *had* to be signed, and they were. Whether they
were signed by the persons whose name appeared on the
top of the document was another question. One such incident, for example, which later drew the attention of investigators, involved the death of a man named Frank
Holzkamper. He died in November 1986, and the conser-
vator of his estate, a woman named Carolyn Anderson
Scholl, asked that his body be cremated by Coastal Cremation. When Holzkamper's name later showed up on a
list of bodies from whom tissue had been donated, Scholl
protested. She denied ever signing a consent form. When
the form itself was examined, it showed that the handwriting on the bottom not only was not hers, but whoever had
signed it had misspelled Scholl's name. The signature
read S-c-h-*u*-l-l.

° ° °

Perhaps by this time, too, all three of the Sconces were beginning to feel pressure from the authorities. It had been a long time coming, but people other than their competitors were beginning to get suspicious. If anything, this was significantly overdue.

In retrospect there were several reasons why David was able to get away with the multiple cremations for so long. One had to do with state law, or rather, the lack of it. A plethora of statutes governing funeral homes existed, but since cremation had not been very popular until recently, crematoriums had escaped rigid regulation. To complicate the issue, the Cemetery Board, which was the agency responsible for crematoriums—probably because most crematoriums were located in cemeteries—had too few regulators. As a result, the ones they did have were terribly overworked.

For this reason, authorities may have been slow to recognize the early signs that everything was not as it should have been at Lamb Funeral Home.

Within two years of taking over the cremation service, David was reporting more cremations than any other facility in the state. By the time his numbers topped 8000 a year—about four times the number of any other crematorium—authorities began getting suspicious. They should have. By looking a little further, it was easy to determine that Pasadena Crematorium had only two retorts. Then, all it took was a calculator to conclude that it was impossible to cremate that many people with that equipment in that amount of time, provided the cremations were done properly.

By 1986, David, in fact, already *was* under investigation by the Cemetery Board. But when one of the agents tried to inspect the Altadena crematorium, he was turned away on grounds that he did not have the authority to make inspections. The action was legal; state law at the time did not give Cemetery Board employees authority to demand to examine a facility.

But the number of cremations was not the only early indicator that something unusual was going on.

In the spring of 1986 a reporter from the San Diego *Union*, Rex Dalton, was working on a series of stories dealing with the sale of body parts to the University of California at San Diego. While he was researching his material, he got a tip that there was a woman who might be able to provide additional details about the subject. Her name: Lisa Karlan.

Karlan met with Dalton and told him the same thing she later told an examiner from the Department of Health Services, Leigh Dusatko. She said she had been fired from David's CIE&TB because she was asking too many questions about the operation.

During the four months she worked there, she said, she saw workers remove almost two dozen whole eyes and box them for sale to UCLA, where they were to be used in research projects. There were at least two corneas removed as well, she said, and they were sold to the Huntington Memorial Hospital in Pasadena to be used as transplants.

Karlan added that she had seen the CIE&TB owner—David Sconce—remove gold-filled teeth from the mouths of cadavers. When enough had been collected to make a sale worthwhile, he took them to a gold dealer in Glendora, an old friend he dealt with regularly.

Particularly interesting to Dusatko were Karlan's tales about remains being mixed together in large drums and then doled out whenever such material was needed to be returned to a family.

In his report to his boss, Roderick D. Hamblin, chief of Laboratory Field Services for the DHS, Dusatko recommended the department look more closely at Karlan's accusations to see if criminal charges should be brought against David Sconce.

Ironically, the report was written on June 9, 1986, the same day that George Bristol formally applied for a permit to create the tissue bank. Despite Dusatko's report, the department approved Bristol's application less than a week later. Soon after that, on June 23 and again on July 2, state inspectors visited the CIE&TB site at Lamb Funeral Home and apparently found no evidence of wrongdoing.

About the same time, an investigator from the Pasadena Police Department, after talking to Karlan and Dusatko, tried to inspect Lamb Funeral Home, but, as with the Cemetery Board agent, he was turned away. The reason for refusing him entry was that he did not have a search warrant. Without sufficient cause to apply for such a document, he was forced to let the matter drop.

Pressure was building on another front as well. However, this time it did not involve David; it had to do with Laurieanne.

On August 13, 1986, an auditor from the state Board of Funeral Directors and Embalmers named Skip Jones made a routine examination of Lamb Funeral Home's books. He would not have been surprised to find a number of nonreportable trust accounts among the records, but he was definitely not prepared for what he actually discovered. As he flipped through the records, he was shocked to find 172 preneed accounts that had never been reported, an obvious violation of state law.

The accountant walked down the hall to Laurieanne's office, then spent the next ninety minutes with her going over state regulations and explaining why such accounts had to be recorded. He followed up the visit with a letter, which Laurieanne responded to on September 12. In an ingratiating mea culpa response, Laurieanne apologized for the errors and promised to "rectify" the situation. As one step toward a solution, she said, Lamb's was discontinuing its preneed policy. If any of her customers demanded preneed services, they could open their own accounts listing Lamb's as beneficiary, which would be virtually the same thing except Lamb's would not have access to the money until after the account holder died. To demonstrate her contrition for violating the law, Laurieanne also enclosed a check for $50 toward payment of the penalty for not reporting the accounts.

During his examination of the books, Jones also found that Laurieanne had not claimed what was allowed the funeral home under the law as a fee for administering the accounts. During their conference he pointed this out to her as well, explaining that she was shortchanging herself by not taking advantage of the permissible expense.

However, what he did *not* know, was the fee that she was extracting was much higher than that prescribed in the statutes. Auditors did not learn until much later that Laurieanne had been transferring actual interest from those accounts—rather than the relatively minuscule 2.5 percent allowed—to her own special account, and that the transferal was being done automatically every quarter. The amount that Laurieanne siphoned off eventually totalled $100,365, of which all but $15,365 was split up among the Sconces. Lamb Funeral Home—Jerry and Laurieanne—received $27,000 of the money. Their younger son, Gary, got $20,000. David got $4000 directly, plus another $34,000 which was listed as being paid to Coastal Cremation. The only nonfamily disbursement was to a firm called Cremation Equipment Service, which got $15,000 for supplies. The remaining $365 stayed in the account. There was no indication of any wrongdoing by Gary Sconce or Cremation Equipment Service in connection with the payments they received, plus David was never charged.

Except for one thing, Laurieanne may have been able to claim later that the transfers were done innocently, in her ignorance of the law. While that would not have removed her responsibility, she could have claimed it as a mitigating circumstance. But even after her long session with Jones in which he carefully explained the law, the transfers were not stopped. Between the day Jones made his initial examination and the time the auditors found the transactions, an additional $7500 was transferred from preneed accounts into Laurieanne's special account.

As if things were not bad enough, they soon got worse.

Back in October 1984, David had applied for permission to build his second crematorium near Shafter, outside Bakersfield, in the San Joaquin Valley. It was there that he planned to freight bodies from the San Francisco area for cremation.

In David's mind, that was to be the facility that would put him over the top; it was going to help him permanently secure his position as the crematorium king of California. But the one thing he had failed to figure into his plans was opposition in Shafter. The local citizens did not like the idea of a crematorium going up in their midst, and activists in the group scheduled a series of well-attended demonstrations protesting its construction. As a result, zoning authorities refused to grant David a variance, in effect telling him to take his retorts someplace else.

That's when David settled upon Hesperia. It also is when he decided, fearful of a repeat of what had happened in Kern County, to camouflage his actions by telling Hesperia authorities the tall tale about manufacturing tiles for the space shuttles. He was careful not to make any reference to a crematorium in the name of the proposed new facility, which he christened after his second wife's father, Oscar Sallard.

Why David did not take into consideration the fact that the cremations would cause a terrible stench is unknown. It may have been because all his cremations before had been performed in a proper crematorium—in retorts built specifically to cremate bodies. At Altadena, the retorts had been equipped with specially designed chimneys which kept the odor from being released into the air. But his retorts at Hesperia were homemade devices constructed from a design for industrial kilns, and were not equipped with the special crematorium chimneys. Of course, if they had been built as cremation retorts and equipped with crematorium chimneys, officials would have immediately become suspicious when they examined the facility to approve his permits. Also, when David built the facility in Hesperia, he probably did not intend to use it as much as he did. His original plans may have been to use Oscar's Ceramics only occasionally, keeping it as a safety valve to take care of the overflow from the Altadena facility until he could find a site for a Bay Area facility. But then he got sandbagged by two workers.

As John Hallinan would later testify, a little after midnight on November 23, 1986, John Hallinan and Bob Garcia, who were toiling on the bulldog shift at the Altadena crematorium, decided to get high on rock cocaine. About three A.M., feeling no pain, they decided to *really* load up the two retorts; to shatter once and for all the record for the number of bodies cremated at one time and set a new one that would never be broken. Sweating and shoving, laughing and cursing, they jammed thirty-eight bodies into the two ovens. In order to get the last one in, Hallinan had to snap its legs.

That broke the record, all right. It also broke David's back. Proud of their accomplishment, the two lit the gas furnace and staggered off to Garcia's house to smoke some more dope. But they had put so many bodies in the ovens that the cadavers blocked the chimney and the heat could not escape. As a result, the whole apparatus went up in flames. By the time the fire department arrived, both ovens had been destroyed. After that, David no longer had a choice about using the Hesperia facility. He would have to go full-blast there or close down operations altogether. He chose to go full-blast.

PART FOUR

The Road to Ventura

15

After the January 1987 raid on Oscar's Ceramics, the action that proved to be the beginning of David's downfall, it took investigators more than five hours to sort through the grisly material, to confirm what they initially suspected: an undetermined number of bodies had been incinerated in two industrial-sized pottery kilns doing duty as illegal crematorium retorts. Furthermore, they determined that the person apparently responsible for the operation was David Wayne Sconce of Pasadena.

That was the easy part; the hard part was deciding what they could do about the situation. Obviously, skulduggery was involved, but the law was not going to allow them to do much more than slap David on the wrist. While it was a felony in California to dismember a human corpse, performing multiple cremations was only a misdemeanor. So all the San Bernardino authorities could lean on David with was a collection of minor charges which, in the long run, meant virtually nothing. He could be back in business somewhere else in a week.

But if they felt cheated because his offenses were only misdemeanors, they could take some consolation in knowing that until 1984 what he had been doing was not illegal at all. The only reason they were even misdemeanors

then, in 1987, was because the public had become outraged over two blatant cases, neither of which involved
David.

The first case to spur public indignation involved the
Harbor Lawn–Mount Olive Mortuary and Memorial Park
in Costa Mesa, near San Diego. That case was eventually
settled after insurance companies agreed to set aside $14
million to compensate some 25,000 persons whose relatives or loved ones were cremated at the facility, most of
them allegedly in multiple cremations.

The second case did not even involve cremation directly, but rather what happened afterward. As cremation
had grown in popularity, it had led to an increased demand for "spreading." Rather than burying the remains or
keeping them in a vase at home, a number of relatives of
persons who had been cremated asked that the remains
be spread in scenic areas—into the harbors and bays, or
over the state's most majestic mountain range, the High
Sierras. Frequently, the requests were made by the deceased before he or she died.

Since funeral directors and cremation service operators
did not have sufficient staff to take care of such requests,
"spreaders" came into being. These "spreaders" periodi-
cally visited funeral homes and cremation services, picking up remains, which they then contracted to scatter at
specific locations. One such spreader was a pilot named
B. J. Elkin, who serviced close to a hundred funeral
homes and cremation services in the Bay Area. When Elkin was paid to scatter remains over the ocean or the bay,
he gassed up his light plane and flew off to do the job. But
when he had remains that were to be spread over the
Sierras, he seldom got beyond the foothills. Instead, he
loaded them in the trunk of his car and drove to the nine-
acre plot he owned in Amador County, where he dumped
them on the ground.

Other landowners finally complained so loudly that investigators were sent in to examine the claims. What they found were a number of piles of pulverized bone sitting on top of the ground like residue from a Boy Scout jamboree. Experts were called in to examine the debris, and they determined that the site contained remains of more than 5300 persons.

Relatives who had believed that what was left of their loved ones had been taken to the High Sierras subsequently filed suit seeking compensation for injuries they had suffered because of Elkin. The courts agreed with the plaintiffs, ruling that people—that is, relatives of the deceased—contracting with a funeral director or cremation service had a right to expect that their wishes would be carried out. The courts then ordered the payment of almost $53 million in damages to the relatives—$31 million to be paid by Elkin and the funeral directors, and the remaining $22 million to be paid by cremation service operators.

But neither of those cases, unlike the one involving David, involved potential criminal activity as well. When investigators examined the material at Oscar's Ceramics, they were revolted by what they found, but they also were disheartened when they realized that they could do very little to make David accountable. But from what they had seen, they felt sure that David's activities had gone beyond multiple cremations. If they dug deeply enough, they were certain they would be able to find evidence linking David to one or more felonies. The question was, how deeply did they have to dig?

On Thursday, January 29, 1987, nine days after the raid on Oscar's, deputies from San Bernardino County knocked on the door at Lamb Funeral Home. Since they were unaware of the depth of the operation in Pasadena —and since it was beyond their jurisdiction anyway, except as it pertained to what happened in San Bernardino

—they were looking mainly for documents that would shed more light on what had been going on in Hesperia.

As it happened, the search warrant included Jerry and Laurieanne's residence, which was above the funeral home. When they knocked on the door, Laurieanne met them with a Bible in her hands. And as they searched the apartment, she was one step behind them, reading loudly from scripture and condemning their intrusion.

Before they finished their search of the funeral home, they uncovered a cache of gold-filled teeth, which they correctly suspected could only have come from cadavers. That was what they had secretly been hoping to find: evidence of a possible felony. When the deputies left the funeral home a few minutes later, they took David and Jerry with them, in handcuffs. Father and son were taken to the Pasadena jail and booked for investigation of theft of the gold teeth. Although they were quickly released on $1500 bail, investigators felt their search had been a success.

But that was only the beginning.

On Wednesday, February 11, a force of thirty-five men representing the San Bernardino, Los Angeles, and Orange counties sheriffs' departments and the coroners' offices from San Bernardino and Orange counties—which was involved because documents recovered in Hesperia hinted that one of the cremated cadavers may have come from an Orange County community—showed up with warrants at four locations where they suspected additional evidence might be found: Lamb Funeral Home; a building in Santa Fe Springs that was used as a headquarters for the CIE&TB; an address that turned out to be only a CIE&TB mail drop; and the residence of Lawrence Lamb. However, the officers turned up little of value on that sweep. No new charges were filed.

But by then the Sconces had begun to fight back. The first thing they did after David's and Jerry's arrests was hire a high-powered attorney, a well-known lawyer from Pacific Palisades named Roger Diamond, who specialized in handling cases for porn shop operators and environmentalist groups.

Diamond began earning his money by calling a news conference and bitterly denouncing law enforcement authorities and reporters. Branding the searches "Gestapo tactics" and an "outrage," the lawyer angrily labeled reporters "vultures," and accused them as well as the investigators of harassing "innocent people."

Despite Diamond's protestations, the case against the three began to build. A week later auditors sent in to examine the funeral home books discovered how Laurieanne had manipulated the transfer of $100,000-plus in interest money to her special account.

Other leads turned up as well. Gradually, tediously, investigators filled their notebooks. As the net widened, it became obvious that the case was too big, too widespread, to be handled in San Bernardino County, especially when it looked as though the center of activity was in Los Angeles County. This realization was the impetus for a meeting in the Pasadena courthouse, a meeting that brought together the various persons involved in the case up to them. It also brought in one totally new participant, a prosecutor named Walt Lewis.

At first he had no idea what was going on. Walt Lewis, in fact, initially feared he was getting slaphappy. From every direction names and facts were being bounced off him, until he felt like the backboard at a Lakers warmup session.

". . . Clear evidence of multiple cremations . . . Galambos . . . Jim Dame . . . a cup full of gold teeth . . . Ron Hast . . . skimming . . . preneed accounts . . . Steve Nimz . . . Jerry . . . mining body parts

. . . "Mom" . . . Dave Edwards . . . bodies stacked like cordwood . . . barrels of human remains . . ."

He listened and his confusion grew; his head was whirling. Oh Lord, he asked himself, what did I do to get into this?

Seated around a table in the law library on the ground floor of the Pasadena courthouse were almost a dozen men, men whose names had been as unfamiliar to Lewis a few minutes earlier as those then being tossed around the room. He glanced again at the sign-in sheet that had circled the room and ended up in his hands. Who *were* these people? Lewis asked himself.

Concentrating on the organizations they represented rather than their names, he ran down the list one more time. Present, he noted, were delegates from the sheriffs' offices and the coroners' offices in both Orange and San Bernardino counties. Someone from the San Bernardino County Department of Environmental Health Services was there, too, as was someone from the state department of consumer affairs. At one end of the long, polished wood table was a man from the fire department in Hesperia, although Lewis was not sure exactly where Hesperia was. At the other end was someone from the San Bernardino Air Pollution Control District. Somewhere in the group was an auditor from the state Cemetery Board, and somewhere else was a detective from the Pasadena P.D.

In spite of his initial bewilderment, Lewis felt a strong surge of professional excitement. For a man who thought he had seen everything in his nineteen years as a prosecutor with the Los Angeles County District Attorney's office, he instinctively knew that what was unfolding in front of him was a one-of-a-kind situation, a case so grotesque that Stephen King—much less Walter Lewis, deputy district attorney—could not have dreamed it up on his most imaginative day.

A slight, unassuming man with graying hair, a soft

voice, and large, sad, blue eyes, Lewis had been totally unprepared for what he had innocently walked into. An hour earlier on that morning in mid-March, 1987, he had been slouching peacefully in his second-floor office, the comparatively commodious sanctuary of the assistant head deputy of the Pasadena branch of the L.A. D.A.'s office. Almost dozing, Lewis had been distractedly disposing of a stack of dull documents when, unexpectedly, his boss, Beverly Campbell, stuck her head in the door.

"What are you working on?" she asked pleasantly.

"Not much," he had replied, thankful she had not caught him in a yawn. "Just cleaning up some paperwork."

When he said that, Campbell smiled enigmatically. Lewis would never forget that. Nor would he ever forget what she said next. "There's a bunch of people in the library," she commented wryly, "Why don't you go see what they want?"

What they wanted, he quickly learned, was direction. For the last six weeks the men gathered around the table had been trying to unravel a convoluted case that dealt with a series of exotic crimes uncovered as a result of a search of a manufacturing facility in Hesperia, which, Lewis subsequently ascertained, was across the mountains in San Bernardino County.

However, Oscar's was not, as originally suspected, the beginning and the end of the operation. It had become increasingly apparent to investigators as they went along that Oscar's was only a newly-grown tentacle on a monster whose den was not in San Bernardino County at all. Rather, its trail led outward from San Bernardino County to all points of the compass. Clearly, the scope of the scheme carried it beyond the capabilities of local officials. That was why those dozen men were there. They wanted to know what charges should be filed and who had jurisdiction. They were urging that the investigation be passed on to an organization with a much longer arm, perhaps the attorney general's office, which could operate throughout the state. Failing that, it should at least be assumed by the L.A. D.A.'s office, since it looked as though the operation was headquartered in that county, specifically in Pasadena. For that reason it seemed logical to brief the local district attorney. That was where Lewis came in.

As he listened in growing astonishment to the discussion flowing around him, Lewis was both fascinated and revolted. Over the years, he had dealt with just about every variety of depraved human there was, every kind of deviant that could be produced in a sprawling metropolis like Los Angeles, from child molesters to psychopathic killers. During his career he had tried uncounted rapists, thieves, and murderers. And he had done it in an efficient, businesslike manner.

After being exposed to criminals and their crimes for an extended period, the individual incidents ceased to make a major personal impact: Lewis could deal with a brutal killer and the crime as objectively as a postal clerk could sort the mail. Naively—although he would, by most standards, be considered anything but naive—he thought that he would never again be shocked at learning about the depths to which some people could sink. But he was wrong. Never before had he been exposed to allegations as abhorrent as the ones being leveled in the law library. But as nauseating as the details were, Lewis found himself unaccountably propelled by a compulsion to root out the entire intrigue; to find the source of the mutant growth and expose it to the sunlight.

Looking back many months later, Lewis was not sure that if he had been given a choice, he would have become involved. True enough, in the L.A. D.A.'s office options were a rarity: the DDA's played with the cards that were dealt them. And Lewis had been chosen, no matter how haphazardly, for the assignment. But as assistant head deputy, he could have passed the file along. Traditionally, the chief aide's role is that of a paper shuffler. By taking the job, the assistant agrees to an unwritten rule to put aside courtroom ambitions. But the more Lewis heard about the case, the more hooked he became. Before he left the law library that afternoon, he had decided to insist upon being allowed to prosecute, a position he partially justified to himself by claiming that it was his *responsibility* to follow through. Truth be told, once he heard the outline, he knew that as a career prosecutor he could no more have turned down the opportunity to pursue this strange case than a fireman could refuse to respond to an alarm.

Never before, at least not since he shed the idealism of the young lawyer, had Lewis become personally involved in a case as he would in the following months. His decision to prosecute would prove a fateful one, one that would come back to haunt him in a very literal sense.

In the long run his determination would prove both a blessing and a curse. His prosecution would be diligent; too diligent, in fact, for his own physical and psychological good. But his investigation also would be exhaustive, carrying him and a score of others down paths none of them could possibly have foreseen, leading to difficulties none of them could have anticipated. The results would be traumatic and long-lasting. Before his involvement was complete, lives, including his own, would be irrevocably changed; the case would impact upon the DDA as no other case had ever done, and probably as no other case ever would.

Also in the room that day, sitting quietly off to one side, was a dark-skinned, rather fierce-looking man with chiseled features and straight black hair, a visual descendant of Geronimo or some other Apache chief. His name was Dennis Diaz and he was a Pasadena police detective. At the time, he was thirty-nine years old and a veteran of eighteen years with the department, a man who had seen life from both sides of the squad-room railing.

He had begun his career as a patrolman and worked in uniform for thirteen years before transferring to the detective division. For four years, from 1982 to 1986, he had answered assault and homicide calls, then he went back into uniform for a year before returning to the detective division. He had only been back in plainclothes for a few weeks when the Sconce case broke. As the newest man in the division, he did not yet have a permanent assignment when the case started developing, so he found himself tagging along as the official Pasadena P.D. observer to the investigators from the other counties.

As Diaz listened, following the debate as avidly as Lewis, his dark eyes darting from one speaker to the next, it became increasingly evident that the case was going to be dropped in his lap, his and Lewis's. It took the others less than an hour to come to the same conclusion. Everything they had collected, they decided, was going to be handed over to the Pasadena authorities.

Despite the material that had already been gathered, the case at that stage was little more than an outline. Except for the charges resulting from the discovery of the gold-filled teeth, the only formal accusations against David were the ones that existed from the first three misdemeanors—performing multiple cremations, co-mingling of remains, and the harvesting of body parts without permission—and one felony, for polluting the air. Jerry was still charged with theft, and he and Laurieanne faced embezzlement counts. But that was pitifully thin material on which to base a case that obviously involved much more. Diaz sighed; he would have to begin at the beginning if he was going to build a file that would result in prison sentences for the Sconces.

The detective need not have worried. As he began working his sources, he found a surfeit of people willing to talk, especially about David. An important witness interviewed early on was former employee Jim Dame, who— apparently fearful that he was going to be dragged into the mud—contacted investigators and offered to tell what he knew in return for an informal assurance he would not be prosecuted. Over the course of several interviews, Dame divulged details about the funeral home operation and pointed Diaz to Steve Strunk.

Strunk told Diaz he thought David had paid to have several competitors beaten up, but he could not remember the names of the victims. A few days later, however, he telephoned the detective saying the names of the victims had come back to him. They were Ron Hast, Stephen Nimz, and Tim Waters. The men who administered the beatings, he said, were Dave Edwards and Danny Galambos.

Armed with pictures of Edwards and Galambos, Diaz went to see Hast and Nimz. The funeral home director and his friend gasped when the detective flashed the photographs. That's them, they said immediately, those were two of the three men who beat them up. From there it was not difficult for Diaz to uncover the third man, Andre Augustine.

Diaz, however, was frustrated when he tried to track down Tim Waters. When he was told that Waters was dead, his interest soared. Then it dipped when he read Dr. Holloway's autopsy report and saw where the pathologist had ruled that Tim's death had been a natural one. Shrugging, Diaz moved on to the assault of the late cremation service owner. And that was when the prosecution got really lucky.

Since Diaz did not have the authority to fully investigate Tim's beating, because it had occurred in Burbank and out of his jurisdiction, Walt Lewis got on the telephone.

When the DDA checked with Burbank P.D., he had unbelievable good fortune. Officers summoned to investigate the attack on Waters more than two years previously had found an empty milk carton on the sidewalk outside Tim's office. On the chance that it might someday be useful, they filed it away in the evidence room. Keeping his fingers crossed, Lewis asked that the carton be dusted for fingerprints. When the results came back, Lewis and Diaz broke into huge grins: the prints were those of Danny Galambos.

From that point on, events began to snowball. By May, Diaz was confident he had enough evidence to build strong cases against all three Sconces. He was whistling when he trotted the bulging file across the street to Walt Lewis's office.

16

David and his parents, it seemed, had made a lot of enemies over the years, many of whom had apparently just been waiting for a chance to tell what they knew about the Sconces. Lewis and Diaz were determined to give them that chance. But what was really amazing to the prosecutor was that every time one of them came forward with a tale to tell, that particular story was more grotesque than the one that preceded it. It seemed to Lewis as if he were diving into a bottomless pit of slime.

The situation was so complex, it would take Lewis several months to fully comprehend the scope of the Sconces' activity. Even then it continued to evolve, with new accusations invariably surfacing, frequently on a daily basis. By late May 1987, as the date for the Sconces' arraignment drew steadily nearer, the list of charges against Jerry, Laurieanne, and David resembled an Amtrak timetable; when he walked into the courtroom to present his case, Lewis had a roster of forty-one charges. In the following weeks, even as he argued for the right to bring them to trial, the list continued to grow as Diaz uncovered still more information. Before he was finished, Lewis amended the charge list three times and the total number of counts grew to sixty-eight.

For the DDA the circumstances were extremely nerve-wracking. Preparing for trial was one thing, but trying to get ready when the charge list continuously shifted was quite another. Despite his long experience, Lewis had never before handled such an unstable case. "I felt like I was on a bucking bronc and I couldn't get off," he said later.

To complicate the situation even more, Lewis was under a tight deadline. If he failed to get some of the charges on the record before mid-June, he stood to lose some of the misdemeanor counts because the period for filing would elapse.

As Lewis worked frantically to put together the list of charges resulting from the operation of the funeral home and the crematorium so it would be in a format that would withstand courtroom scrutiny, Diaz and D.A. Investigator Gerald Loeb, who had been assigned to help in the case, simultaneously were trying to zero in on the charges that had to do with activity away from the funeral home, such as David's alleged involvement in the attacks against Hast, Nimz, and Waters. At that time, the possibility that Waters had been murdered was a tantalizing but elusive suggestion, one that was crippled by lack of proof that his death had actually been a homicide, since the autopsy report had clearly spelled out death by natural causes. Diaz felt that he and Loeb stood a much better chance of building a substantial case against David on the beatings than they did of tying him into a death that may or may not have been a murder. But even on the beatings, the detectives lacked one important component: David's own version of events.

Balancing the desire to question him about the accusations were other factors that made them hesitant about approaching him directly. For one thing, they were reluctant to tip their hands. Though confident that the accusations were valid and eventually could be proved, they knew that David was not yet aware that they were investigating him for assault. There also was the question of his physical absence. If he had been in Pasadena, where the investigators could keep an eye on him, they might not have vacillated about arresting him so they could grill him about the attacks. Unfortunately for them, however, he was safely out of their grasp. Soon after he and his father were charged and released, David had taken his wife and children to Bullhead City, Arizona, just across the California state line. By June, not only was he some 200 miles away, but he was in another state, and that could present serious jurisdictional problems in attempts to get him to court in Los Angeles County.

Lewis and the investigators agreed that the less David knew about the case they were building against him, the better would be their chance of bringing him to trial. Also, they knew that in a matter of days David was going to have to return to Pasadena to plead to the funeral home charges, and until then they did not want to spook him with talk about the assaults. Still, the temptation to discover how he might react to the accusations was great. So they settled for the next best thing to questioning him themselves: they had someone else ask him while they listened in.

After Galambos, Augustine, and Edwards were confronted with the evidence against them in the beatings of Hast, Nimz, and Waters, they decided, in a rush to save their own skins, to offer their services to the prosecution, hoping the effort would be remembered when their cases came to court.

Galambos, in his haste to be helpful, had spilled to Lewis the essence of the conversation in which David allegedly admitted that he had murdered Tim Waters. Edwards subsequently substantiated Galambos's claims to a large degree by saying that David had made similar remarks to him. But at the time investigators were trying to put their case together, it was all very vague. What the investigators needed most at that stage was something from David—virtually anything—that would show how he might react to accusations that he had engineered three assaults and, not incidentally, a possible murder.

Diaz and Loeb devised a plan. Since David had been relatively close to Edwards, the investigators decided to ask Edwards to telephone David and feel him out about these aspects of the case. Edwards was in a bind; he could hardly refuse. On June 5, three days before David was scheduled to appear in court in Pasadena to be arraigned, Edwards called him in Arizona using a telephone equipped with a tape recorder. At his shoulder was Loeb.

"Hello," Edwards said nervously once David was on the line.

"Dave?" David responded, surprised because he had not heard from Edwards since he quit his job at Coastal Cremation late in 1986, before the incident at Oscar's Ceramics. "How are you doing?"

"Not too bad," Edwards replied.

"I was going to say," David told his black friend, "that I hadn't heard from you in a coon's age, but that would be tactless."

Edwards, apparently not amused, tried to explain why he had called.

David's guard went up. When Edwards did not react as he expected to his attempt at humor, he suspected that his friend may have been talking on a tapped line. "How's stuff over the phone these days?" he asked, giving Edwards the opportunity to signal him if he knew the call was bugged.

"I'm not real sure," Edwards answered slowly.

That was enough for David. "Speak hypothetically," he instructed.

Ignoring the order, Edwards got straight to the point.

He and Galambos had been fingered for the attack on Hast and Nimz, he said, and Galambos was cooperating with the authorities. "Danny said yes to everything," Edwards explained.

"Well, it doesn't matter," David answered calmly. "He could be saying that to save his ass."

"Of course he is," Edwards answered somewhat indignantly.

"You know," David replied, "it comes right down to it, it's your word against Danny's."

But that wasn't the worst of it, Edwards pointed out. "They asked him about Burbank," he said, indicating to David that Galambos also was being questioned about the beating of Tim Waters.

"Oh, big deal," David replied.

Edwards was not sure that David understood. "The big guy," he added.

"Yeah," David assured him. "That's okay."

Edwards still was not sure that David had grasped the implications of what he was trying to say. "That's okay?" he asked incredulously. "The guy's gone!"

"Yeah, he's history," David agreed calmly. "But see, now I heard that [a third person] was telling a bunch of people about three weeks ago at the Cemetery Board meeting that he knows it was me that had him beat up."

"Yeah," prompted Edwards.

"Okay? So big deal," David said. "I mean, I don't care who would say that. They're going to have to prove it."

"Yeah," Edwards repeated, hoping to draw more out of his former employer.

"Even if Galambos said, 'Yeah, he did it; he paid me,' I'll say, 'Okay, well, you know, I didn't. I don't know why he's saying that.' "

Edwards, convinced that David still was not getting the point, made it plainer. "What we're afraid of," he added, "what Danny's afraid of, and what I'm afraid of, is that they might try to say that he had something to do with him kicking off."

"No!" David replied more urgently, the light apparently dawning. "Uh-uh. Uh-uh. He didn't! Waters was a paranoiac from a long time ago."

Startled by David's reaction, Edwards let the conversation drift to a discussion about David's lawyer. But then he maneuvered it back to Tim Waters.

"I know Danny's going to say something about the thing in Burbank," he said. "What if they try to say that he had something to do with that, with him kicking off."

"Well, you weren't around with that," David replied, seemingly clearing Edwards while confirming, however imprecisely, that he had information about Tim's death.

Edwards sighed inwardly and shot an I-told-you-so glance at Loeb. "I know that," he said hastily into the telephone, "but knowing Danny, he's going to say you had something to do with that."

David's caution returned; he wanted to get off the subject entirely. "No!" he told Edwards. "Big deal if he says [that]. I didn't, you know. They can't prove I did, because I didn't. So I don't care."

Edwards looked at Loeb and shrugged. The gesture said he believed that he wasn't going to be able to get David to say any more. Loeb nodded in agreement.

Edwards and David made small talk for a few more minutes, then David broke it off. "Give me a call if you want to talk," he said affably.

Although David had not admitted anything directly in the conversation, Lewis became very excited when he read the transcript, especially when he got to the place where David had said, "Well, you weren't around with that," referring to Tim's death.

From that point on Lewis was convinced that David

A FAMILY BUSINESS

was not only a creep who would steal teeth from the bodies of dead people, but also was a vicious thug who would have people beaten up and maybe killed for no reason stronger than they posed a threat to his illegal activities. The DDA was convinced that David belonged in jail, and he was going to do what he could to make sure that's where he was going to be.

Earlier, Lewis had talked briefly with Roger Diamond, the Sconces' attorney. When Diamond asked Lewis what kind of bail the prosecutor would seek if he talked his clients into surrendering, Lewis thought a moment and said he would be happy with $5000 each. But that had been before he read the transcript and listened to the tape of David's telephone conversation with Edwards. That put the situation in an entirely new light.

As he sat listening to David matter-of-factly discuss how he was going to lie about vicious assaults on innocent people, Lewis's sense of revulsion grew. Up until that time he had not understood exactly how dangerous David could be, but after playing the tape, he decided that David was *very* dangerous indeed; too dangerous to be walking the street.

There was another thing to consider as well, Lewis reminded himself: David's move to Arizona. If David were released on bail, Lewis could not be sure that California would ever get him back. In fact, he recalled, snapping his fingers, David had even mentioned something to that effect when he was talking to Edwards. Flipping through the transcript, Lewis found the passage:

D.S.: *You just take care of yourself.*
D.E.: *Yeah, you too.*
D.S.: *Yeah, well I'm out here in Arizona. You know, if they want to come chasing me down across state lines for some kind of misdemeanor thing, that's their business.*

Lewis tossed the papers aside. David was saying that if the authorities wanted him, they were going to have to come get him. The possibility that he might bolt was too big a risk for the DDA to take. If he ever got David in his grasp, did he want him slipping out?

On June 8, Lewis took his seat at the prosecutor's table, still debating inwardly about what he should do when it came time to ask for David's bail. He had told Diamond he would request only $5000 each for David, Jerry, and Laurieanne. But that was before he knew the whole story. He could live with $5000 for the parents, Lewis told himself, but David was another matter. As he pondered these issues, deep in thought, Lewis was startled by a voice whispering in his ear. Spinning around, he saw that David had slipped onto a bench behind the prosecution table and was trying to make conversation with him. Lewis was too shocked to do anything but gape. In his years in the courtroom, he had never been approached before arraignment by a person he was getting ready to charge; it was a virtually unheard-of situation. Normally, a person accused of a crime will sit on the opposite side of the courtroom in an effort to maintain as much distance as possible from the prosecutor. Usually they are only too content to let their lawyer do the talking.

"This is all a mistake," David said softly, flashing a quick grin. But only his lips were smiling; his eyes were icy cold. "This whole thing is crazy," he said. "Just give me a chance and I can explain it all."

Lewis's mind was a blank, numbed by David's audacity. When he recovered his wits, the DDA's mind was made up. If he had previously waffled about the bail request, David's action had taken him off the fence. If he could possibly do anything about it, he decided, he was going to see that David did not go free at the end of the day.

Soon afterward, when Judge Elvira Mitchell called the luncheon recess, Lewis dashed from the courtroom. Taking the stairs to his office, he summoned a secretary and begged her to give up her lunch hour to type an amended list of charges against David. To the original inventory, the prosecutor added solicitation of the murder of Lawrence and Lucille Lamb, plus the assaults against Hast, Nimz, and Waters. Once that was done, he asked the secretary to retype the bail request, changing $5000 to $500,000. "That ought to do it," he said with determination.

Clutching the revised documents in his fist, he hustled back to the courtroom just in time to give them to Judge Mitchell as she gaveled the court back into session.

As he slipped into his chair, he realized that he had neglected one thing. In his haste to amend the forms, Lewis had not taken time to seek out Roger Diamond to explain what he was going to do. It wasn't that he *had* to do it, but it would have been a lawyerly courtesy. As it was, the first Diamond found out about the change was when Lewis submitted the amended papers.

Predictably, when Diamond heard that Lewis had raised the requested bail amount on David a hundredfold, he was furious.

After glancing over the revised charge sheet, Judge Mitchell announced that she agreed with the prosecutor. Unless David could meet the high bail, she said, he was going to jail. She did, however, agree to a defense request for a formal hearing to air arguments from both sides on the issue. The proceeding was scheduled for two weeks in the future.

Lewis, who had been sitting tensely at the prosecution table, relaxed when he heard Judge Mitchell agree to his request. He felt a glow building inside himself. He had followed his conscience, and knew he had done the right thing.

His mood of self-satisfaction was quickly shattered,

however. As he gathered his papers and looked up, he found David staring at him with undisguised hatred.

David had come into the courtroom that morning expecting to be back in Arizona in time for dinner. Instead, he was about to be taken away to a cell and he had no idea when he would be free again. As he was led out of the room under guard, he turned once more to glare at Lewis. "You lied to me," the look said, "You lured me into a trap with a promise you never planned to keep." It was something that David would neither forget nor forgive. Lewis did not know it at the time, but he had just moved to the top of David's hit list.

17

If David believed that Judge Mitchell was going to change her mind about lowering his bail once details of the charges against him were revealed in open court, he was soon disabused of that notion. Any hope that he may have entertained about seeing Bullhead City again anytime soon quickly evaporated in the face of a flood of damning testimony from his former employees, colleagues, and people he had called friends.

Lewis had used the two weeks since the arraignment to line up witnesses to support his high bail request. Once the session got under way, it was apparent that he had utilized the time well. The tales the witnesses spun about the son of two of Pasadena's more respected businesspeople, as limited as it was to meet Lewis's specific purpose, were decidedly unpleasant. It was not as overwhelming as later testimony would be, but at that stage Lewis was not building a case for a conviction. The purpose of the June 22 hearing was not to determine David's guilt or to allow the prosecution to present a panorama of the case during the preceding four years, but only to present enough information to help Judge Mitchell decide if David's bail had been set unfairly high.

It was Lewis's job to convince her that David needed to

be locked up until he was either ordered to stand trial or the charges against him were dropped. Otherwise, he contended, if bail were reduced and David were freed, others would be in serious physical danger. There was the additional possibility, Lewis argued, that if David were allowed to walk out the door, Los Angeles officials might never see him again.

Conversely, Diamond's argument would be based on the supposition that David could be trusted not to flee. As a member of a family whose Pasadena roots went back three generations, David was not likely to disappear.

Under the rules governing such procedures, Lewis got the first shot. He called his first witness. Then another, and another, and another. For four days prosecution witnesses paraded before Judge Mitchell describing their experiences with the pleasant-looking, blond-haired man staring fixedly at them from across the room. If they were intimidated by his presence, their testimony did not reflect it.

• David Shively, the policeman involved in the investigation of two burglaries of David's former girlfriend's house in 1976, told how David showed no remorse for the break-ins. It was almost as if he considered his actions justified by the circumstances, the officer claimed. In his opinion, he added, David was a man obsessed with vengeance and retaliation, a drive that could be precipitated by almost anything, but usually by a perceived insult. It did not seem to matter if the affront was real or simply imagined.

• Former employee Jim Dame testified that when he asked David why he was not concerned about the possibility that former employee Steve Strunk might go to the authorities and tell them about what he had seen at Lamb Funeral Home, David snapped: "If anyone deters me from providing for my family, I wouldn't stop at killing them." Dame added that he had been present during an argument between Lisa Karlan and David, and that David had told him afterward: "That girl has gone too far, and one of these days she's going to wind up dead."

• When she got on the stand, Lisa Karlan detailed her particularly stormy relationship with David during the time she worked for him at CIE&TB and related how he had threatened her life when she hinted that she might report him to the authorities. She took the threat seriously, she added, because David had once told her how he planned to track down a man that he believed had cheated him, and when he found him he was going to "get him" and then "take care of whatever remains were left." She interpreted that to mean that he planned to incinerate the body in one of the retorts.

• Dave Edwards, supporting earlier testimony from Hast and Nimz themselves, told how David had furnished him with the pair's address, their physical descriptions, and the license number of Hast's car, so he, Galambos, and Augustine could find them and beat them up. He added that when he reported back to David about the success of the attack, David had told him, "Good, I'll have money for you." Edwards also related how David had asked his help in finding someone to kill his grandfather, Lawrence Lamb. David wanted to see him dead, Edwards explained, because Lawrence had told his daughter, Laurieanne, that he was going to sell the funeral home and that had "made his mother cry."

Regarding Tim Waters, Edwards testified that

David had originally told him that Tim had died of a heart attack, but later offered another version. In the second story, Edwards quoted David as telling him how he had met "the fat guy" in a restaurant and that when he left the table David "dropped something in his drink."

• Dan Galambos said when he mentioned the attack on Nimz and Hast, David told him how "happy" he was with the results. Galambos said David also told him that he planned to kill his grandparents by poisoning their drinking water, but if he couldn't do it that way, he wanted to hire someone to do it. When David asked him if he would be willing to kill someone, Galambos told him no. However, David pressed the issue and asked the weightlifter if he knew anyone who might be available for such a job. Galambos said he again told him no. When Lewis asked the 245-pound ex-football player what he thought of David, he replied, "He's a scary and dangerous guy."

• Richard Gray, who had been Tim Waters's best friend until he decided to open a competing business, said that when he asked David and his father if they had heard about Tim being attacked in his office, the two of them "looked satisfied," and David had quipped that Tim "got what he deserved." Then David added: "Now maybe Tim Waters won't talk so much."

• Andre Augustine, who had helped Galambos and Edwards beat up Hast and Nimz, said that when he saw David after the incident, David seemed "joyful or happy." When Lewis asked Augustine if he felt threatened by David, the 265-pound ex-athlete said that unless he had to meet him on a one-to-one basis under street-fighting conditions, he was afraid of him. Why? Lewis asked. Because David did not forget, Augustine replied. "Pretty much anything David says he will do, he will do."

When the testimony was finished, Lewis slumped in his chair, exhausted but confident that he had made a good case for David's high bail.

Diamond rose. "I am sure," he told Judge Mitchell, "that Mr. Lewis will concede he didn't expect to get exactly what he was requesting" as far as bail was concerned. "Maybe something lower than that—" he began.

Lewis bounded to his feet. "For the record—" he started to say, only to be cut off by Judge Mitchell.

"Mr. Diamond," she said, leaning forward, "I will be very, very sincere with you. If it were me, based on what is in the [list of charges], I would have asked for more than $500,000 [bail]."

Lewis sank back in his chair, sighing inwardly in relief. He had made his point.

"What is set forth in this request," the judge continued, tapping a stack of papers, "causes me more concern than you can imagine. We are not here to litigate what is set forth in that report. I am here to determine whether or not there is sufficient bail to make sure, one, that Mr. Sconce does not flee the jurisdiction, and two, whether or not there is a safety situation as far as the public is concerned."

Diamond tried to argue. "It is all based on alleged threats and statements made a long time ago," he protested. "We are not talking about threats to intimidate." He was prepared to say something else, but Judge Mitchell interrupted him again.

"I am very concerned," she repeated, shaking her head. "I really am. I am concerned about the allegations that are set forth in this document, and, as I said, based on my reading of the document, I would be inclined to make the bail higher than the bail that has been requested by the district attorney's office."

Lewis smiled to himself. Holy cow, he thought, she really would have agreed to a higher amount if I had just asked for it.

The judge, however, had her attention focused on Diamond. To make absolutely sure the defense attorney understood her position, the judge added, not unkindly: "It is a serious situation, counsel, and I would not be comfortable if anything occurred because I decided that I was going to reduce the bail, or I was going to decide to release him on his own recognizance."

Diamond turned to David, shrugging his eyebrows. She's made up her mind, the gesture said, there's nothing further we can do right now. Far from considering it a lost cause, however, Diamond already was making plans to explore other avenues and to try different legal approaches. We may have struck out here, he acknowledged, but there are other judges and there will be other days. Leaning over, he whispered words of encouragement to David. But David was not concentrating on his lawyer; he continued to glare at Lewis.

For David, there would indeed be other judges—a lot of them, as it turned out—but not one of them would reduce his bail. In fact, a few months down the road even the chance for bail would be removed altogether. After that, he would not have an opportunity for freedom until he was judged on the accusations. At that point his only chance of seeing Bullhead City in the immediate future would be if he were acquitted.

Sitting in Judge Mitchell's courtroom, half listening to Diamond, David knew only fury. The judge's decision must have angered and frustrated him, but his real rage seemed to be directed at Walt Lewis. If it had not been for him, David felt, he would never have found himself in such a pickle to begin with. One day, he vowed, Lewis is going to pay for this. In the meantime the path was clear: he planned to fight. If anything, Judge Mitchell's decision had increased his determination. Lewis may have won the first round, David told himself, but the battle was just beginning. Recalling a lesson he had learned on the football field, David was reminded of that truism in contact sports: If you can't go over an obstacle, go around it. And he had an idea about how he just might be able to go around the prosecutor.

18

Lying on his bunk, staring at the ceiling of his cell, David's thoughts churned with possibilities. Let his lawyer worry about appeals and suppression hearings and motions protesting illegal searches, he thought. In the meantime he had a scheme of his own. Diamond would not agree with his plan, he knew, so he was going to have to do it himself. But that was no problem. All his life, he had been able to talk his way out of any jam he had gotten himself into, and this time was not going to be any different. It was just going to take a little more planning, was all.

For more than two weeks he plotted. His plan was to go to the prosecution and try to work a deal. If his lawyer wouldn't do it, he would move on his own.

When Lewis was handed David's note requesting an interview, which came to him via one of the jailers, he was delighted. If Lewis had learned one thing in his years as a prosecutor, he felt, it was to *always* listen to a defendant's story. By articulating a position, a defendant put himself on record, even if what he said was obviously false. Since Lewis himself, as the prosecutor, could not take part in the interview, he sent Detective Dennis Diaz.

For his part, Diaz was flabbergasted when he learned

that David was requesting an interview. Certainly, he thought, David must know what I think of him. Although the two had never had a conversation, Diaz had interviewed too many people about the Sconces for him to be anything but absolutely convinced David was guilty of the charges pending against him. "He brags a lot," Diaz commented to a fellow officer one day, "but he has done what he brags about."

The detective had been investigating David for some four months, and while he had a good idea of what the man was like, it was all based on secondhand information. He was curious about what it would be like to talk to him man to man, the two of them sitting across a table from each other, so he could form his own opinion.

Diaz knew that David could be extremely charming, that when he wanted to, he could be polite, articulate, and as down-to-earth as the guy next door. He had evidence of that already, and not just through his conversations with people involved in the funeral home operation. Just a few days previously he had heard through the law enforcement grapevine that David had everybody in the system convinced about what a nice guy he was, that the deputies in the county jail were amazed that he was locked up, because his claim to innocence sounded so convincing. Diaz had problems with this. He could understand how a bleeding-heart liberal might fall for David's spiel, but it was totally beyond him how David could have so thoroughly snowed a group of experienced fellow officers as well.

On the morning of Wednesday, July 15, 1987, Diaz and another investigator named Ricky Law met with David in a lawyer's meeting room at the Castaic Wayside Honor Ranch—a grim, prisonlike facility which belied the term "honor ranch"—about twenty-five miles northwest of Pasadena, where David was then being held.

While he had not come to the meeting expecting to

hear the truth from David, Diaz was nevertheless taken aback by the first words out of David's mouth.

"It's just unbelievable," David began affably, treating Diaz more like an old friend and confidant than an antagonist, "I can't believe the intellect in jail. It's actually incomprehensible. I could never understand how it could be in jail. I honest to goodness say thank God for jail, because some of the people I've seen in here, they don't belong anywhere else."

Diaz stared at him. "I can imagine," he mumbled, stifling an impulse to laugh at the irony of the comments.

"I can't imagine some of these people being out in the world," David continued, oblivious to the looks of disbelief he was getting from the investigators. "It's just tough," he whined. "I'm telling you, there are fights, loud talk, lights on twenty-four hours a day, showers every three days . . ."

Diaz and Law let him ramble, stopping him only occasionally with a request to elaborate on something he said or prompting him with a verbal nudge. If he were going to tell them anything of value, it would have to be at his own pace and in his own time. The best he could do, Diaz figured, was give David full rein. Sooner or later he would get to the point.

Diaz was right. David eventually did get around to what he really wanted to talk to the investigator about, but by the time he got there, he had blown such a smokescreen that Diaz would not have believed him if he said the sun rose in the east. The interview turned out to be a real trip for Diaz, and like many journeys, half of the excitement had been in getting there.

The first thing he wanted to tell them, David said, was that he was meeting them behind Diamond's back. Diaz knew that and had planned for it. Just to make sure that David did not try later to claim that the meeting was forced upon him and therefore violated his rights, Diaz whipped out a statement that had been drawn up in advance by Lewis and asked David to sign it. It acknowledged that David had agreed to the interview without an attorney being present.

"Sure," David agreed amiably, "I'll talk to you without an attorney. He hasn't talked to me in two weeks anyway. I know he will be mad about this, but I'm reasonably intelligent and I don't believe I'm going to do anything to discredit anything. I just want to talk to you guys because I haven't had a chance to talk to anybody."

What he wanted to talk about, he said, was how everyone had lied about him. "What I'm interested in, before this goes any farther, basically, gentlemen, is I'm interested in cooperating with you."

Diaz looked at him evenly. *Sure you are,* he thought, *if you think it will help you walk.*

Not surprisingly, David's version of events differed considerably from what Diaz had been told by others. According to David:

• It was not he whom Lisa Karlan used to argue with almost constantly when she worked at CIE&TB, but George Bristol. "George hired her; George fired her," he said.

• He had not been involved in any depth in the operation at CIE&TB. The money supporting that facility had come from a man named Randy Welty, who also owned a small chain of adult bookstores. According to David, Welty suggested establishing the business and was willing to finance it, but he insisted that everything be in David's name. At the time, David said, he needed money to build Oscar's Ceramics, so he went along with the idea, accepting

$30,000 in traveler's checks from Welty. "It more or less paid for all my bricks to build [the retorts at] Oscar's."

But David insisted that he took no active part in the operation and was not paid by the company. "I never ran the bank. I never talked to doctors. I never placed any corneal tissue, or removed any tissue. I never drew a check from the tissue bank. I never received any compensation whatsoever from the tissue bank for any activities at all." The day-to-day operation, he added, was handled by Bristol and another employee.

• Dave Edwards had been in a near panic when he telephoned him on June 5.

Apparently unaware that Diaz had a tape of the conversation, David contended that Edwards had called him looking for a place to hide because he was afraid he was going to be arrested.

"And I told Edwards, I says, 'If you come out here, they'll just extradite you.' And I go, 'Most of the stuff that I'm facing now has turned into misdemeanor stuff anyway, so there's no real big deal about showing up.' He just wanted to come to Arizona. I says, 'I don't have the room, I don't know anybody out here, and you can't do it.' "

• It was Edwards's idea to beat up Hast and Nimz, not his, and they carried it through on their own, not because he had paid them to do it.

He said Edwards was angered by Hast's telephone call to Laurieanne in which he threatened to publish rumors of multiple cremations. Edwards, David said, was very fond of his mother and had been disturbed because Hast's telephone call had upset her. Also, Edwards felt that if the crematorium were forced to close down because of anything Hast did, he would not be able to get his brother a promised job driving one of the vans.

If it had been him, not Edwards, who was angry with Hast, David said, he simply would have met with the funeral home director and talked him out of it. "I wasn't going to go down there and kick the guy's butt."

• He never removed gold-filled teeth from cadavers or told anyone else to. If he saw gold bridgework, he said, he would remove it and he or Jerry would dispose of it, but that was all.

"So, basically, you never pulled anybody's teeth?" Diaz asked.

"No," David said.

"Then" Diaz asked, "why is it we found so many teeth?"

"Where are the teeth that were found?" David wanted to know.

"I've got them," Diaz replied. "They were in a cup exactly where people said they were going to be. On a desk. It may have been your mom's desk."

"There were a lot of people," David answered smoothly, "who had access to the stuff there. And I made no bones about hiding what I did. Everybody saw me taking dentures or stuff like that out, and my dad and I would toss it. We'd keep it on the table in the sifting room, and when we would remember to get it, we'd take it and we'd go dump it. It was my legal right to do that by the cremation order."

Besides, David added, he had been told by an old family friend, Mike Engwald, who owned a gold exchange company, that dental gold was virtually worthless. "He told me it wasn't worth anything because it wasn't truly gold; that it was a mixture of a bunch of inert stuff and it wasn't really worth the trouble of taking it out."

Engwald also had warned him that there were federal regulations governing the sale of gold, and if he tried to peddle the precious metal, he ran the risk of being found out by the IRS.

"He told me I should take great steps in preventing anybody from taking any because if it ever came back, it would hurt me and my business."

"And obviously you never sold any gold to him then?" Diaz asked, tongue in cheek.

"No!" David answered firmly.

• Multiple cremations were something always mentioned by anyone who wanted to make trouble for a crematorium owner.

"I take it you're going to say that you never cremated more than one body at a time," Diaz asked skeptically.

On this point David turned cautious.

"Ahhh," he began, collecting his thoughts. "I'm not going to say that," he finally answered. "I'm not going to say I didn't; I'm not going to say I did. I'm going to take the Fifth on that right now. It won't do me any good to say one way or another because you know in the state of California it is legal to cremate more than one [body] at a time if you have consent, if you have a release." He did not want to discuss the issue further, he said, until he had collected all his records and could determine when he had consent and when he did not.

I'll be damned, Diaz said to himself, that's the closest this guy has come—maybe it will be the closest he ever *will* come—to admitting anything. And what does he pick? A misdemeanor.

• The accusations that he had sought the murder of his grandparents were almost too farfetched to talk about.

Lawrence Lamb, David said, was a lovable man, a "funny old guy," who at eighty-one still insisted on driving the hearse to funerals even though his driving skills left a lot to be desired. Every time he took the wheel, David said, the officers in the motorcycle escort quaked in fear. One time, David added, his grandfather took the funeral procession to the wrong cemetery, and that was a hoot. But as far as planning to kill him, the idea was ridiculous.

However, he added ominously, Dave Edwards seemed to have a lot of problems with his grandfather.

Edwards had been present one day when one of the escort officers warned David that he had better not let Lawrence drive anymore because he was not safe on the road. When Edwards heard that, he turned to David. "He said, 'When's that old buzzard going to kick off?' and 'Isn't your mom going to inherit this whole place when he kicks off?' "

David explained that the business was set up as a trust fund, and when Lawrence died the money would be divided among all the children, not just his mother. "Edwards goes, 'Oh gosh, it's a shame, you know.' He goes, 'Too bad, man, your mother works hard.' "

A few days later, David said, Edwards brought him a copy of *The Poor Man's James Bond*. "He goes, 'Here, you ought to read this, man. This has got all kinds of good shit in it.' "

David said he put the book aside and never looked at it. And he certainly never talked about adopting any ideas from it to use in getting rid of his grandfather.

"Why would I benefit from getting rid of my grandfather?" he asked Diaz. "It wouldn't make me any money. It would hurt everybody in my family. I would run the risk of being in jail the rest of my life. You know, I don't do things like that."

• He was still angry about the size of his bail.

He could not understand why his bail had been set so high, while the bail for his parents had been set so low. Actually, he added, they were accused of more serious crimes than he, such as embezzlement.

"Conspiracy for assault," he sneered. "Even if that was a viable charge, the bail of half a million dollars is ludicrous. Absolutely ludicrous. To say that I'm a threat to these people who I haven't seen or spoken to in over a year was appalling. I couldn't believe it. I looked at my dad and I started getting tears in my eyes. I go, 'What is going on here? I came in here to voluntarily surrender.' Why did the D.A. say I was going to have a five-thousand-dollar bail and it wasn't five minutes before you raised it?"

Diaz glanced at his watch. By then the interview was almost one and a half hours old, and they still had not done more than skirt around the most important issue: the death of Tim Waters. Let's get to it, Diaz thought impatiently, let's cut to the real reason we're here.

But, as Diaz had figured, it was going to have to progress at David's pace, not his. Before David would get to Tim Waters, there was one other person that he wanted to discuss: Dan Galambos. David could not find enough bad things to say about his former friend.

19

To begin with, David confided, Galambos was a *very* violent person. "Let me tell you what he did one night at a Kings game," he said, launching into a series of mind-numbing Danny Galambos stories.

According to him, the Kings were playing the Buffalo Sabres when Galambos became so enraged at one of the Sabres that he tried to climb onto the ice to attack him. He had to be restrained and dragged back into the stands. "That was the reason they installed Plexiglas behind the visitor's bench. It was because of Danny Galambos."

As a result of that incident, he added, Galambos was banned from the arena for the rest of the season.

It was, however, not his only violent outburst in the Forum. To listen to David, the arena was one of Galambos's favorite places to exhibit his aggressive tendencies. He would hit people just because they told him to sit down, David said. "I mean, he'd walk up four or five rows and smack them."

David also told about how Galambos went to the house of his then-current girlfriend to demand to know why she wanted to break up with him. Her father answered the door and told Galambos to go away, then he slammed the door in Galambos's face. Galambos became so angry that he tried to punch the man through the glass doorfront, severely slashing his arm and wrist.

"I mean," David said, "the history of Danny Galambos and violence is not new at all."

In addition to being violent, David added, Galambos was personally offensive. "He invited himself to my river house one time, you know," David said. "He stood on the bow of my boat in the middle of the lake and peed in front of all the girls. 'Hey, girls, look at this,' he said, and then he walked around naked in the early morning hours with all the people and their wives to see because he doesn't care. I sent him home because he was so obnoxious."

David paused to reflect; then, in marvelous understatement, he added: "The guy is absolutely not one of my close friends. He never has been."

Diaz shrugged. He had no idea if there was any substance to these wild stories. He couldn't care less.

By this time Diaz and Law were getting pretty tired of the string of anecdotes about Danny Galambos. Maybe David was, too, because he suddenly shifted from talking just about Galambos to how Galambos was connected to Tim Waters.

Diaz's interest picked up. Although David danced all around the issue, never quite coming out and saying that Galambos may have killed Tim, he hinted at it very strongly.

Diaz could appreciate that. He realized that David had to be careful with what he said and how he said it. It was part of the game; like football, except the stakes were a lot higher. David wanted to tantalize the detectives with hints of secret knowledge, but he didn't want to give away too much because Galambos was his main bargaining tool. Diaz, on the other hand, could not show too much interest because that might give David additional leverage in the negotiating he knew was going to come. He was well-aware of what David was doing; in fact, he had predicted it was the reason behind the request for the meeting. But he could not afford to plunge in too quickly. Let him get to it in his own way, he cautioned himself.

Power horse-trading was what it was. And David proved to be a shrewd dealer. He had set the scene well, feeding the investigators just enough details to make them curious, to hint that there was much more to the story than he had divulged so far, while simultaneously building up Galambos as a credible heavy. His next step was to cut himself loose, to disabuse Diaz of any belief the detective might have that he, David, could possibly have been involved with Tim Waters's death.

"I never met Tim Waters," David told Diaz and Law, sounding as sincere as a Jesuit. "I never spoke to Tim Waters. I never saw Tim Waters until that photograph in court. Tim Waters was not an account of mine. I didn't care one way or another about him. I didn't make any money from him, you know. I never knew Tim Waters at all."

With those tidbits firmly on the record, David leaned forward and lowered his voice.

"But I'll tell you something," he confided. "There's an individual out there whose business was cut in half by Tim Waters. And this same individual had a real hard-on for Tim Waters and told me [about it]. There were other people who heard telephone conversations with this individual and Danny Galambos arranging [to pay] Tim Waters a visit."

"You're not speaking of Richard Gray, are you?" Diaz asked.

David mumbled ambiguously.

Shit, Diaz thought, I wish I could pin him down.

"Richard Gray was a friend of Tim's," the detective pointed out.

"Yeah," David commented noncommittally. "Best of my understanding he was."

At that point David must have figured it was time to back off a little, let the detectives chew on what he had said. He dropped the Galambos issue and instead went off on a tangent, talking about multiple cremations and the pilfering of dental gold.

Diaz gave him his head. He'll come back to it, he told himself. And David did.

"You still don't have the Waters thing together at all," David said several minutes later. "You got the wrong guy in jail. I've got no motive. I didn't know the man."

If you didn't have him assaulted and maybe murdered, why do others say you did? Diaz asked.

"I'll tell you why," David replied eagerly. "It's because the other guy told them to tell [investigators] that I said it —the other guy that you still don't have in proper custody that should be in jail."

David said the "other guy," who he still had not specifically named, went to Tim's funeral to make sure he was dead, and then he came to him to tell him about it.

Again Diaz asked if he was talking about Gray, since Gray had testified at the hearing before Judge Mitchell that he had mentioned the attack on Tim to David and his father.

David smiled. "Dick Gray was talking a lot about Tim Waters back then," he replied coyly, "and about how he was scared of him and he didn't know what to do."

"Right," Diaz prompted neutrally.

"You know," David said, his tone changing, moving into his salesman's mode. "What should I do? I'm telling you there's another guy who was there, right there with me, who heard all the same stuff and who had a hell of a motive and talked about a lot of things involving Tim Waters and wanted to do Tim Waters dirt, and then contacted Galambos about doing Tim Waters dirt."

Did he provide Galambos's name? Diaz asked, knowing what the answer would be.

Definitely, David replied. "He asked me about the big guy. He wanted to know who were those big guys at the hockey game who went and beat up Ron Hast. That's how he found out about Galambos."

There would never be any evidence to substantiate David's hints that Galambos or Gray might have been involved in killing Waters.

Diaz studied David. "Did you ever have the habit of bragging?" he asked.

"Oh, yeah," David chuckled, "I talk like an idiot."

"Is it possible that you would have said the thing about Tim Waters just to say it?"

"No, no," David said hurriedly. What happened, he explained, was this: He, Galambos, and Edwards were at a Kings game, and he mentioned that he had heard that Tim had died. David said Edwards expressed surprise. "He died?" he asked David. But before David could answer, Galambos screamed, "Hey, everybody, business must be slow; Dave's out drumming up business on his own again." The memory infuriated David. "The guy yells like this at the top of his lungs at the hockey game," David told Diaz, either actually indignant or faking it very well. But before he could answer Galambos, he continued, Edwards jumped into the conversation.

David quoted him as saying, "Ah, you must have read that book I gave you, huh? You're really getting into that stuff, aren't you?"

To the detectives, David denied that he answered Edwards directly. But, he added, that was how the whole thing about him being tied to Tim Waters and to the controversial book, *The Poor Man's James Bond*, got started.

He would have spoken up in court, David continued, but Diamond wouldn't let him.

Why was that? Diaz asked.

"Because he doesn't want me to give Randy [Welty] up?" he said. After a brief digression, David elaborated: "I'm sitting in jail with an attorney who won't let me give up the guy who paid for all the tissue stuff and authorized it and instructed it to be done and shipped it and collected the money from it and set me up and everything. So I'm sitting here because he doesn't want to get involved because he's in the porno business."

Again Diaz pondered what David had told him. Was David claiming, Diaz asked himself, that his lawyer, Roger Diamond, would not let him—David—testify because he might try to blame Randy Welty for any problems with the tissue bank? At the time the significance of what David was claiming was lost on the detective. However, it clicked weeks later when Diaz learned that Diamond had represented Welty in another case. What David had been saying was that, in his view, the reason Diamond advised David not to testify was a fear that his testimony might possibly damage another of Diamond's clients. Because of this potential conflict of interest, Diamond was later not reappointed as David's lawyer. But it was only temporary. He would be back, with David's support, when it did not appear that anything David said would have an impact on Welty.

David paused for breath. Apparently deciding the timing was right, he got to the *real* reason he had asked for the interview with Diaz.

"I don't have a whole lot to do but sit in jail and think about this," he said, hoping to engender some sympathy for his cause. "Now, guys," he added in a reasonable, buddy-buddy tone, "I want out of jail and I'll give you who did Tim Waters."

Diaz nodded. About damn time! he thought.

"So basically," the detective said, "I guess maybe the bottom line is, if we would get you out, then obviously you would give up whoever the person is that actually hired Danny to kill Waters."

"Yeah." David nodded. "And I'll prove it, and I'll give you two witnesses besides that heard him arrange it on the telephone, and then I'll sit there and I'll cooperate with you."

Diaz was considering how to respond when David asked him to turn off the tape recorder. Puzzled, he reached over and flipped the switch.

"Now let me ask you something," David said conspiratorially. "Can you get me something to eat? I want a burger or something. The food in here is *so* bad."

Diaz was not sure whether to laugh or cry. He flipped the recorder back on.

"Obviously I can't make any promises," he said slowly, definitely not referring to food. Any bargain would have to come from Lewis, the detective added.

"You know," David said, speaking of Lewis, "I don't think he likes me a bit."

Diaz mumbled something about Lewis being under pressure because it was such a high-profile case, but David would not let it go; he wanted to go back to the issue of his possible release. He *knew* about Walt Lewis, he implied, meaning he thought Lewis was out to get him, and he thought he knew what he was going to do about him. But he wasn't about to share that with two detectives.

"I think it would be winnable from both sides if I were out," he said encouragingly. "You'd win a little, I'd win a little, and then what you want to accomplish would be accomplished because you'd get the right people, and I'd get what I want to accomplish because I'd get out."

To hear it that way, it sounded very rational, which was

exactly what David was hoping. Apparently he thought he had Diaz convinced, because his tone softened.

"You know," he said congenially, referring to the illegal crematorium at Hesperia, "the only thing I feel guilty about is not telling the county of San Bernardino what I was doing up there."

Having made a gesture toward friendship, he got back to business.

"Let's speak honestly here," he suggested briskly. "This is a very weak case, and I know it's a weak case as far as actually pinning the blame on me for this tissue stuff."

"It's not as weak as you think," Diaz pointed out, his dislike for David peeking through. "And I'm going to be a little up front with you too. It's stronger on your mom and dad than you."

David seemed surprised. "As far as the tissue?"

"I don't want to talk about what it is that we have," Diaz said, mentally kicking himself for maybe saying too much already, "but I have your dad and mom stronger [than you] on direct involvement with the illegal taking of tissue without consent."

With that, they were off on another tangent, and it was several minutes before they got back to David's offer.

"Here's what we could do," David proposed, settling down for some more bargaining. "Just lower my bail to a hundred thousand or something so that I can bail myself out, and then immediately upon bailing out I'll go with you and give you a deposition. Immediately! And then I'll tell you about Waters."

For a moment no one said anything, but David picked up on Diaz's hesitancy. He let the conversation wander some more before he came back with another offer. Rather than having his bail lowered, he suggested that probation might be appropriate.

"As long as I hear that I'm going to have probation,

then I'll be more cooperative with you in respect to what's going to transpire from this day forward," he said. "I mean, if I know I'm not going back to jail, if I know that I'm going to be able to go home with my family, then that's all I want."

To sweeten the pot, he threw in a little contrition. "I want to get into a completely different line of work," he confessed. "Eventually I want to move away somewhere and just start my life over again, get back into going to church and stuff and being the way I was before."

When Diaz continued to balk, David poured it on even thicker. "Dennis," he said, looking the detective in the eye, "truly, I'm a good person. I'm not going to fabricate anything to get out of jail, because eventually it would come out anyway and it would only be to my detriment. I realize that. I never did anything or say I'd want to hurt my grandfather."

And again he denied involvement in the Hast, Nimz, and Waters beatings. "I can give you motive and I can give you reasoning," he said, adding pleadingly, "I just want out of jail. I'll talk to anybody if they get me out of jail."

"All right," Diaz replied evenly. The session was over. It had lasted almost exactly three hours; they had worked straight through lunch. The talking was over, but there was still tension in the air. David broke it. Look at the bright side of spending the whole morning here, he urged: "I missed lunch." Then he added with a laugh, "Thank goodness."

All the way back to Pasadena, less than an hour's drive in the early afternoon when the freeway was not jammed, Diaz weighed the value of the discussion. Ricky Law, the detective who had accompanied him to the interview, was not familiar with the case, so the two didn't talk about what David had said. For the most part, Diaz was alone with his thoughts, which was precisely what he wanted right then. As he mentally reviewed the experience, he became certain of one thing: Walt Lewis was not going to go for any deal. And, while that had been the main item on David's agenda, Diaz looked at the discussion from an entirely different perspective. He had gone into the interview anticipating that his meeting with David would be a learning experience. And it certainly had proved to be that. It had given him a tremendous opportunity to study David, to measure the man, and to determine what kind of opponent the prosecution was facing.

David had been clever, Diaz admitted. In fact, he had been even sharper, smoother, and more charming than the detective had expected. He could understand how David had won so many supporters among his jailers. But that made him even more dangerous, he reminded himself. If David could win over cynical law enforcement officers who dealt with all types of criminals on a day-to-day basis, no telling what he could do with naive civilians. In the detective's mind, David was a man totally without conscience, a man who could commit the most vile acts but never feel a twinge of regret or remorse. He was one of those people who had an excuse for everything. No matter what happened, it was always someone else's fault.

Maneuvering down I-5, Diaz concluded that David was a classic sociopath, definitely *the* most sociopathic person he had come across in his almost two decades of police work. But deciding that David was without morals was a relatively easy conclusion to come to. What to do about him was something else. The prosecution would proceed; he was confident of that. But what would happen when David eventually got his chance to tell his story to a group of vulnerable jurors or a sympathetic judge was anyone's guess. Diaz decided that he wasn't going to take any bets on that one. The way he figured it, it was going to be too close to call.

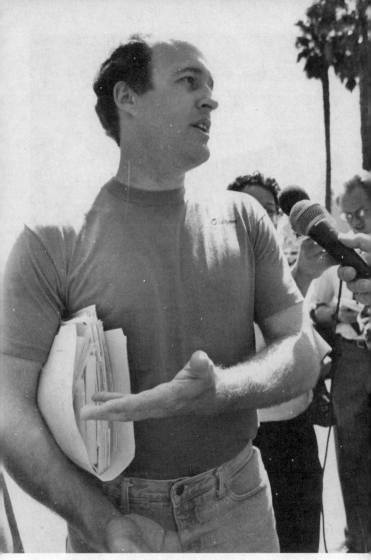

The All-American football hero turned Cremation King of the West—David Sconce, who was arrested for unethical funeral home practices and later pleaded guilty to having his adversaries beaten up. *(Photo by Stacey Gore)*

Jerry and Laurieanne Sconce, David's parents. Laurieanne assumed control of the Lamb Funeral Home as her father, Lawrence Lamb, drew closer to retirement. She gradually pulled her husband and son into the business. *(Photo by Stacey Gore)*

Now the Pasadena Funeral Home, the former Lamb Funeral Home is now attempting to recover its reputation, which had been compromised by David Sconce's improper business practices. *(Photo by Sara Englade)*

The Pasadena Crematorium, the Sconce-owned facility that did cremations for the Lamb Funeral Home. *(Photo by Sara Englade)*

Timothy Waters, the owner of Alpha Society, a rival cremation service. The cause of his sudden death in April, 1985, remains unknown, although the coroner has ruled that it was due to natural causes. *(Photo by Stacey Gore)*

Dave Edwards, an ex-football player who was hired by David Sconce to beat up his business rivals. *(Photo courtesy The University of the Pacific)*

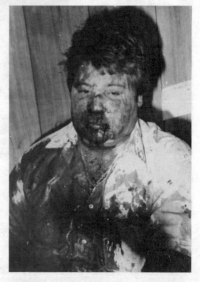

Tim Waters, after having been assaulted by Daniel Galambos and one other man in February of 1985. *(Photo by Stacey Gore)*

Superior Court Judge Terry Smerling, who took over the case against the Sconces. David and Jerry were arrested for multiple cremations, commingling of human remains, and other improper activities. Jerry has still not been tried on any of the charges against him. *(Photo by Stacey Gore)*

Los Angeles County Deputy District Attorney Harvey Giss, who was scheduled to prosecute David Sconce for the murder of Tim Waters. He was later forced to drop the charges due to lack of evidence. He hopes to be able to prosecute Sconce for conspiracy to murder Elie Estephan, another rival funeral home director. *(Photo by Stacey Gore)*

Co-prosecutor Kevin De Noce, also scheduled to present the case against Sconce in connection with Waters's death. *(Photo by Stacey Gore)*

David Sconce with defense attorney Roger Diamond *(left)*. *(Photo by Stacey Gore)*

Sconce in court, up on charges that he had murdered Tim Waters. *(Photo by* San Diego Union/*Roni Galgano)*

Jerry, Laurieanne, and David's brother Gary in the courthouse, just before murder charges accusing David of murdering Waters were dropped. *(Photo by Stacey Gore)*

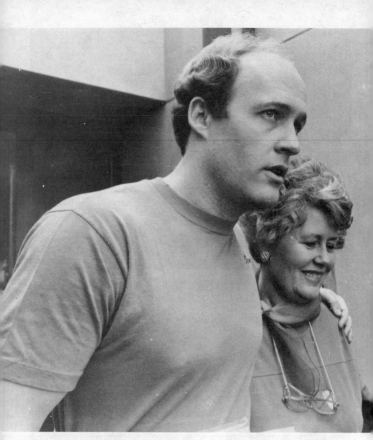
David and his mother leave the courtroom, the murder charge against him dismissed. *(Photo by Stacey Gore)*

* * *

Something that apparently did not occur to Diaz or anyone else at that juncture was the irony of the thrust of David's argument. Everything that he had proposed to Diaz regarding a deal revolved around his alleged knowledge of what had happened to Tim Waters. But at that point Tim Waters technically was a nonissue. His death was still listed as a natural one. Police had a confession from Galambos in which he admitted attacking Tim, so the assault issue was settled. And right then there was no other point to consider. Officially, Tim Waters was not a murder victim.

20

Diaz had been exactly on target in his assessment of how Lewis would react to David's proposals; in the DDA's opinion, no one was going to ever get the truth out of David, and a deal was totally out of the question. When a transcript of the Diaz interview appeared on his desk, Lewis picked it up and got no further than the first page before he broke up laughing. Oh, God, he guffawed, this is great. This is really great. David Sconce saying "thank God for jails." David's trying to sound so innocent, Lewis mumbled, continuing to cackle. He laughed until he was afraid his co-workers might think he'd gone round the bend. Then he wiped his eyes, threw the transcript onto an empty chair and picked up a stack of statements that he had to go through to start preparing the case for court. Reading the words of those who had worked for the Sconces, he quickly lost sight of the humor he had enjoyed just moments before.

A week later Lewis emerged from his office and David from his cell for a brief confrontation in court, just long enough for David to plead not guilty to the charges of soliciting the murder of Lawrence and Lucille Lamb, an accusation that the grandparents and David's parents felt was ludicrous. Then both the prosecutor and the accused resubmerged into their separate prisons to await the next encounter. It came on August 3 before Judge Victor Person.

Required to appear along with David were his parents, Jerry and Laurieanne. All three had been summoned for the opening of a court proceeding designed to determine the disposition of the myriad charges against them. Each had his own lawyer: Diamond represented David; Edward Rucker represented Laurieanne; and Thomas Nishi, Jerry. The Sconces had pleaded not guilty to the accusations, so the next move was up to the court. Would they be ordered to stand trial? Or would the charges be dismissed? That was up to Person.

Although the forty-one-year-old jurist, who pronounced his surname Purr-sahn, carried the title of Municipal Court Judge, a job description more accurately would have read Preliminary Hearing Judge. Since March 1986, some five months after he had been appointed to the bench by Governor George Deukmejian, Person's only judicial role had been that of conducting preliminary hearings. Sometimes he handled as many as sixteen in a single day.

Frequently referred to by lawyers as probable cause proceedings, preliminary hearings have a single purpose: to give a judge the opportunity to determine if the prosecution has sufficient reason—probable cause—to bring a defendant, or defendants in this case, to trial. In many states prosecutors rely on grand juries to perform the same function. Typically, a panel of civilians—a grand jury as opposed to a petit or trial jury—meets in secret to examine evidence compiled by a prosecutor. If the group feels the evidence is strong enough to warrant a trial, it issues an indictment, a formal listing of charges, which then is handed up to a trial court. Although California has a functioning grand jury system, it has been largely ignored by prosecutors since the state supreme court ruled in the mid-eighties that a defendant, even if he had been indicted by a grand jury, was still entitled to a preliminary hearing. To district attorneys, it seemed senseless to hold two sessions if one would suffice. As a result, the preliminary hearing became the proceeding of choice. In fact, as a matter of course, every felony charge was aired at a preliminary hearing, a policy that kept the municipal courts extremely busy. Because of the demand, some municipal court judges did nothing but hold preliminary hearings. Person was in that group.

For the most part, preliminary hearings are comparatively brief, ho-hum affairs. Commonly during such proceedings prosecutors present only enough material that they feel is necessary to convince the judge that there is a "strong suspicion" the defendant committed the offense. The object is to get the judge to order a trial, not to try the defendant at a hearing. While the defense also has the right to call witnesses and present evidence, it seldom is used to any appreciable extent. Defense attorneys figure if the district attorney has much more than a smidgen of evidence, there is going to be a trial anyway, so why tip their hand?

But defense attorneys have one big advantage at a preliminary hearing: they can cross-examine prosecution witnesses. This, again, is unlike a grand jury proceeding, where the panel hears only the prosecution side of the case. In fact, the defense is not even allowed in the room when the grand jury is hearing the prosecution's evidence. The judge in a preliminary hearing does not rule on guilt or innocence. His function is to act as referee, making sure that the hearing proceeds in an orderly fashion and that the lawyers keep within their defined legal boundaries. Once the evidence is presented—which in run-of-the-mill criminal cases does not take very long—it is up to the judge to decide if the case should be moved up the ladder for trial. All in all, most preliminary hearings are fairly uncomplicated affairs; in more cases than not, the judge goes along with the prosecution. Since so little evidence is needed to determine probable cause—usually no more than it takes for a police officer to decide to make an arrest—the outcome of most preliminary hearings tends to be predetermined. But nothing in the Sconce case up to then had been simple, and the preliminary hearing would not be an exception. And while most preliminary hearings are culminated rather rapidly, the Sconce hearing would drag on interminably.

From the beginning, Person realized the Sconce hearing was going to take longer and be more complex than any hearing he had been involved with previously. However, he did not anticipate just *how* long and *how* convoluted it was going to be. Before it was over, it would set a record as the longest preliminary hearing in the history of the Pasadena Municipal Court. Testimony began on August 3 and ran through December 18. During that time, the prosecution presented ninety-nine witnesses whose words filled some 125 volumes, enough to make a pile of transcripts more than three feet tall. After the testimony, Person spent another five months reviewing the record, so the hearing was not officially over until he issued his ruling on May 9, a little more than nine months after it began.

In every court proceeding, and the Sconce hearing was no exception, there is a subtle factor at work that commonly effects the outcome: the mix of personalities of the opposing lawyers and the defendants, as well as the quirks of the judge.

Before he was appointed to the bench, Person was a deputy district attorney for twelve years. As a result, he probably tended to lean toward the prosecution in any given case. At least, this was his reputation, and as a result, most prosecutors who came into his courtroom regarded him as a sympathetic fellow traveler. On the other hand, defense attorneys, particularly public defenders, viewed him as blatantly prejudiced against them.

The Sconce case was not going to settle the argument. While it seemed as though Person gave Walt Lewis tremendous latitude in the breadth of the evidence he was allowed to present, the judge's supporters argued, not unreasonably, that this was justified because it was an especially tangled case and the crimes were unusually vile. In such a situation, the argument went, the more evidence that could be presented, the better. Another judge, even one without a DDA's experience, might have allowed the prosecution the same freedom.

There was one other thing that made the Sconce preliminary hearing, if not unique, at least highly unusual. As soon as the hearing opened, Diamond renewed his request for a reduction in David's bail. Commonly, such pleas are considered at a separate hearing, but facing an unwelcome potential delay in getting the preliminary hearing started, Lewis suggested that the two proceedings be combined.

The proposal had considerable merit. That way witnesses would not have to be called twice: once to testify about David's dangerousness, and again to testify about broader issues that had to do with the criminal cases itself. Person agreed. In the end it was a momentous decision. While it undoubtedly extended the time the hearing would take had bail not been an issue, it also cleared the way for a rare, broad display of evidence, much more than would have been allowed in either a bail reduction hearing or a preliminary hearing if they had been held individually.

In one way, this was a boon to the prosecution, since it allowed Lewis to present a more comprehensive, more cohesive case. But it also helped the defense because in the long run it proved quite beneficial to the Sconces. After the hearing, when the transcripts were forwarded to the superior court judge who would conduct the trial, he already had before him, just by reading the record, a remarkably detailed outline. If circumstances had been different, this fact might have helped the prosecution rather than the defense. But as it turned out, it was a disastrous blow for the district attorney's efforts.

In the beginning Lewis was delighted with Person's decision to wed the two proceedings. Instead of being restricted to introducing just enough material to show that there was probably cause to bind them over for trial, he had license to literally bury the court in a mass of detail. With the bail reduction hearing being shoehorned in, Lewis was free to roam across a very broad landscape in his efforts to show that David not only probably committed the crimes of which he was accused—with his parents in collusion and possibly in active participation in the funeral home crimes—but that he was one vicious character besides.

However, Lewis discovered quickly that it was not going to be all clear sailing; the prosecutor still had more than a few problems. The biggest obstacle he faced, and one that would prove almost overwhelming in the weeks to come, was that his case was far from static.

Because the situation was so complicated, the investigation had to be exhaustive. And although it had been under way for seven months, it still wasn't finished; new leads kept popping up with regularity. Even as the preliminary hearing progressed, Diaz brought Lewis new information on the Sconces' illegal activities virtually on a daily basis. Lewis had no idea, from one day to the next, how many more witnesses he was going to have to subpoena, or that the list was going to grow like an athlete on steroids.

The result was often controlled confusion. For Lewis it meant laboring in the court by day and in his office by night. Instead of being able to reserve the evenings to prepare his presentation for the following day, he was forced to spend that time dealing with new witnesses and new evidence.

By the time he was just a few weeks into the hearing, Lewis already had lost count of the number of nights that he dragged himself home too exhausted to do anything except fall into bed. Except for one thing. Usually at the end of such a day, seeking irony where he could find it, he rallied enough to repeat to himself, like a mantra, Laurie-anne's comment to her son about the extraction of gold-filled teeth: "How much AU did you get today, honey?" It kept him going. If I ever write a book about this, he told himself, that is going to be the opening line.

21

Actually, the least of Lewis's worries was momentum. Once it began, the hearing barreled along like an eighteen-wheeler thundering across the Mojave. It created a force of its own, plowing a distinctive, disturbing furrow across the tranquil facade that the City of Roses presented to the world. Once Lewis started calling his army of witnesses into the courtroom called Division 6, the alleged atrocities that had been occurring at the city's preeminent funeral home/crematorium became a prime topic of conversation from Victorville to Ventura. For salacious detail, it could not be topped; the parade of horrors seemed to have no end.

In his methodical fashion, Lewis had organized his material—at least as best he could in view of the tidelike surge of witnesses—so that testimony would move, as closely as possible, from one topic to another in what he hoped would eventually be a seamless circle, or more accurately, an unbroken noose, around the collective necks of Jerry, Laurieanne, and David.

On the whole, his plan was admirably successful. For a few days witnesses trooped in telling stories primarily about multiple cremations. Then another group came in and talked about the sale of body parts. And then another about the forging of ATC forms. And so forth. But since every topic had its own scandal attached, it became a spectator's haven. On any given day a citizen with a couple of hours to kill could pop into the courtroom and be almost certain of hearing some titillating details. There was, in fact, so much to choose from, it was difficult to say which was the most shocking. Every area that Lewis explored had its own sad side.

At the beginning, though, he seemed cautious. Like a runner launching on a marathon, he had to first establish a pace before he could settle into a regular rhythm. As a result, he began with the rather tedious material, the kind that was unlikely to stimulate many headlines: the forgery and embezzlement charges. Doggedly, he proceeded to demonstrate the basis for those accusations.

A man named Clarence Turner and his sister-in-law, Jean Bodenshot, testified that Lamb Funeral Home had taken care of the arrangements for the funeral of Turner's wife, Helen. When investigators compiled a list of organ donors, one of the names on the sheet was Helen Turner, and according to the paperwork, Clarence had signed the consent form.

However, when Clarence took the stand, he denied ever giving authorization for organ or tissue removal. It was something he never would have done, he said, because his wife had died of cancer and he would have worried about a recipient getting a diseased organ.

His claim was backed up by Bodenshot, who had actually made the arrangements with Laurieanne. She testified that organ donation had not even been discussed.

The prosecution's handwriting expert, Georgia Hanna, testified that Turner's purported signature was an apparent forgery. Although she could not determine who *had* signed Turner's name, other than it was *not* Clarence Turner, she felt that the signatures of the two witnesses to his signing—Jerry and Laurieanne—were both signed by Laurieanne. This implied that she also signed Turner's name, or at least was aware of fraud by claiming to be a witness to a signature she knew was not authentic. Laurieanne later told a reporter that the law allowed her to sign someone's name if she had received consent over the telephone. But Turner denied this as well.

In the same vein, a woman named Claudine Johnson denied that she had agreed to the removal of organs or tissue from the body of her sister, Clara Hildebrandt, and that the signature on the consent form was not hers. More damning evidence was developed by Diaz that showed that Hildebrandt's heart had been removed *the day before* Johnson met with Laurieanne at the funeral home, allegedly to sign the form permitting organ removal. Hanna testified that, in her expert opinion, Johnson's name had been forged by Laurieanne, who also signed her own name, and Jerry's, as witnesses.

The third case involved Carolyn Anderson Scholl, the woman whose name was misspelled in her purported signature on the consent form. According to her, Laurieanne had mentioned the tissue bank but she had never asked if any of Frank Holzkamper's organs were to be donated. If Laurieanne *had* asked, Scholl said, she would have refused. The only document she signed for Laurieanne, Scholl said, was an ATC form. At no time, she testified, did Laurieanne tell her that by signing the ATC form she was also authorizing organ removal.

When she was shown a donor consent form purportedly carrying her signature, Scholl denied ever having seen the form before, much less signing it.

A few minutes later Hanna testified that she was "nearly positive" the "Schull" signature was in Laurieanne's hand.

These cases, while admittedly dreary in comparison to what was to come, could not simply be ignored.

"The forgeries alleged in these . . . counts constitute a fraud not only against the immediate next of kin of the deceased whose signatures were forged, but in a larger sense . . . against the public," Lewis argued. Furthermore, he continued, the import was broader yet because the recipients of the organs also were defrauded in the sense that they thought they were getting material that had been donated, not stolen.

To put this testimony into context one had to remember that the forgery case against Laurieanne almost certainly would be contested hotly when and if Laurieanne was ever forced to stand trial on the charges. The evidence against her was authenticated primarily by the prosecution's handwriting expert. At trial, Laurieanne's lawyer undoubtedly would call experts of his own to refute Hanna's claims. Laurieanne's conviction or acquittal on the forgery counts probably would rest largely on whose experts were the most credible.

However, the situation was different in the embezzlement case, where the district attorney's evidence against Laurieanne was much stronger. The main prosecution witnesses in that phase were Skip Jones, the auditor for the State Board of Funeral Directors and Embalmers, and Lillian Garcia, a savings supervisor at the institution where Lamb Funeral Home's preneed accounts were on deposit.

In the embezzlement phase, Lewis was not dealing with arguable interpretations of loops and swirls in a person's signature, but with actual documents filed and signed by Laurieanne in a bank officer's presence.

When the DDA called Garcia to the stand, she said that the special account—No. 01–847664, or for easy reference in the court, the "664 account"—was opened on February 15, 1984, and was designed specifically to receive interest money from Lamb Funeral Home's 172 preneed account holders. After March 20, 1986, the money was transferred to the account automatically at the end of every quarter.

Eventually, Garcia said, the total in the 664 account grew to $100,365.52, of which an even $100,000 subsequently was disbursed to Lamb Funeral Home, David, David's brother Gary, and an equipment service. That money included some $23,000 from two new preneed accounts which Laurieanne had not opened, as required by state law, within thirty days. These accusations spun off as separate charges against the couple.

In his argument before Person, Lewis contended that both Jerry and Laurieanne participated in the money transfer scheme, and that the practice persisted even after state regulations had been explained to Laurieanne in exhaustive detail by Skip Jones.

Also, the prosecutor added, the fact that Laurieanne's brothers later replaced the $100,000 after they took over operation of the mortuary, did not make up for the fact that Jerry and Laurieanne had broken the law by diverting the money in the first place.

"If a guy gets caught after robbing a bank and then he gives the money back, that doesn't mean he will not be charged with bank robbery," Lewis explained.

By this time Lewis was starting to find his stride. Having established that there were some strange things going on at Lamb Funeral Home, he proceeded to demonstrate just *how* strange. Without breaking his gait, he segued smoothly into the issue of multiple cremations, calling a string of witnesses to corroborate his accusations.

Former employees Jim Dame, Steve Strunk, and Leon Packard testified that remains would be scooped from large metal barrels into boxes that were to be returned to next of kin. Ostensibly, the containers held the remains of their loved ones.

"There was like a table where there was empty boxes with name tags on them," testified Strunk.

How many boxes? asked Lewis.

Strunk replied that there were twenty or thirty. "They were filled up with ashes that were scooped out and placed into each one."

"Did you ever see Laurieanne Lamb scoop out ashes from the trash can and place it in boxes?" Lewis asked.

"Yes," Strunk replied.

"And did you see that on more than one occasion?"

"Yes."

In addition to Laurieanne, Strunk testified, he also had seen David and Jerry perform similar operations "numerous times."

Once, Strunk added, smoldering remains were tossed into a Dumpster, and when the trash bin caught fire, Laurieanne extinguished it with a garden hose.

It was Strunk, too, who gave damaging testimony about the habit among all three Sconces of referring to dental gold as "AU."

"When you heard Laurieanne Sconce use the expression 'AU,' can you think of a particular incident?" Lewis asked.

"Yes," Strunk replied, adding that the incident occurred in the back room of Lamb Funeral Home and she was talking to David. "The exact words I heard were 'How much AU did you get today, honey?'"

"And what did David respond?"

He showed her a styrofoam cup, Strunk said, which was half filled with gold teeth.

Besides showing his mother gold teeth that had been extracted from the mouths of cadavers, Strunk said he also had heard Laurieanne and David talking about the contest among the workers to see who could shoehorn the most corpses into the two retorts.

Strunk also testified that he took a take-back to one mortuary, supposedly representing one of its customers, before the body had even been cremated.

Dame said when he first went to work for David, his job was that of an ash sifter. It was his duty, he continued, to take the remains that were delivered to the funeral home in large metal trash cans and spread twenty to twenty-five pounds worth on a long empty table. He then would carefully go through the dark gray substance searching for bits of metal, which he would discard. Since the remains were still in fairly large chunks, the next step of the operation involved putting the material in a commercial cement mixer which contained two shot puts. When the mixer was turned on, the metal balls would tumble and crumble the pieces of bone.

"Did you ever get this ash from any place other than a large trash can?" Lewis asked.

"No," Dame replied.

When asked what conclusions he drew from this practice, Dame replied that he believed that when ash was packaged to be returned to survivors, it never came from just one body.

When his father died, Dame said, he pleaded with David to cremate his body alone. David promised to take care of it.

Asked to describe the incineration process at Pasadena Crematorium, Andre Augustine said:

"There were racks in the crematorium and bodies were on the racks. I saw David take bodies off the racks, put them on his shoulder, and load them into the retort." He put them in head first, Augustine said, one on top of another. "If they weren't all the way forward in the retort, he would go around to the other end, use a hook and pull them up to the front of the oven."

"Is the hook sharp on the end?" Lewis asked.

"Yes," Augustine replied.

"Where did the hook go into the body?"

"Either through the neck underneath the jawbone or under the shoulder."

"Did you ever see the hook go in the mouth and through the cheek?"

"Yes."

John Hallinan described a similar scene.

"Now when you would stack these bodies into the retort, would they be layered?" Lewis asked.

"Yes."

"How many layers of bodies would you have before they were burned?"

"I would say at least between two and four layers," he said, explaining that the usual process required using a piece of plywood as a temporary shelf. "We would place the bodies over that and then we would use that to push the bodies up. After that body was in place, then we would move the piece of plywood on top of that body and push the next body up. We'd continue until we worked our way up."

"And you were able to stack five high?" Lewis asked.

"It depended on the size of the bodies."

"What is the most amount of bodies you were able to get into a retort?"

"To my recollection, twenty."

It was Hallinan who had been working the morning the Pasadena Crematorium caught fire.

"Do you recall approximately what time you started loading bodies into the two retorts on the evening of November 22, 1986?" asked Lewis.

"It was approximately eight P.M.," Hallinan replied,

adding that it took them about five hours to get all the cadavers inside.

"And do you remember how many bodies you were able to get into each retort, or altogether how many bodies you were able to get in both?"

"Thirty-eight," Hallinan replied matter-of-factly.

The former funeral home worker said that he and co-worker Bob Garcia lit the ovens soon after they finished packing them, then left the building to go to Garcia's house to "get intoxicated on rock cocaine."

While they were gone, he said, the retorts caught fire and were subsequently destroyed.

The fire occurred early in the morning of November 23, 1986. Eighteen months later, when he was helping Lewis prepare the case against David, Detective Dennis Diaz testified that he went to the crematorium to see how badly the fire damage had been. What he found, he said, was that the roof of the building had caved in and the inside of the building was filled with rubble. The retorts, which had not been cleaned since the fire, were filled with human remains to a depth of ten to twelve inches.

Diaz said he took some bone samples from the retorts and delivered them to a forensic anthropologist named Judy Suchey. When she was called to the stand, she testified that her examination of part of the remains brought to her by Diaz showed that at least three bodies had been included in the sample.

How did she know that? Lewis asked.

Because, she said, there were three distal left humeri in that particular sample bag, and each person has only one distal left humeri, which is the lower part of the upper arm bone.

* * *

Hallinan's testimony caused Lewis to miss a step; it produced for the first but not the last time during the hearing an unplanned deviation in the prosecutor's strategy.

Late on the night he testified, Hallinan telephoned Lewis saying he was upset by something that had occurred after he left the courtroom. Lewis listened to his tale, then told him he was going to call him back to the stand early the next day and let him tell his story to Person.

The following morning the DDA wasted no time getting to the heart of the issue. What happened to you last night? he asked Hallinan as soon as he was settled in the witness chair.

Shooting a nervous glance at David, Hallinan said he was sitting at home when his telephone rang. He answered, and a man asked to speak to John. When he identified himself, the voice said: "You are pissing off some of your friends. They say you are a big rat, and they say that I have been hired to take you out. They said if you want to start, you can zipper your mouth and not show up tomorrow. If you don't, you'll be a statistic."

Did you recognize the voice? Lewis asked.

Another nervous glance at the defense table. "No," Hallinan said.

22

After Hallinan, Lewis was back on schedule. As he had done with the issue of multiple cremations, Lewis elicited testimony on another phase of the Sconce operation: the removal and sale of body parts.

He began by offering into evidence a document that contained the names of twenty-three people. At least one organ had been removed from each of the people on the list, he said, organs that then were sold by the CIE&TB. Organs from at least seventeen of those on the list were taken without permission, Lewis added. Plus he knew of at least nine other bodies from which parts were removed without consent. In all, the prosecution was able to document thirty-two bodies from which organs had been removed, twenty-six of them "by the use of fraud, deceit, forgery and outright theft."

In some cases, Lewis said, consent forms were signed only *after* the organs had already been removed. This activity was carried out under the authority of ATC forms which the DDA argued were inadequate, or without any forms at all.

"Considering the facts of this case," Lewis argued, "the people contend that the defendants, having been in the funeral business for many years, were well-aware of the vulnerability of the families of the deceased. The evidence clearly shows that the defendants . . . displayed a callous disregard for the feelings of these families in their most difficult and delicate times. The evidence in this case shows that the defendants . . . took grossly unfair advantage of the numerous families of the deceased persons who had the misfortune of trusting the bodies of their loved ones to the care of these three defendants."

To back up his contentions, he called a string of witnesses, both former employees and next of kin.

• Leon Packard testified that Jerry told him, in Laurieanne's presence, that if any customer ever asked about the "to remove tissue" clause in the ATC form, he should tell them it referred to the need to remove pacemakers, and when pacemakers were removed, it was inevitable that a "certain amount of minute tissue" would have to be removed as well.

• Former employee Louis Quinones testified that Laurieanne gave him a stack of ATC forms in November or December, 1986, and told him they were revised documents which needed to be distributed to their customers. Laurieanne added, Quinones said, that it was not necessary for him to point out the revisions when he delivered the forms.

• Stanley Dickey of the Dickey Mortuary in Fontana testified that if he had known that Lamb Funeral Home operated a tissue bank, he would not have used them for cremations.

Lewis also called the directors of thirteen funeral homes that sent bodies to Pasadena Crematorium/ Coastal Cremation. Each of them testified that they were unaware that organs were being removed, since they had never been told by David, Laurieanne, or Jerry that they needed to counsel next of kin about organ donation. Neither were they told, they said, that the Sconces were interpreting a signature on an ATC form as authority to remove organs, including eyes and corneas.

"In view of the evidence produced in this case is it reasonable to believe that all three defendants simply forgot to tell all these funeral directors that when they obtained the signatures of the next of kin on the Authority to Cremate forms that their signatures, in addition to authorizing cremation, also authorized unlimited organ removal?" Lewis asked rhetorically.

"No," he said, answering his own question, "this is not a case of forgetfulness. This is a case of premeditated fraud and deceit. The three defendants clearly did not want the funeral directors to know what was going on."

Lewis also called witnesses who testified that Jerry, Laurieanne, and David took an active role in organizing and operating the CIE&TB.

Marion Steen, for instance, said she loaned Laurieanne $15,000 in September 1985 to help her get the tissue bank started.

And funeral director Gregory Zook said he had wanted to invest but by the time he was ready to write a check, Laurieanne told him they didn't need any more investors.

Zook also testified that David once excitedly described how much money could be made from a tissue bank, claiming that he planned to make a half-million dollars just from the agreement with Carolina Biological Supply.

A man named Freeman Fairbanks testified that he blindly signed an ATC form proffered to him by Laurie-

anne when he was making arrangements for the cremation of his sister, Golda McCauley. He was not asked to
read the form or told what it was.

"As I recall," he testified, "Laurieanne made up a contract, the charges and so on and so forth, and I signed
that. And she showed me another form that she says was
an Authority to Cremate and asked me to sign it and I
signed it."

"Did you read the form before you signed it?" Lewis
asked.

"I'm sorry to say I didn't," Fairbanks replied.

"Did you get a copy of the form after you signed?"

"I don't have one, no."

After signing the form, he said, he asked to see his
sister's body one more time, but Laurieanne said that was
not possible. "She said I couldn't see her because she'd
already been prepared for cremation, 'wrapped' was the
word I believed she used." In actuality, bodies are
stripped of all clothing and other "unnatural" devices,
such as prostheses, jewelry and dental bridgework, before
they are put in the retort. They are, however, "wrapped"
in a cardboard sheet in an effort to preserve some mod-
esty.

"Did she tell you that your sister's eyes were taken out
the day before?" Lewis asked.

"No way!" Fairbanks replied. "She certainly didn't."

The prosecutor queried Fairbanks about an organ donor's card, if Laurieanne had ever asked him if his sister
had one.

"I can't say for sure," he replied, "but someone asked
me if she had a donor's card, and to my knowledge she
did not."

"Did you ever consent to donate any organ or eyes of
Golda McCauley?" Lewis asked.

"Definitely not," Fairbanks replied.

Lewis walked to the prosecution and returned with a

sheet of paper, which he handed to Fairbanks, explaining that it was a form used to log research tissue.

"On the back," Lewis said, "it has Golda McCauley's name at the top and it says date and hour of death, 5/27/86 at 1900, date and hour of procurement, May 27, 1986 at 2020 hours, and date and hour of preservation, 5/27/86, 2030 hours, and time between death and preservation, 1.5 hours. Have you ever seen that before?"

"No," Fairbanks said softly.

Although David had told Detective Diaz that the CIE&TB had been financed by Randy Welty, George Bristol, who had been hired by David as the technical expert to set up and operate the facility, said he never doubted that the three Sconces were running the operation.

"How would you determine whether in the case of any particular body that there was consent from the next of kin to take organs or tissue?" Lewis asked Bristol when he was on the stand.

"Well, we would look at the bodies, David or I or Eddie [Marshall] would. And we would see if they were okay to remove organs as far as being fresh enough, [that is,] not exhibiting stages of decomposition. Then we would write down the names on a scrap of paper and bring it in to either Jerry or Laurieanne to see if we had clearance to remove it."

"And did you get clearance from every body from which you removed organs or tissue? Did you first get clearance from Laurieanne or Jerry?"

"Yes," said Bristol.

Lewis wanted to know if he or the other workers made any distinction between bodies that had been brought in from Lamb Funeral Home or from other sources.

"There was a difference in consents usually," Bristol replied. "Because Lamb cases that we worked on, a lot of those were burials, to be embalmed cases, where the crematory cases, a lot of them, came from other funeral homes and they were on cremation authorization."

"How would your conduct with respect to taking tissue vary depending on whether the case was a burial case or a cremation case?" Lewis asked.

"Well," Bristol answered carefully, "there are certain things that we wouldn't remove on burial cases because if the scalpel slipped or something it would affect the viewability of the body."

Lewis asked if whether a body was destined for cremation or for burial made a difference in who Bristol went to for permission to remove organs.

"We would usually go to Laurieanne if it was a burial case because she was in charge of the ceremonies and she was the one to be in contact with the family," he answered.

Switching from the general to the specific, Lewis began questioning Bristol about the agreement to procure a large number of organs for the Carolina Biological Supply Co.

Bristol replied that he kept a special list of organs destined for the company so Laurieanne would have a list of donors to provide for state inspectors. However, the list was made up long after the organs had actually been supplied.

"Why did you wait so long to make that list?" Lewis asked.

"We were very busy," Bristol replied. "Much of the time we did not have time."

The initial list, Lewis determined, carried twenty-three names and represented the first shipment of tissue from the CIE&TB to Carolina Biological.

"What kind of tissue are we talking about?" Lewis asked.

Bristol shrugged. "Either primary organs, brains, hearts and lungs and so forth."

"Was at least one such organ—either a brain, heart or lung—removed from every person named on the list?"

Bristol nodded. "At least one."

Flourishing a sheaf of papers, Lewis identified the documents as shipping lists which identified organs sent at various times to Carolina Biological. The documents were dated between October 27, 1986, and November 21, 1986. One shipment consisted of eight boxes containing 48 brains; another was made up of four boxes with another 24 brains; one shipment included 40 pairs of lungs; another 81 hearts, and one box, shipped on October 27, contained only one organ, a spinal column.

"How did you happen to pick Carolina Biological?" Lewis asked.

"I'm a scientist," said Bristol. "I have worked in biology and everything forever, and I know that they are the largest supplier of specimens for anatomical study."

The organs that were sent to the company, Lewis asked, what were they to be used for?

They were destined to be used in research, Bristol replied, as opposed to transplant.

"When you started fulfilling the Carolina Biological order, was there any discussion between you and David Sconce with respect to doing research tissue, that is, procuring research tissue instead of procuring transplant tissue?"

"Yeah," said Bristol. "I thought the better way of going was transplant. That's what I am trained for."

"Is that what you thought you would be doing when you were hired by Coastal?"

"Yes," Bristol replied. "But I remember David telling me that we don't have transplantable tissue. We are going to have to work with what we have. And that's why we went into the research and teaching tissue."

Lewis had one other document he wanted to proffer. It was a purchase order from Carolina Biological made out to the CIE&TB and it called for the delivery of 500 brains, 750 hearts, and 100 lungs.

"Did you ever see this purchase order?" Lewis queried.

"No," said Bristol.

"Was there any discussion about the money to be made from research tissue?" Lewis asked.

"Yeah," said Bristol, "we believed we could do quite well with it."

"And did David say anything to that effect? What did he say?"

"Well, he said something like he had all the bodies that we ever needed."

From Bristol, Lewis switched to men who had worked for David at the crematorium, men who could testify to the allegedly common practice of removing gold-filled teeth. For sheer unpleasantness, that testimony was as strong as anything that had come before.

Leon Packard, Jim Dame, Dave Edwards, Andre Augustine, and Lisa Karlan all said they saw David pry open the mouths of cadavers and remove teeth. Once, said Augustine, he saw David remove ten to fifteen teeth from four bodies that were waiting to be cremated.

Packard testified that several times he saw David take containers of teeth and put them in the file cabinet behind Laurieanne's desk.

Packard also said he once asked David why he took the teeth, and David replied that it would be silly to let the gold burn up in the retorts. "It helps pay your salary."

On one occasion, Packard said, he went with David to Glendora, where David's friend, Mike Engwald, ran a business called "Gold, Gold, Gold." David had a container of teeth with him, and when they got to the shop, he and Engwald disappeared into a back room. When David returned a few minutes later, he had a stack of bills in his hand. He peeled off five $100 bills and gave them to Packard, saying that represented the raise that he had promised him.

Lorraine Moore, who once worked for Engwald, testified that David came into the shop at least three or four times a week—and sometimes as often as several times a day—carrying containers of gold-filled teeth.

Engwald usually paid David in cash, she said, frequently leaving the money in a sealed envelope with David's name on it. On one occasion, at Engwald's direction, she wrote David a check for $1200.

According to Hallinan's testimony, David was not the only one at the crematorium profiting from the removal of gold teeth. Bob Garcia also would extract them, he said.

Hallinan said Garcia put some of the teeth into a bottle which he turned over to David, but some also went into his pocket. Later, Hallinan testified, when he and Garcia were alone in the building, Garcia would take the teeth out of his pocket, put them on a hard surface, and pound them with a hammer until he had pulverized the dentine. Then he plucked out the gold and put it back in his pocket, throwing the bits of tooth in the trash. Later he would take the gold to a shop and sell it.

Garcia, Hallinan added almost as an afterthought, also had a passion for clothes, which he would remove from cadavers and either wear himself or sell.

Switching abruptly from teeth and clothes to another incident, Hallinan had an even more gruesome tale to tell.

He said he was working one day when another worker took a fancy to a gold ring on the finger of one of the cadavers.

"He attempted to get it off by pulling, but the finger had grown too much or expanded," he testified. "So at

that point he figured there was another method. That's
when I went into the next room."

"You didn't assist him?" Lewis asked.

"No."

"Did Garcia assist him?"

"As far as holding the finger," Hallinan acknowledged.

"Do you know what happened to that ring?"

"No, I don't."

Even as the parade of witnesses continued, there were
other factors at work that demanded Lewis's time and
attention. There was one situation, for instance, that
struck particularly close to home. As far as Lewis was
concerned, it irrevocably changed not only the entire
complexion of the proceedings, but his life.

23

On October 1, almost two months after the preliminary hearing began, Lewis asked for a private meeting with Person in the judge's chambers. Behind the closed door, Lewis explained that there were developments taking place that had a direct bearing on the case and he wanted Person's guidance on how to continue.

About three weeks previously, Lewis said, he received a telephone call from an inmate at the county jail tipping him off that David was trying to hire someone to commit a series of murders. The alleged potential victims included the prosecutor himself and David's grandparents. Lewis would later learn as well that there was another potential victim: Elie Estephan.

As for wanting *him* killed, a much-shaken Lewis reported, David was said to have two motives. One was the bail issue; the other was his mother. Apparently David continued to feel that he had been tricked by the prosecutor into coming into court thinking the requested bail would be $5000, only to discover that Lewis in fact was asking for $500,000 bail. If it had not been for Lewis, David reasoned, he still would be free. As far as David was concerned, Lewis was leading a personal vendetta against him.

What seemed to bother David as much if not more than the bail issue, however, was how upset his mother was by Lewis's aggressive prosecution. As David had told Dave Edwards when he asked the ex-football star to assault Ron Hast, "He made my mother cry." Lewis was doing more than make Laurieanne cry; he was humiliating her and trying to send her to prison.

Lewis had come to Person, he told the judge, because the defense had also heard about the leaks and wanted the prosecutor to turn over a list of the prisoners that investigators were talking to. Lewis, however, wanted Person to keep the defense at bay until investigators had a chance to complete their job.

Person did not find the request unreasonable. He would take care of the defense, he promised, until the investigation was over.

In mid-November, eight weeks after Lewis got the first telephone call and six weeks after his meeting with Person, the issue came into the open. Ironically, it was not because of the D.A.'s investigation, but because the defense decided to take the offense by attempting to discredit the prosecution's inmate witnesses' testimony before it could be offered. The action was good news for Lewis. Since it was the defense that had raised the question, Lewis was able to call his witnesses without having to turn over his investigative notes to the Diamond, Rucker, and Nishi. It was a small but significant victory for the DDA.

In the end, Lewis ended up calling still another string of witnesses to describe how David was trying to contract for the various killings.

One of the first to testify was Rogelio Rojas, an inmate barber who regularly trimmed David's hair.

While he was snipping David's locks one day, Rojas

said, David casually asked him if he knew anyone who would be willing "to take out a few people for money."

Who did he have in mind? Rojas asked.

Two people specifically, David replied. One was a man who had testified against him, Dave Edwards. The second was the prosecutor, Walt Lewis.

According to Rojas, David never went into detail about any actual plans to have Lewis killed, but instead he "just said that he wanted to try and find some people that were willing to do it for any amount of money."

And where did he expect to get this money? Lewis asked.

By selling some property he owned, Rojas said David replied; that, and with the proceeds of his grandparents' estate. If they could be killed as well, their money would go to his parents and they, in turn, would give him what he needed.

Rojas said he told David he would see what he could do, but he said he never pursued the issue any further.

Inmate David Gerhardt testified that David asked him if he could refer someone who would "put a hit" on Lewis and on his grandparents, who he claimed were "quite wealthy." If the elderly couple could be "knocked off," Gerhardt quoted David as saying, possibly by poisoning their mineral water, his parents would inherit all their money.

In return for his services, David promised Gerhardt that when he was released, he could move into the mortuary and stay there as long as he liked. He would even give him a job working in the funeral home.

Steve Warren, who had been a cellmate of David's at one point, said David mentioned to him one day that he wanted to have Lewis killed.

"And did he say why he wanted to kill me?" Lewis asked.

"For the strain and trauma that you were putting his folks through," said Warren, who added that David was particularly upset because of the way the prosecution was affecting his mother.

"What did he say?" Lewis prompted.

"He said that she had had a nervous breakdown and she was going through menopause."

"And how was that connected with wanting me killed?"

"What he said was, it's not so much what you are doing to him, it's what you are putting his parents through."

"And he didn't say what the district attorney's office is putting the parents through, or the police. He said me personally?"

"Yes," Warren replied, adding that David was very explicit about what he wanted to have done to Lewis. "He said he would like to put you in a sack and hang you from a hook [and] beat you until you were black and blue and then put you—throw you—into an incinerator." As an alternative method, Warren said, David suggested that he would like "to tie you up to a cactus and skin you and let the ants crawl over you."

Finally, Lewis asked, did David say anything about how such plans might be carried out?

"He said," Warren answered, "that if I was released and you were to disappear, that I would be taken care of."

"How did you respond to that?"

"I told him I didn't want any part of it."

When investigators went to the jail to begin talking to inmates, they also found inscribed upon the wall of David's cell, in two-inch high letters, the sentence: "Lewis will die." An expert called by the prosecution testified it was David's handwriting.

David did not deny the scribbling. It was intimated that the sentence had originally read "Lewis will die of AIDS," but someone anxious to see David get in trouble had erased the last two words. Investigators noted, however, that "Lewis will die" was inscribed within a tightly penciled oval and there would have been no room for the rest of the message.

Inmate George Philpott testified that David mentioned to him at least three times, once when they were playing cards, that he would like to have Lewis murdered. He also mentioned, Philpott said, that David wanted to arrange the murder of a fellow inmate—Gerhardt—who by then had fallen out with David.

Philpott said he told David he had better be careful about what he said because if he were to be overheard by one of the guards, additional charges could be filed against him.

And inmate Jack Dubois testified that David had talked to him at least five times about having Lewis murdered. He brought it up often enough, Dubois said, to make him believe that David was serious about it.

Quoting David, Dubois said that he wanted Lewis dead and Edwards "seriously hurt."

When David asked him if he knew anyone who could carry out his plans, Dubois said, he replied in the affirmative.

"Money is no problem," Dubois said David replied, adding that he could have the cash delivered.

Roger Diamond met with reporters outside the courtroom after Rojas and Warren testified, to denounce their claims against his client. Warren was nothing but a "jailhouse snitch" Diamond asserted, insinuating that he and Rojas made up their testimony so they could get extra privileges while they were behind bars.

Despite Diamond's denials, Lewis continued to have faith in what the inmates had said. Although he eventually had to withdraw as prosecutor because he had become a potential victim, Lewis remained significantly disturbed by the experience. Nothing Diamond would ever be able to say would convince him that David had not been actively seeking his murder.

But Lewis apparently was not the only one on David's hit list.

According to Gerhardt, David told him that he wanted to have his grandparents killed because that was the way his mother could get her inheritance. David planned to accomplish the task, the inmate said, by poisoning the Lambs' bottled water.

George Bristol, Dave Edwards, Andre Augustine, and Dan Galambos also testified that David had mentioned to them at different times that he wanted his grandparents dead.

"He said to me that he hated his grandparents so many times that I can't remember how many it was," said Bristol, who added that David's preferred method of dispatching Lawrence and Lucille Lamb was by poisoning them.

About a week after first hearing David make such remarks, Bristol said he went to Jerry, telling him that his son, David, might be planning to "off the old man."

And what was Jerry's response? Lewis asked.

"He put his fingers to his lips and said, 'Shhhhh,' " Bristol answered.

Despite this testimony, the grandparents, as well as Jerry and Laurieanne, continued to publicly support David, professing to disbelieve the statements. They were, they proclaimed, manufactured by the district attorney's office in an attempt to frame David. Nevertheless, as a result of what he had heard, Lewis filed additional charges against David, accusing him of solicitation of murder—with him-

self and David's grandparents as the intended victims—
and conspiracy to murder, with Elie Estephan as the potential prey. Since David had already been charged with
soliciting the murders of his grandparents, the information furnished by the inmates led to no additional charges
on that count.

Of the two new charges, the conspiracy accusation was
by far the more serious. As far as the courts were concerned, a conviction on conspiracy to murder carried the
same penalty as one on murder: twenty-five years to life.
On the other hand, the solicitation count was comparatively benign. A conviction on that charge carried a maximum sentence of only six years.

Shortly after filing the new charges, Lewis asked for a
meeting with his superiors in the district attorney's office
to discuss his possible immediate withdrawal from the
case. The decision was that Lewis would not withdraw at
that time. The reasoning was that the district attorney had
decided long before not to be pressured into withdrawing
a prosecutor until the current proceeding had been completed. Otherwise a defendant who wanted to delay legal
action against himself could indefinitely postpone it simply by threatening the prosecutor. A number of cases—
this one in particular—are so complicated that it may take
a prosecutor months to prepare. That work could then be
negated by the defendant making a threat. If the district
attorney's office responded to every threat by withdrawing
the prosecutor, it also would be an effective way for a
defendant to effortlessly get rid of a prosecutor he
thought was doing too good a job, hoping that the re-
placement prosecutor would be less efficient.

With the decision made for him to continue as prosecutor, Lewis returned to questioning the inmates. There
were other issues that he wanted to bring out as well, ones
that would send him back to amend the charge sheet yet

again. By the time *those* issues had been probed, David, in addition to the accusations he already faced, also would be charged with bribing a witness, offering to bribe a witness, and solicitation of perjury; Laurieanne with offering to bribe a witness, bribing a witness, conspiring to bribe a witness, and solicitation of perjury; and Jerry with conspiring to bribe a witness and solicitation of perjury. Plus, one other family member, Brad Sallard, David's brother-in-law, would be accused of trying to bribe a witness. The charges came about this way:

Rojas, David's inmate barber friend, who had testified that he did not pursue David's request to help him find a hit man, also swore that David paid him $200 in anticipation that he would lie for him on the witness stand.

However, since inmates are not allowed to have cash, the money was not given directly to Rojas. Rather, according to Lewis, it was left for him in a sealed envelope at the home of his stepmother, Concha Rojas, who testified that there had, indeed, been a plain white envelope containing cash delivered to her house and addressed to her stepson.

Concha Rojas's granddaughter, Anna Marie Aguirre, testified that the envelope was dropped off at the Rojas home by a blond-haired woman who arrived in a white van driven by a man. When asked if she could identify the woman, Aguirre pointed to Laurieanne.

But the real kicker was additional testimony from David Gerhardt, the inmate who claimed that David offered to let him live at the Lamb mortuary and work for the Sconces while he planned the murder of Walt Lewis.

With Lewis pumping him, Gerhardt, who proved to be an extremely articulate witness, spun a tale about a plot that would have been worthy of Len Deighton for its complexity and shrewdness, a tale that would have been extremely damaging to the Sconces if it had been related by anyone but a convicted felon.

Under Lewis's questioning, Gerhardt said the idea had

been dreamed up by David. According to the plan, Gerhardt was to contact the prosecutor and volunteer to testify against David. When he got on the stand, however, he was supposed to say that Lewis and Diaz had put pressure on him to appear in court against David because they wanted to frame the crematorium operator. What the prosecutor and detective were to have done, Gerhardt was to say, was ply him with information from David's confidential file and order him to reveal it on the stand under the guise of information gleaned from conversations between him and David.

In theory, when he testified about the alleged frame-up, the prosecution of David and his family would be thrown into disorder. Maybe, with any luck, it would have to be abandoned altogether.

Gerhardt's reward for participating in this intrigue was to be $2500.

But there was one other condition. Before Gerhardt would get the money, David insisted that he sign a statement summarizing their agreement. This Gerhardt was reluctant to do.

He not only was hesitant to sign the document, Gerhardt said, but he had serious doubts about the efficacy of the plot, telling David there was too much of a chance it could backfire. David, however, had argued that he was going to give Gerhardt such solid information that it would appear that the *only* place it could have come from would have been the prosecutor's file. The information was *so* good, David said, that there would be no way for anyone to cast doubt on Gerhardt's claim that it had come from investigators.

Gerhardt said that when he continued to exhibit reluctance, David started turning the screws. First, David's wife, Barbara, came to see him and promised to deposit $160 in his jail account as a down payment on the full amount. Then Jerry got in touch with him, verifying that the deposit had been made. Then he was visited again by Barbara, who brought along her brother, Brad Sallard. On that visit, Gerhardt said, they gave him a bag full of dimes. Later, he added, Laurieanne sent him gift packages containing socks, underwear, and a *Penthouse* magazine.

To substantiate the inmate's *real* testimony, Lewis introduced two letters that Gerhardt said he had received from Laurieanne.

One, dated September 1, 1987, was designed to encourage him by quoting a passage from Ephesians which dealt with King David's imprisonment and the biblical figure's ability to endure. The letter also urged Gerhardt to testify honestly. It was signed with a religious platitude.

The second letter, dated the next day, September 2, addressed David as a "friend." It quoted from a hymn that was part of the Chapelbelles' repertoire and gushed platitudes about angels and God's promises. Laurie signed it with their nicknames, Mom and Coach Sconce.

Lewis further corroborated Gerhardt's claims by calling a woman, Stephanie Moten, who worked in the cashier's office of the L.A. County Jail. She said that on September fourth a man who identified himself as "Mr. Sallard" deposited $160 into Gerhardt's account.

Lewis did not offer any corroboration for Gerhardt's testimony regarding the alleged roles of Barbara and Jerry in the bribery attempt. Barbara, Jerry and Laurieanne were not charged. Charges against Sallard are still awaiting a probable cause hearing.

24

The defense, naturally, was anxious to demolish the testimony of the inmates who had spoken against David. One attempt to do this came from David himself.

When Warren had been on the stand detailing the alleged murder plot against Lewis, he also told how David had mentioned to him his involvement in another proposed escapade, one that came about, Warren said, when he and David were discussing ways of murdering people. David suggested that poison might be the perfect weapon, remarking specifically that one way to accomplish the job might be to use leaves from the poinsettia plant, which could be added to an innocent-looking salad. Another, he said, was to use a compound called "zytel." When Warren uttered the strange-sounding word, David straightened in his chair. "Hook, line, and sinker," he muttered sotto voce.

At the time, Detective Diaz happened to be sitting on David's immediate left. In Pasadena Municipal Court, the defense and prosecution tables abut end to end, in effect forming one long table. Seating at the table was fairly standard. Going from right to left, looking from the bench, was the prosecutor, his chief investigator, the defense attorney, and the defendant. The defendant's attorney, in this case Roger Diamond, would usually be sitting next to Diaz, a buffer between the prosecution team and the defendant, but Diamond had difficulty hearing in his right ear and so had moved to David's other side. This put Diaz in a unique position, literally, since David had a habit of keeping up a steady stream of patter during the proceedings.

At first, when he made the comment regarding Warren's testimony, Diaz thought David was speaking to him.

"Pardon?" the detective said.

David whispered that Warren had fallen into his trap, that he, David, had fed Warren the word "zytel" just to see if he would repeat it. And he had. Diaz glanced sideways at David. What the hell *is* this? he asked himself. David was claiming on one hand that he had never talked to anyone in jail about anything remotely related to murder, but on the other hand he was saying that he baited a trap *during a conversation about murder,* so that one of the snitches would repeat what David wanted said, thereby proving what David suspected—that he was being ratted upon. From Diaz's viewpoint, the very fact that David fed Warren the word "zytel" was an admission that he *had* been talking to fellow prisoners.

Had he fed Warren the word before he realized that he was going to be turned in? the detective wondered. Or was it afterward, in an attempt to cover up? As far as the detective was concerned, David's back-door admission that he had talked at least to Warren about murdering others strengthened rather than weakened what the inmates had said about his potential dangerousness. David's affirmation only gave credence to their testimony.

Apparently, Person agreed. When Lewis asked the judge on December eighteenth to revoke David's bail order—that is, to make it impossible for him to be released even if he could have come up with the $500,000—Person went along. Lewis's request also marked the end of testimony. At that point Person gathered his papers and gaveled the court into an indefinite recess. He wanted to study the transcripts and the evidence, he said, to determine how to proceed.

Five months later, on May 9, 1988, Person summoned Jerry, Laurieanne, and David, along with their lawyers and Lewis, back into the courtroom to hear his decision. What he said surprised no one: that he had determined that there was sufficient evidence to bring the Sconces to trial. But the fervor of his response was unexpected.

Person began reading his thirty-seven-page ruling sedately enough by acknowledging the uniqueness of the case. "It has raised a number of legal and factual issues of first impression in this state," he said. "In fact, the complaint in and of itself weaves a pattern of allegations which this court believes to be unique in the history of law of the state of California and perhaps in this nation."

In what would prove to be incredible understatement, he added: "I am fairly certain that before the legacy of this case is final, that the appellate courts and perhaps this state's supreme court will be reviewing this case and the many issues raised by it."

Then Person began expressing his alarm at the situation described during the four months he had sat listening to the parade of ninety-plus witnesses. As he progressed through his ruling, his comments became increasingly scathing.

Although he admitted he was appalled by the nature of the testimony—words powerful enough to have "made the strongest stomach feel uneasy"—he had been considerably impressed by the character of the witnesses and the solidity of Lewis's presentation.

"Only very few of these witnesses had, in this court's opinion, any arguable motivations to fabricate testimony for these proceedings, and in most instances where the court may have had some doubts in its mind, these witnesses were generally corroborated substantially by physical evidence presented here or by the testimony of other witnesses," he said.

As one witness followed another, he continued, he began to perceive the breadth and depth of what had been occurring behind the mortuary's closed doors.

"The picture beginning to emerge," he said, "was one of a family funeral business with a long and proud history in the Pasadena community and with family generations passing it down to one another, which for some reason or reasons started to be motivated by a desire at almost any cost to procure the largest number possible of human remains for cremation by outbidding its competitors, and once having succeeded in cornering of the local market for cremations, viewing its perceived triumph by deciding to cast aside morality as well as legality in virtually every aspect of its expanding enterprise in the handling of human remains thereafter."

It was these "unholy and unfettered" ambitions, Person added, that led to the stunning array of charges on his desk, charges "ranging from conspiracies of various types, forgery, grand theft and embezzlement, to wrongful handling of trust funds, to falsification of death certificates, to mass cremation, to commingling of human remains, to unlawful removal of body parts from human remains, to, in David Sconce's case, grand theft auto, receiving stolen property, to conspiracy to commit felonious assaults upon competitors as well as those who had threatened to reveal the unlawful practices rumored to be occurring in the family enterprise, to robbery, to solicitation of murder of his grandparents as well as the district attorney who is prosecuting the case against him, to bribery, to dissuading witnesses from testimony, to solicitation of perjury, to witness intimidation, and, as to David Sconce and Laurieanne, bribery of a witness, and finally, as to each defendant, conspiracy to obstruct justice."

Person paused, apparently overwhelmed anew by the magnitude of the accusations.

"Clearly," he began again, "the picture emerging was not unlike the portrait hidden in the attic of Dorian Gray in that as more and more evidence was presented, the uglier the picture became. The picture, like that of Dorian Gray, was hidden to all except the Sconce family. Outwardly, with the possible exception of David, members of the funeral industry as well as their customers believed that the Lamb Funeral Home was one of the most revered of all such businesses in the area. Only after they expanded the scope of their business in the sale of organs, which was virtually unknown to all who did business with them, did outsiders who had compassion for the potential customers begin to see what the portrait really looked like behind the scenes."

Why the Sconces operated as they did, Person said, he had no firm idea. "The court does not have the benefit of knowing for certain what was going through the mind of each of these defendants. [But] it does have the benefit of the circumstantial evidence as to the motivations of these defendants in taking the course of action which was taken in furtherance of their enterprise." And those motivators, he added, appeared to be "avarice and amoral ambition." These, he clearly implied, were, in his opinion poor precepts upon which to base a business, particularly one that served a vulnerable public.

Barely containing his outrage, Person pointed out the inherent weakness of the Sconce argument that organs were freely donated.

"Not one document received into evidence or any testimony in support thereof in this matter persuades this court that any donor or other authorized person voluntarily intended to make a gift of any body part to the Lamb

Funeral Home, Coastal Cremations, Inc., or Coastal International Eye and Tissue Bank." As far as the practice of removing organs, Person said, "It was clearly done without authority of law."

It was his opinion, he added, "that no contract was entered into by any of the donors or other authorized persons by virtue of the execution of Authority to Cremate forms where said forms were in fact made out by the appropriate donors or otherwise authorized persons.

"The court finds beyond a reasonable doubt that the Authority to Cremate forms which contained any of the variations of the phrase 'to remove tissue' did not lawfully authorize defendants herein to remove corneas, whole eyes, hearts, lungs, or brains."

However, it would not be very long in the future before Person's opinion on this issue was directly contradicted in a way that would leave prosecutors and others who had followed the case deeply shocked. But in May 1988 it was Person's opinion that counted.

Citing the fact that David, when he applied for a permit from the state to open the tissue bank, claimed that his plans were limited to working with eye tissue only, Person said:

"How could approval to remove eye tissue ever be in good faith presumed to be approval to remove brains, hearts, or lungs? The defendants argue that the approval was general . . . to remove whatever organs they wanted. This court respectfully disagrees with that position. All it does in this court's opinion is reveal that the defendants wanted to appear to be in compliance with the rules by obtaining some kind of approval as required, but then to set their own parameters for the scope of the approval in light of the lucrative business that could be done with the additional forms of organs."

In addition, Person added, the Sconces tried to deceive their own employees into believing that appropriate authority had been given for removal of organs. "Even then," he said, "one of them, Lisa Karlan, was persistent in her belief that the Authority to Cremate form was not legally sufficient to do so and was ultimately terminated for, among other things, her adherence to the position that the entire record reveals was a logical and legally sound one."

In Person's opinion, the Sconces' actions had been neither inadvertent nor unintentional. "It is clear to this court," he said, "that these defendants worked hand in hand to commit fraud and deceit upon the donors or other authorized persons by violating their fiduciary duty to those persons by the active, intentional concealment or nondisclosure of the material facts which were in the defendants' exclusive knowledge with the actual knowledge that there was concealment intended to deceive those persons who signed the Authority to Cremate forms with the 'to remove tissue' clause.

"On the surface," Person concluded, "the Sconces treated the affected customers with dignity and respect, and all believed they had been treated fairly. However, the Sconces' unspoken plans to profit by the sale of human organs and tissue, which they believed would probably never be discovered, were blatant actions that exhibited the propensity to take unfair advantage of unknowing persons in perhaps their most difficult moments."

If Person had been the trial court judge, the Sconces undoubtedly would have been called accountable, in toto, for the long list of alleged transgressions. That was beyond his responsibility, however. His job was limited to ruling on the probability that they had committed the crimes with which they were charged. About that, he had no doubt. But that was the end of Person's involvement. From his court the case transferred to superior court, where it eventually landed on the desk of Judge Terry Smerling.

Philosophically, a more direct opposite of Person could not have been found. When Smerling finished reviewing the same evidence that had been presented before Person, his conclusions were markedly different. Once Smerling began working on the case, it no longer was recognizable as the same one that had landed on his desk. In the end, Smerling, who *did* have the responsibility to call the Sconces accountable, gave them everything except the keys to his car.

Before then, however, David had one more chance to explain to investigators his involvement in the series of events that had been outlined in the preliminary hearing. That time, though, the investigator was not Diaz, but a Detective Robert Hopkins, who had come into the case late and via a rather circuitous route.

A twenty-four-year veteran in law enforcement, Hopkins was a member of the police department in Simi Valley, which is in Ventura County rather than Los Angeles County, where the charges outstanding against David were filed. Hopkins got involved because the Ventura County and Los Angeles County district attorneys offices had decided to look more closely at events surrounding the death of Tim Waters.

That, too, had come about in a rather roundabout way. When Steve Warren was testifying about zytel, he explained how he had expressed his skepticism to David about the efficiency of poison as a murder weapon. However, David had told him not to worry, he had already proved a poison would work with "that Waters guy," Warren testified, quoting David. When Warren said that, Lewis jumped as if he had been poked with a cattle prod.

25

Unknowingly, Warren had hit on a particularly sensitive point when he brought up Tim Waters. In his own mind, Lewis had believed that Tim had been murdered and that David was involved. But proving it was something else. He had been trying for months to penetrate the shield that seemed to surround the case, but he had had little luck. There was no doubt that David initiated the February 12, 1985, attack on Waters; he had Galambos's confession regarding that, plus Dave Edwards's admission that he had gone to Burbank to do the same thing and had abandoned the plan only because there was too much risk that he would be arrested. Also, there was unassailable physical evidence that Tim had been severely beaten. But assault was not murder; building a case for Tim's murder would be much more difficult. Before he could even consider developing a case against David in connection with Tim's death—even though both Galambos and Edwards swore that David had bragged independently to them about killing Tim—Lewis would first have to be able to substantiate that Tim's death was indeed a homicide. The stumbling block there, of course, was Dr. Holloway's report, which stated that Tim had died of natural causes.

Long before Steve Warren suggested a connection,

Lewis had been on the phone with Dr. F. Warren Lovell, who had been Holloway's boss. Lewis correctly felt that discourse with Lovell had to be handled with utmost diplomacy. Lewis was a DDA in Los Angeles County and Lovell was the coroner in Ventura County, therefore Lovell was under no obligation to go out of his way to help the prosecutor. As far as Ventura County was officially concerned, Tim had died a natural death. The county had enough murders to handle as it was without having to go out of its way to find one more.

Choosing his words carefully, Lewis asked Lovell if his former assistant possibly could have made a mistake during his autopsy. "Is there *anything* in the file that might suggest that Tim's death might have been a homicide?"

While Lewis kept the line open, Lovell retrieved the file. Twirling a pen, the prosecutor waited impatiently. In the background he could hear Lovell flipping pages. After what seemed an interminable period, the coroner grunted. "That's strange."

Lewis dropped the pen. To date no one he had talked to had ever even hinted that something might be amiss.

"What's strange?" he asked cautiously.

"We never ordered any toxicology tests done," Lovell said.

Lewis thought he was going to scream. He wanted to make a case for murder by poisoning, and no one had done any toxicology tests on the suspected victim.

"Can we do it now?" he asked very carefully. "Can we exhume the body?"

"No need to that," Lovell replied cheerily. "We routinely file tissue and fluid samples on all the bodies we autopsy."

"Would those samples still be there?" Lewis asked, his hopes rising for the first time.

"Let's see," Lovell said. "Waters died in 1985. We keep

the material for five years. Yes, the samples should still be here."

"Can you do the tests?" Lewis begged. "Can you run the tests and tell me if he was poisoned?"

"We don't have the proper equipment, but I'll send the material to Foster City and see what they can come up with," Lovell said, referring to a crime lab near San Francisco. It was reputed to be one of the best facilities of its kind in the county.

"Great," said Lewis. "Let me know what they find."

Lovell dispatched the specimens on October 6, 1987. At the same time, he began the paperwork to back up his action. Lovell's instincts told him something was not right as well, and he wanted to make sure all his bases were covered. On November fourth he countermanded Holloway's natural-death ruling and filed a new report listing both the cause of death and the manner of death as "undetermined." As imprecise as that sounded, the action was significant because it acknowledged officially that there may have been more to the incident than was initially believed.

As the weeks slipped by and Lewis became more involved in the preliminary hearing, he pushed Tim Waters to the back of his mind. He never quit wondering about the incident, but he was too busy to do a lot of about it. Occasionally, when he had a few minutes, he checked in with Lovell just to see if he had heard anything from the lab, and the answer was always no. Then one day he got some encouragement.

"I got a report yesterday," Lovell told him when he phoned. "I was just about to call you."

It was, Lovell explained, a good news/bad news situation. The bad news was that Foster City technicians had been unable to find any trace of the usual poisons like arsenic in the material that had been supplied from Tim's body. It is a common belief that toxicologists can put specimens from a victim into one end of a mysterious machine and have a list of the contents come out the other. Unfortunately, that is not so. Toxicologists can run a series of tests on tissue and fluid samples and say with a certain degree of certainty whether one or several substances are present, but they have to have an idea of what they're looking for to begin with. Generally, tests on a suspected poison victim are designed to look for a very few common substances. If there are no positive reactions on those tests, toxicologists then either assume the victim was not poisoned or had been killed with something unusual. Any further tests have to be conducted almost on a substance-by-substance basis. It is not unlike trying to thread a needle in the dark.

"Oh," Lewis replied unhappily when he heard Lovell's summary, his heart sinking yet again.

But, Lovell said optimistically, much to Lewis's relief, he was continuing to pursue it. "I've asked the lab to do some more tests anyway," the coroner added, "just in case it was something more exotic. I'll let you know."

"Okay," Lewis replied, his mind already on his witnesses for the next day.

Again there was a long gap between conversations. Even when the two did talk, Lovell had nothing new to report.

Finally Lewis took a reluctant step: He bypassed the coroner and went directly to the lab. When he finished talking to the director of the department that was conducting the tests, he was dejected. Well, at least I have an answer, he told himself. Cheerlessly, he dialed Lovell's number. As soon as the coroner was on the line, Lewis began apologizing.

"I didn't really want to go over your head," he said, "but time was getting critical for me and I felt I needed an answer."

"That's all right," Lovell replied graciously. "What did they find?"

"Nothing, I'm afraid," Lewis explained. "We know Waters was extremely overweight, so he undoubtedly had a heart condition and probably was taking medication for it, most likely digitalis. The only unusual substance Foster City could find in Waters's samples was something called digoxin, which apparently points to digitalis."

There was a pause. *"Digoxin!"* shouted the normally soft-spoken coroner. "That's it!"

"What's it?" Lewis said, surprised by the coroner's reaction. "What do you mean? If Waters had been taking digitalis, they naturally would have found digoxin."

"But Waters *wasn't* taking digitalis," Lovell replied.

"That doesn't really matter," Lewis replied. "Maybe it was some other kind of medication. In any case, Foster City said Waters was not poisoned with digitalis because the amount of digoxin in his system was not enough to be fatal."

"That isn't what I mean," Lovell said excitedly. "The digoxin itself didn't have to be fatal. I just finished reading an article in one of my journals that dealt with an elderly woman who had died from a self-inflicted dose of oleander."

Lewis was totally confused. "What does oleander and an old woman have to do with Tim Waters?" he asked.

"Oleander is a deadly poison," Lovell said, explaining that when someone ingests it, it affects the heart—interrupts its rate and rhythm, in fact—and that leads to death from heart block.

"I still don't see the connection with Tim Waters and digoxin," Lewis persisted.

Lovell then explained that if the tests conducted at the Foster City lab turned up digoxin when the person whose blood was being analyzed had not ingested anything with digoxin in it, the inescapable conclusion was that the person had ingested oleander.

Lewis wanted to put his head on his desk and sob. Oleander! he cried silently. My God, something as simple as oleander.

Truly, California has been blessed in many ways, not the least of which is its fortuitous conjunction of climate and soil which makes the area one of the world's most prolific, agriculturally and horticulturally speaking. Fruits and vegetables grow in shocking profusion, covering fertile acre upon fertile acre. As for flowers, they are everywhere: in pots and window boxes, beds and borders, parks and playgrounds. Flowering shrubs decorate the entrances to government buildings and office complexes, high-rise apartments and humble adobes; they line the shoulders of highways and brighten the neutral grounds. Flowers are to California what crabgrass is to Indiana.

Undeniably, the flowers are beautiful. But what many people don't realize is they can also be deadly. There is, for example, the beautiful lily of the valley with its white, bell-shaped flowers and orange-red berries. It can kill in a matter of hours. There is hemlock, which grows wild in most places. Hemlock leaves used in a salad are as deadly as curare, the infamous Central and South American poison popular in crime fiction. A subtle danger from hemlock comes not so much from the chance of someone ingesting its leaves, but in unknowingly eating quail that have fed on the seeds. The poison, universally known because it allegedly was the base for a fatal cocktail for Socrates, has no effect on the quail, but the ingested flesh of one bird can paralyze a man.

The popular azalea can be a killer as well; the state flower of West Virginia and Washington is remarkably lethal. What makes it potentially more hazardous is that its funnel-shaped blooms seem to have a special attraction for children, who often try to suck the nectar. If they do, they can be dead in six hours.

Even the beautiful poinsettia, the Christmas flower, can be perilous. Although there have been few documented cases of death caused by the plant, ingestion of the leaves can cause excruciating abdominal pain with vomiting and diarrhea. David knew something of what he spoke when he mentioned this plant to Steve Warren.

And then there is oleander. Known to scientists by its Latin name, *nerium oleander*, it has other names in other places. In some areas it is called Jericho rose. In Hawaii it is oleana or olinana. In Mexico, rose laurel. In Cuba, rose bay or rosa francesa; and in Haiti, laurier desjardins. In some places, the name derives from its properties rather than its appearance. In Italian and Arabic, the name for the plant translates as "ass killer," and in Sanskrit as "horse killer."

In less temperate areas oleander is a popular house plant, but in warmer, subtropical places, such as the southern, southwestern, and western United States, as well as much of Asia, Africa, Australia, Greece, and Italy, it grows well outdoors, a bush frequently reaching a height of twenty feet or more. The leaves are dark green, long, and narrow. The flowers, which are themselves not large but grow in grand clusters, are a beautiful pink, red or white. In areas where it grows readily, oleander is frequently planted as an ornamental, decorating not only public and private gardens, but miles and miles of California freeway. Around Los Angeles and its environs, in the region the residents call the Southland, oleander is ubiquitous, a colorful, easy-to-care-for, delightful-to-look-at perennial that can, and does, show up everywhere. There is no doubt, visually speaking, that it is a handsome addition to the landscape.

Unfortunately, it is also extremely lethal. Every part of the plant, from its milky white sap to its willowy branches, is capable of causing agonizing illness and death. The most dangerous parts are the blossoms and seeds. If they are ingested, they are guaranteed to cause, at the very least, debilitating illness. Particularly dangerous is the water in which cut branches have been placed, such as the liquid in a vase that has been holding a floral display. Drink that, and the foolhardy imbiber had better check to make sure his will is up-to-date. Chew a handful of leaves and the result is the same.

After the blossoms, seeds, and leaves, the toxicity drops off slightly but not significantly. Honey made by bees feasting on oleander nectar can be toxic. If the plant is burned, the smoke also is toxic. And there is a story, perhaps apocryphal but nevertheless very possible, about a Boy Scout who used an oleander stem to roast a wiener, a killer hot dog, so to speak. Whether this actually happened is irrelevant; it *could* happen. The mystery writer Lucille Kallen used just such a method for murder in her book, *The Piano Bird*. And Sue Grafton used powdered oleander leaves as a murder weapon in *"A" Is for Alibi*.

Several cultures are especially savvy to oleander's death-causing potential. In Europe it is often used to exterminate rats. In the subcontinent, in countries like India and Pakistan, oleander is a common tool for murder or suicide.

Under the system by which fatal poisons are commonly ranked, there are four major classifications: the hyperacute, which causes death immediately; the acute, which takes a little longer; the subacute, which is slower still; and the chronic, which causes death by accumulation. Oleander fits into the acute or subacute categories. Nevertheless, it acts swiftly enough to be lumped into a subgenus the experts call the "sudden death" or "drop dead" class. In this context the actual *time* it takes to kill someone is academic.

Symptoms, which usually appear quickly, are sweating,

nausea, vomiting, and bloody diarrhea, followed by loss of muscle coordination. Victims also often see colors that are not there. In almost all cases there is severe heart palpitation, which frequently convinces the victim, not altogether incorrectly, that he is suffering a coronary. The final stages are coma and death, caused by the poison's effect on the heart.

In all its forms, it is odorless colorless, and tasteless, besides being virtually untraceable. Chances are, a toxicologist searching blindly for traces of a poison in a person's blood or tissue almost certainly would *not* stumble upon oleander. Unless the toxicologist had an idea of what he was looking for, he most likely would find—and then only by utilizing special techniques—digoxin. That probably would lead to an erroneous conclusion that the person had overdosed on digitalis, which might very well have happened in the Tim Waters case except for Lovell being particularly aware of the properties of oleander.

Such a mistake would be totally excusable. Both digitalis and oleander are what scientists refer to as a cardiac glycosides; that is, medicines that affect the heart. In fact, oleander's ability to produce this potentially beneficial substance has led to several efforts to incorporate oleandrin, the active substance in the plant, into a legitimate drug. One major pharmaceutical firm recently conducted an extensive series of experiments to make a marketable product from oleandrin, but then abandoned the search, apparently because the idea was not proving feasible.

There are still a lot of unknowns surrounding oleander poisoning, because the research done in this country has been both small and not altogether pertinent to what happens in situations such as that involving Tim Waters. Virtually all of the studies that have been done have focused on the properties of oleand*rin,* the pure form of the poison, rather than on the oleand*er* plant.

In some countries oleander is used as a healer rather
than a killer. In Haiti and India, for instance, it is popular
with herbal doctors for treating a variety of health problems ranging from indigestion, ringworm, and malaria to
leprosy and venereal disease. It also is commonly used to
help induce abortions.

When scientific investigators began looking into Tim
Waters's death, they could find, in this country, only one
other case connected to death-by-oleander, and it involved an herbal doctor in Florida's Haitian community.
In that incident, a female member of the community went
to the local medicine man seeking a potion that would
help her gain weight. He prescribed oleander to be administered both orally and rectally. The woman became ill
very quickly. Even though she received treatment at a
local hospital, doctors could not save her.

In addition, there has been at least one documented
case in this country of oleander being used as a means for
suicide, although it would not be surprising to learn that it
happens more often than authorities think. The March
1982 edition of the American Medical Association *Journal*
detailed the death of a ninety-six-year-old California
woman, who, according to the article, had exhibited signs
of depression and had told family members that she
would like to end her life. Two weeks before Christmas,
in 1980, they found her on the floor of her room, weak
and very sick. Although they called for help immediately
and she arrived at the hospital only fifteen minutes later,
it was too late. Within forty minutes she was pronounced
dead. An autopsy determined that she had chewed and
swallowed from five to fifteen oleander leaves.

It was the article describing this case that Lovell had
auspiciously stumbled across just before Lewis told him
that digoxin had been found in Tim Waters's specimens.
Of course, in Tim Waters's case, proving oleander poison-

ing was going to be much more difficult because he did not conveniently die with oleander leafage in his stomach.

On December 9, two months after sending Tim's samples to Foster City, Lovell drafted an official report on the results of the tests as far as they pertained to the Waters case.

"If an individual were poisoned with an oleander leaf [or alcoholic beverage in which an oleander leaf had been soaked,] he could die from this," Lovell wrote, "and the findings in the blood of digoxin would be about that of the blood level found in Mr. Waters."

There was still another hurdle to clear, however. The lab at Foster City had found digoxin, the presence of which Lovell felt was caused by ingestion of oleander. But to make this connection in court, there had to be more definite authority. To help establish such substantiation, Lovell turned to the country's foremost expert on oleander poisoning, a Ph.D. named Frederic Rieders, the founder and director of a Willow Grove, Pennsylvania, organization called National Medical Services.

Lovell sent Tim's specimens to Rieders—a sample of his blood and a small vial of bile taken from his liver—in December 1987, about the same time he wrote his report based on the Foster City findings.

It took Rieders more than nine months to perform and verify his own tests. By then, testimony in the preliminary hearing for David and his parents had long been over. But that did not matter. There is no statute of limitations on murder; David could be charged with killing Tim Waters at any time.

On August 9, 1988, Rieders wrote Lovell saying his lab had come to four determinations after examining the Waters specimens:

1. The tests had detected oleandrin.

2. The tests did *not* find any other "potentially death-producing kinds or concentrations of . . . exogenous toxicant." (Translation: there was nothing else in his system that could have killed him)

3. Oleandrin is a "sufficiently cardiotoxic glycoside . . . to be capable of causing death."

4. Analysis of the specimens "established with reasonable scientific certainty the intake, absorption and distribution of the oleander poison by this individual prior to death."

Rieders's conclusion: "In the absence of other similarly competent or more competent cause or causes, the oleandrin findings provide a competent, independent mechanism and cause of death in the captioned case." In other words, nothing else appeared to have killed Tim Waters, so it had to have been the oleander.

In Pasadena, when Walt Lewis was told of Rieders's report, he rejoiced; his persistence had paid off. Although he was totally out of the picture as far as possible prosecution went, he felt he had a very large personal stake in what happened to David Sconce. If Lewis could see David charged and convicted of Tim's death, he would feel completely vindicated. But the first thing a person learns in dealing with the criminal justice system in the United States, especially in California, is that patience is not only preferred, it is required. If the old saw about the wheels of justice grinding slowly holds for America as a whole, it could be modified in California to proclaim that movement is infinitesimal, sometimes even nonexistent. In actuality, David would not be charged with Tim Waters's murder until February 1990, nineteen months after Rieders submitted his report, some sixty-two months after Tim's death. Proceedings leading to a trial would not begin for for more than a year after that.

But even before receiving Rieders's report, investigators suspected that Tim Waters had not expired as naturally as Dr. Holloway believed. With that in mind, Detective Hopkins decided to battle the freeway traffic for a ride into downtown Los Angeles on the off chance that David might open up to him.

26

There were several significant differences between David's interview with Diaz and the one with Hopkins. The first was the circumstances under which the two meetings were held. While David had initiated the interview with Diaz, it was Hopkins who sought the second meeting. And where Diaz had openly placed his recorder on the tabletop during the conversation, Hopkins, apparently fearful that David would be less than enthusiastic about agreeing to speak into a tape recorder, decided to make a surreptitious tape. A week before the scheduled interview, Hopkins called the L.A. County Jail and made arrangements to huddle with David in one of the attorney's cubicles *and* to bring along a recording device, which he planned to conceal in a specially adapted briefcase. It was a decision that would come back to haunt him later when David's attorney would try to have the recording tossed out.

Another noticeable difference was in David's attitude. While he had been sociable, even jocular, with Diaz, he was downright hostile to Hopkins. In fact, virtually the first words out of David's mouth were bitter: He seemingly found it impossible to contain his anger about the prosecution's use of inmate informants—called K-9's in the Los Angeles jail system—during the Pasadena preliminary hearing.

"How can you guys in good faith sit there . . . and believe what the six fucking asshole K-9's came forward and said about this situation?" he asked even before Hopkins and a detective he had brought along, Jess Estrada, had introduced themselves.

Hopkins, a mild-mannered, amiable man, tried to soothe him, explaining that was the reason for his visit, to talk about what the inmates had said about Tim Waters.

"You can't charge me with this thing because I didn't have anything to do with it," he snapped. A few minutes later, however, he half-heartedly apologized for his outburst.

"I am usually not this abrasive, guys," he said. "I have been cooperative ever since I have been in jail . . . but it's burning me, it's hurting me, and I haven't done anything but tell the truth."

Hopkins repeated that he and Estrada were from Ventura County, not Los Angeles County.

"There are no charges against me in Ventura County," David said, "and there never will be. I'm not worried about that. Even if there were, I'd shove it down all your throats because I didn't have anything to do with this."

As he had with Diaz, David again denied that he knew Tim Waters.

"Not even in your business dealings?" Hopkins asked.

"Not in my wildest dreams," David responded, "have I ever met, seen, or spoken to Tim Waters, ever."

As the interview progressed, it was increasingly apparent that the detectives and David were working toward opposite goals. Hopkins wanted David to talk about Tim; David wanted to talk about the inmate informants. The session evolved into an odd compromise, with Hopkins following his agenda and David following his, and only occasionally did their interests overlap.

At the beginning, David wanted to get his feelings off his chest, directing most of his venom toward David Gerhardt. "He is the most notorious con man, lying, conniving, manipulative K-9 in this jail," David said. Knowing this, he said, he was amazed that Walt Lewis had believed Gerhardt's story, especially the part about him allegedly offering Gerhardt a place to live when he was released. "Oh, right," he said sarcastically. "I am going to let [Gerhardt] . . . move into the one-bedroom apartment with my wife and two kids. Let's put him in front of a jury and see who they believe. I can't believe the cops believe these jailhouse rats," he added. "I can't fathom why they believe it."

"Did you ever mention the poisoning of Tim Waters to any of these people?" Hopkins asked.

"Never!" David answered emphatically.

"Did you ever mention to any of these people the beating of Tim Waters?"

"No!" he said. "I didn't talk about Tim Waters."

Well, if he had not mentioned Tim, Hopkins asked reasonably, how did they come up with all the information about him?

"Through my transcripts," David insisted. "Through my transcripts."

Hopkins looked at him dubiously. "I don't think the transcripts were that detailed," he pointed out. "They come up with some very detailed information that all seems to fit. It all seems to correlate."

David asked what kind of detailed information Hopkins was talking about. "The parts that dealt with Waters's poisoning," Hopkins responded.

"Waters wasn't poisoned," David shot back. "Waters died of natural causes."

"Okay," Hopkins replied condescendingly.

"That hasn't been established at all," David responded. "That's still a fishing expedition in fantasy land, and both you guys know it. You know, you can say what you want, but Tim Waters died of natural causes. I know who had it out for Tim Waters," he said, touching on the subject he had brought up with Diaz in hopes of working a deal for bail.

Hopkins asked if he was talking about Richard Gray.

"No, I'm not going to talk about this," David said. "This is a viable part of my defense."

"Okay," Hopkins said agreeably.

Then David proceeded to talk about it. "You know, when are people going to want to wake up and smell the coffee and really realize what's going on here? What motive would I have to hurt Tim Waters? I didn't compete with him. I didn't do any business with him or for him or against him or anything. I didn't compete with anybody in the cremation industry. See, that's been a big stigma attached to me from the start. I didn't have any competitors."

Hopkins let him ramble, then he directed the questions back to Tim, asking David again when he met with him.

"I have never met him at all," David repeated. "Where is this going? Ultimately, do you guys seriously think this guy was poisoned? Or are you spinning your wheels? Because this guy died of natural causes."

Although Dr. Rieders would not turn in his written report on his laboratory findings in the Waters case for another month, the Pennsylvania scientist apparently had given a verbal report to Lovell, who seemingly had passed it on to Hopkins. But the detective did not want to play that card yet. He wanted to push David some more before revealing his information.

Despite your protests, Hopkins told David, authorities had eight people who had testified that David admitted poisoning Waters.

"No," David said, contradicting him. "You've got six jailhouse informants that don't know their head—"

"Well," Hopkins interrupted, "we've got Edwards, who testified that you told him you dropped something in Waters's drink."

"So?" David said.

"We've got Galambos testifying that you told them that you poisoned Waters by putting something in his drink."

"So?" David repeated.

Hopkins shrugged. "Okay," he said, "we've got Gerhardt . . ."

That sent David off on another tirade that lasted for several minutes. "All I need," he said finally, "is twelve rational people on a jury. That's all I need."

Hopkins decided to give up half his information.

"You know that Dr. Lovell changed the cause of death, don't you?" he asked.

"No, I didn't know that," David said in surprise. "To what?"

"Well, right now it's undetermined," Hopkins said.

David smiled. "Bullshit," he said. "Foster City hasn't come up with the cause of death yet, and they are the leading forensic pathology lab in the nation. If they haven't ascertained the cause of death, there *is* no cause of death . . . If Foster City can't come up with something, then no one in the world is going to come up with something."

Hopkins figured it was time to play the trump card. He told David that Foster City had determined that Tim had ingested oleander and they sent their findings on to Rieders for confirmation.

"No, wait a second," David said. "They discovered digoxin."

"You are right, they first discovered digoxin," Hopkins said, putting a slight emphasis on the word "first."

"Digoxin is consistent with many substances," David said.

"Okay," Hopkins replied. "Through other tests and analyses they discovered oleander in the blood. Dr. Rieders has now determined positively—positively determined!—that the cause of death was oleander poisoning."

David was disbelieving. "Positively?" he asked. "Digoxin!" he added.

"No," Hopkins insisted. "Oleander." Not only did the scientists find evidence of oleander, Hopkins added, but they determined that oleander was the cause of death, and that there was nothing else that could have killed him. Hopkins wanted to emphasize this so David would be sure to grasp the significance of the test results. "Then this situation down here in L.A. County arises and eight people testify that you told them that you poisoned him," Hopkins said.

"Throw six of them out right away," David said, unflustered by the information that Hopkins had imparted.

"Well, you throw out who you want."

"I will. And I'll discredit all those guys. I'm not worried about that."

Hopkins gave David a questioning look. Eight people who testified that you admitted poisoning someone and you're not worried?

"Then charge me with it," David challenged.

"Okay, listen a minute," Hopkins said calmly. "They come to me and say this guy died in Ventura County—"

"You wouldn't be here if you thought I did something," David interrupted. "You wouldn't be here right now talking to me. You would just charge me with it."

"What do you think the chances are of eight people saying that you poisoned Tim Waters, and some of them even describing a method of poisoning that is consistent with oleander poisoning, and we have someone who died in 'eighty-five. It's all been signed off, and we send his blood away and, by God, he did die of oleander poisoning."

"Then put me with him," David said defiantly. "Put me with him. Give me a motive to want to do anything to the guy, a guy I never met or talked to in my life. Give me a motive."

"Well, I mean—"

"What motive? What motive?"

"The fact that he was spreading—"

"Spreading rumors? People were writing things about me? These guys all got together. It's called a term I am sure you are familiar with if you are familiar with informants. It's called 'getting in the car.' They get two or three guys in the car, they all try to say the same thing so they can add weight to it. Prosecutors nowadays are using it more to jerk bail and to add different charges. They still use it to buttress weak cases."

Hopkins let him work off his anger, and then approached him again from a different angle. "What I am interested in, really, Dave, is that you know that there is testimony that there was a second person involved in your meeting with Waters in the restaurant."

David refused to play. "I never met Tim Waters at a restaurant," he contended again. "I never met Tim Waters. Never! Ever! Never!"

"There was a second person—" Hopkins began.

"There was a person that didn't like Tim Waters at all," David said, moving in the same direction he had with Diaz. "There are a couple of them."

Hopkins wanted to know if David would talk to him about those people.

"This is very relevant to my defense later on," David said. "It is important to show why I didn't do what these people say I did. It's very important, and if I knew for a fact that you guys were not going to talk to the Pasadena police, I would tell you this right now. I'd give you the person who had the motive, why he had the motive, what he talked about, and four other people who heard him talking about it. I'd tell you why he wanted to have Tim Waters whacked." His condition for talking, he added, was bail. "Give me bail so I can fight my case from the street."

Hopkins said he had no authority in Los Angeles County, that he could do nothing about the charges against David there.

David looked at him skeptically. "No, but you could talk to people."

"I can't make you any deals," Hopkins said.

"I'll help you guys," David said. "And then you can pound the guy who had this done because I even went with this guy to the Holiday Inn to talk to Tim Waters, but he wasn't there. I went there with this guy for the specific reason of talking to Tim Waters not about my business but about what this guy wanted to talk about."

"Do you want to tell us about that," Hopkins pushed. "I would think, see the way the D.A. up in Ventura is looking at this, we've got you wrapped up pretty good just on what we have."

"No, you don't," David volleyed. Staring at Hopkins he softly voiced a challenge. "Fine, then," he said slowly. "Then wrap me up. You aren't going to because I didn't do it."

Again the discussion wandered off, but ten minutes later Hopkins brought the issue up yet another time. "Are you saying that sometime in the future you might give us that information?" he asked.

"Yeah," David said. "Work with Pasadena and have them give me reasonable bail so I can go free. I want to put every mother's son in front of a jury and let us cross-examine those assholes. I am living for that day. I don't think the D.A. is stupid enough to put them on, but if he is, more power to him. You get me a workable bail, I'll give you the guy and the motive and four other people who heard him talking about it with Tim Waters. It ties Galambos into it too."

If Hopkins had a choice, it would be for David to share his information with him right then. I'll give it one more try, he thought. To David, he again tried to emphasize the importance of the Rieders report. "And I am not bullshitting you, David."

"Spend the county's money all day long," David responded.

"We're not bullshitting you," Hopkins added. "We're being up front with you. That's why the tests took so long. He eliminated any other possible cause of death."

"He did?" David replied acerbically. "Okay. If you got that, then come on with it. That's all I can say: Come on with it. I know I had nothing to do with it. I don't positively know that he wasn't poisoned because I didn't know him. But I know I didn't have anything to do with his death in any way, shape or form, so it doesn't bother me."

David, however, was unwilling to let the interview end without touching on his two favorite topics: conditions in the jail and Walt Lewis.

First, the jail: "Roaches this big," he said, holding his fingers several inches apart. "They fly. I have never seen a cockroach fly in my life until I was over in [the] old county [jail]. And, you know, queens. I never seen guys with breasts before. Running around with hard-ons, chasing each other around in the shower. I never saw that until I was over at Old County. I could write a book about this place. Most of the cops here, I don't know how they put up with the scum that they have to deal with on a daily basis. They are incredibly patient. Some of them have attitudes, but most of the cops try. That is a salute to them."

"I'll give your attorney a call," Hopkins promised.

"Or call the clown, the new D.A. who is taking this case over," David said. "I don't have a real high opinion of Walt Lewis because of how he slimed me all through the preliminary, and I knew he was sliming me. I knew he was coming down talking to jailhouse informers. I knew all this as it was going on, and I knew what the jailhouse guys were doing to me, and I didn't figure that anybody who could believe all that crap was looking out for my best interests. So I don't hold a high opinion of Walt Lewis." He grinned. "But you knew that anyway, didn't you?"

Hopkins left the meeting with a personal opinion of David that closely matched that of Diaz. But where Diaz had disregarded most of what David had said as sociopathic blathering, Hopkins was more intrigued by his comments.

Specifically, he found it particularly interesting that David was saying two things at once. In one breath he claimed that Tim Waters was not murdered, that he died a natural death. But in the next breath he contended that he knew who had a strong motive to kill Tim, and who in fact may actually have committed the crime.

It was something for him to think about on the hourlong drive back to Simi Valley. David had been very cryptic. The more Hopkins thought about it, the more he wondered exactly who David was trying to finger. Finally he decided it was Steve Strunk, whom David had fired. David seemed to be hinting that Tim was competing with Strunk's father, who owned the Cremation Society of California. Strunk's CSC and Tim's Alpha Society may have been direct competitors, David seemed to be saying, while his own company, Coastal Cremation, was in a different league altogether. Since David was for all practical

purposes the cremation king of California, he professed
not to be worried about the minor irritation that Tim
could have caused him. Hopkins, however, was aware of
no evidence even remotely connecting Strunk to Tim's
death.

But it was not as simple as that in the labyrinth of the
Los Angeles funeral home industry. There were wheels
within wheels. For example, if David indeed was pointing
toward Steve Strunk, there could be several motives for
David to seek to frame Strunk. For one, Steve Strunk was
a potentially powerful witness against David as to what
had been going on at Lamb Funeral Home/Coastal Cremation. For another, David was charged with conspiring
to murder Elie Estephan, the inheritor of Frank Strunk's
CSC—a company that David was reputed to covet. And,
for still another, Steve Strunk might be the only possible
witness who could testify to a physical link between David
and Tim.

Holy cow, Hopkins thought, braking to a crawl in the
freeway traffic, it was enough to give a guy a headache.

27

After Hopkins's interview with David and the publication of Rieders's report, the detective began an exhaustive investigation to try to connect David to Tim Waters's death. Although the detective visited a lot of restaurants up and down the coastal strip of Ventura County searching for someone who may have remembered serving the fat guy and the weightlifter, he came up professionally hungry. The prosecution, in fact, *never* was able to find a witness who would swear to seeing Tim and David together on Good Friday evening in 1985. Three and a half years was just too large a gap, given the vagaries of human memory for a casual event and the rate of turnover in Southern California restaurants.

Going at it from another angle, Hopkins sifted through stacks of reports from the major credit card companies and mounds of canceled checks, hoping David might have left a paper record of the meeting. Again, he drew a blank.

Although the detective was coming up empty in his exhaustive attempts to uncover sources in Ventura County, there were still the funeral home/tissue bank charges pending against David, Jerry, and Laurieanne in Pasadena. The voluminous file on those accusations, the

ones that Judge Person had determined were valid
enough to demand an airing in a court of higher jurisdiction, bounced from desk to desk before settling in the in-basket of Judge Terry Smerling in Department D of the
Pasadena branch of the Superior Court of Los Angeles
County. (Judicial trivia: In California, municipal courts
are called "divisions" and carry a numerical designation;
superior courts are "departments" and have an alphabetical designation.)

David could complain all he wanted about the unfairness of the system in effectively denying him bail, but the
fact that his file ended up with Smerling would prove to
be an unbelievable piece of good fortune. While Person,
the former DDA, had a reputation as a pro-prosecution
judge, Smerling was at the other end of the spectrum;
definitely pro-defense.

A slight, balding man of medium height, Smerling was
born in Los Angeles but went back East for his legal education, graduating from Columbia University School of
Law in 1970. His first job after returning to California was
with the Legal Aid Foundation in Long Beach. After
three years there, he went to the Greater Watts Justice
Center, and in 1977 he became a staff lawyer for the
American Civil Liberties Union.

As an ACLU lawyer he was lead counsel in a highly
publicized class-action suit on behalf of three inmates at
the Los Angeles County Central Jail, *Rutherford v. Pitchess*, which, in 1979, resulted in a sweeping order for reforms at the facility. He also was responsible for another
high-profile civil liberties case, *Youngblood v. Gates*. It
was precisely this activist position that influenced Governor Edmund G. Brown Jr., a liberal Democrat, to appoint
the thirty-seven-year-old Smerling to the bench in November 1982.

From his first job in municipal court, Smerling moved
up to superior court in 1984, serving initially as a trial

judge in the Van Nuys branch. From there he went to a job as an administrator primarily responsible for arranging court calendar dates for petty criminals. Then he was transferred to Pasadena, and it was back to being a trial judge again.

As a trial judge in superior court, as opposed to his position in municipal court and before that as an activist lawyer, it was Smerling's job, in the absence of a jury, to decide on the guilt or innocence of people who came before him. Sometimes he had to sentence those people to jail, although it was a role he admitted he found personally abhorrent. In a 1985 interview with the *Los Angeles Daily Journal,* a publication covering the area's legal and judicial scene, Smerling readily confessed to his personal discomfort in dealing harshly with lawbreakers.

"I'm not eager to put people away in jail," he said. "I'm painfully aware of how bad jails are. I believe, as I did at the ACLU, that jail is indeed appropriate for some people, but particularly for [those] the first time around, possibly just being processed through the system is a sufficient deterrent."

If it had been possible for David to have *hired* a judge, he could not have found one more predisposed to his plight, or one more likely to give a sympathetic hearing to his complaints about the conditions he was forced to endure as an inmate, than Terry Smerling.

During his stint as an administrator in the Van Nuys court, part of Smerling's job was to negotiate sentence agreements with defendants who otherwise would have had to appear in court, thereby being exposed to the possibility of having to serve hard time. Since jail sentences were repugnant to him, Smerling was totally comfortable with "indicated sentences," which are roughly analogous to plea bargaining, since that way he could dole out probation rather than hard time. And with that character trait as a given, it should have been no surprise when the forty-three-year-old Smerling suggested a deal. Listening eagerly to the judge's proposal was David's new lawyer, Guy O'Brien.

O'Brien had replaced Diamond between the time the Sconce case left Judge Person's court and the time it ended up in Smerling's. Diamond was not reappointed to represent David because of a possible conflict of interest after it was discovered that he also had represented Randy Welty, a major financial backer of the CIE&TB, in a case stemming from Welty's role as the owner of several adult bookstores. Since David might later try to blame Welty for his own wrongdoing at the tissue bank, Diamond's exit was viewed as a necessity. That meant a complete turnover in legal counsel, as far as David was concerned, because by that time Walt Lewis was off the case as well. Because of David's threats against him, Lewis had a personal involvement in the case, and that could hinder him in doing his job. He was replaced by a young DDA named James Rogan.

In California a judge can give an indicated sentence if a defendant agrees to plead guilty to all counts against him. The only restriction on the judge is that the sentence he proposes be authorized by law. No one was happier with Smerling's propensity for indicated sentences than O'Brien and the lawyers representing Jerry and Laurieanne, Edward Rucker and Thomas Nishi. Starting on June 30, 1989, Smerling's reputation for handing down light sentences began manifesting itself. On that day, a Friday, Smerling announced the first of a series of decisions. To begin with, he announced his decision to dismiss ten of the charges against the Sconces, many of them dealing with the alleged theft of tissue and organs.

"The motives of the defendants are despicable," he proclaimed from the bench, "but that's not the issue. The issue is whether a crime has been committed."

In his opinion, as it related to the removal of body parts in a majority of the charges before him, it had not. He had decided, he said, that the "to remove tissue" clause in the ATC forms used by the Sconces had provided sufficient authority for them to harvest the material. By signing the forms, he said, the relatives of the deceased were, in effect, becoming parties to a contract. And under contract law it was the burden of the next-of-kin to challenge the "to remove tissue" clause. "The failure to read a contract doesn't justify rescinding the contract," Smerling said.

Interestingly, his view on the issue was exactly opposite that of Judge Person. Fourteen months earlier, in his ruling on the case, Person had said there was *no* contract. "The court finds . . . that no contract was entered into by any of the donors or other authorized persons by virtue of the execution of the Authority to Cremate forms . . ." Person had said.

More important, in a move that would later cause all manner of turmoil, Smerling also announced his decision to dismiss the conspiracy-to-murder charge against David, the one that alleged that David had requested and helped plan the killing of Elie Estephan. It was, in terms of possible punishment, the most serious accusation that David then faced. Although he also was charged with three counts of solicitation of murder—on his grandparents and Lewis—the conspiracy accusation would have been the one to send him to jail for a *long* time. Under California law, conviction of conspiracy to murder carries a mandatory term of twenty-five years-to-life, while conviction of solicitation of murder carries a maximum sentence of three years.

The reason for the wide disparity in sentences had to do with the degree of involvement by the person accused of the crime. "Solicitation" required only that two or more people talk about the possibility of committing murder, while "conspiracy" required actual agreement to commit murder. Smerling said he was dismissing the conspiracy charge because David had abandoned the murder plot before Garcia and Dutton could carry it out. In other words, since the murder never took place, there could not have been a conspiracy to commit it, at least not in the legal sense.

Smerling's pronouncements rocked the district attorney's office, which believed its case was rapidly being ravaged. But the prosecutors' frustration was only beginning; Smerling was barely getting warmed up.

Six days after the first proclamation, the judge announced that he was tossing out twenty more charges against the Sconces. This second round of dismissals dealt mainly with charges stemming from the CIE&TB operation. Smerling said he was discarding them because he had no way of knowing for certain whose body parts had been removed and sold. He also dismissed the charges against Laurieanne and Jerry arising from the Rojas bribery, citing a lack of evidence that they knew of David's alleged plan to bribe Rojas.

In a separate move, Smerling said he had also decided that there would be two trials for the defendants. One trial would focus on the violent incidents such as assault and solicitation of murder, and the other would deal with the remainder of the accusations, essentially separate trials for David and his parents, since Jerry and Laurieanne were not charged with any violent crimes.

But the real shocker came seven weeks later. On August 30, Smerling announced his decision regarding some of the more serious charges against David.

The judge went through the inventory of accusations and put together a list of some of the more serious ones. How he chose which charges to include from the variety of accusations that David faced is still a mystery to everyone but the judge. In any case, Smerling said this: If

David would plead guilty to those selected accusations—seventeen felonies and three misdemeanors—he would fine him $100 and sentence him to a total of five years in prison. Furthermore, and this was the real shocker for the district attorney, if David agreed at some unspecified time in the future to plead guilty to the remaining charges, which included accusations of soliciting the murder of his grandparents and that of prosecutor Walt Lewis, he would get no additional prison time. And, Smerling added, that included the charge of conspiracy to murder Elie Estephan, the charge he had already dismissed before he made his offer.

Apparently, in determining the sentence he planned to impose, Smerling had used the most serious offense on the list, the robbery of Tim Waters, as the base conviction, thus the five years. Although David did not actually commit the robbery, he hired Galambos to do it, and that made him equally accountable. On the remaining sixteen felony charges, David drew sentences of three or four years each. However, Smerling ruled that they would run concurrently. That meant that David would be credited for serving them at the same time he was serving the single five-year sentence for robbery.

In reality, David's sentence would be three years and four months rather than five years, because he would get time off for good behavior. Figuring in the time he had already served while awaiting disposition of his case, David would be eligible for release in October 1990, barely thirteen months distant. Considering that Smerling could have sentenced him to as many as eleven years in prison just on the crimes he was initially pleading to, David got off very lightly, especially given the seriousness and the vileness of the offenses with which he had been charged.

Calculating that his decision needed explanation, Smerling said: "I'm well aware of the facts of this case, having read the preliminary hearing transcript. I certainly can't condone the acts of which you were accused and for which there is substantial evidence. However, I'm also aware of the fact that a filing of a murder case, probably a capital murder case, against you in Ventura County is imminent, that relating to the death of Timothy Waters. That case obviously carries a lot more gravity than this one."

But, he added, he felt that unless he disposed of the charges before him, the murder charge in Ventura might be further delayed. "I think it's important for all concerned, not just you, but to the people of the state, that that case commence and be resolved."

Another consideration in the plea bargain arrangement was the amount of his time—he estimated a minimum of six months—that would be needed to try David on the charges he then faced. "This is an enormous consumption of time," Smerling pointed out. "For those reasons I think my offer is appropriate under these rather unusual circumstances."

Rogan leaped angrily to his feet. He had already made the prosecution's position clear during discussions in Smerling's chambers, he said, but he wanted to get his opposition on the record in open court as well. "The plea bargain," he began, tight-lipped and furious, "is not with the concurrence of the prosecution."

If the relatively light sentence that Smerling had offered David were only for the charges that he was pleading to, the district attorney's office might be able to live with it, Rogan said. But, he added hastily, a number of other charges were involved as well, including the accusation that David had conspired to murder Elie Estephan.

"My understanding," Rogan said hotly, "is that should the people be successful in bringing that count back from the appellate court before this court, Mr. Sconce would have an opportunity to plead to that count and would be given probation on what would otherwise be a twenty-five-to-life sentence. And," he added indignantly, "as I understand the court's rationale for that, the court doesn't feel that under the facts of that case it's worthy of twenty-five-to-life."

Rogan wanted to keep going but Smerling waved him to silence. "Let me respond to that and then you may continue," the judge said.

Rogan sat down, biting his tongue.

Locking eyes with the DDA, Smerling assured him that his assessment of the situation was correct. Turning to David, he reiterated his deal. "My offer to you, Mr. Sconce, is that in the event any counts in this case you're later convicted on, you receive no more time than the five years I just sentenced you to. That does include the conspiracy-to-murder count that I dismissed."

What Smerling was saying rather inarticulately was that if David later pleaded guilty to the charges still pending against him, Smerling would not sentence him to any additional prison time. The offer applied as well to the conspiracy-to-murder charge that Smerling had dismissed earlier, in case an appeals court later reversed his decision. Smerling apparently had very strong feelings about that. The way the law read, if David was convicted of conspiracy to murder, the statute mandated a sentence of twenty-five-years-to-life. The only alternative was to give no prison time at all, only probation. To Smerling, apparently, that was the more just course.

"It's my view, that [twenty-five-years-to-life] is an extremely excessive sentence for the behavior that underlies that count," Smerling said. "I'd be compelled by conscience to give you probation. Actually, a sentencing in between would be more appropriate, but that's not the law."

David was being offered probation on a sentence that

could have put him away for a considerable period of time, solely because Smerling did not believe in harsh sentences.

Rogan, still seething, was back on his feet. "Thank you, your honor," he said perfunctorily. "As I was saying . . . I think that with that type of offer [on the other charges] . . . an appropriate sentence would be in the seven-year range rather than five years because of the multiplicity of actions and the amount of threats and so forth. When we get to the conspiracy count and we throw that in the pot also as a probation—and I say this with all due respect to the court—I feel it's Christmas Day in August for Mr. Sconce."

"I'm mindful of those concerns and I respect them, Mr. Rogan," Smerling said, dismissing him.

Once Smerling had made the offer, it could not be retracted. However, there was one thing that could gum up the works. If David decided to fight the remaining accusations by going to trial, the offer would cease to be valid. If that happened, David would have to take his chances with a jury. But with a promise of not having to serve any additional time, given the fact that evidence against him appeared quite strong, it did not appear likely that David would reject the suggestion.

Smerling also made an offer to Jerry and Laurieanne. If they pleaded guilty to the charges pending against them, the judge would sentence them to only one year each in the county jail. They did not jump on the offer as quickly as David, deciding instead to bide their time and see what happened while they remained free on $5000 bond.

When Smerling took over the case, there were sixty-eight charges pending against David, Jerry, and Laurieanne. At the end of the summer of 1989, he had pared that number down roughly by half. When he finished, the score-card looked like this:

David

Guilty (sentenced to five years):
- Conspiracy to commit assault (four counts)
- Assault with great bodily injury (three counts)
- Robbery
- Grand theft auto
- Receiving stolen property
- Removal of body parts (four counts)
- Mutilation of human remains (two counts)
- Conspiracy to mutilate human remains
- Multiple cremation of human remains (two counts) (misdemeanor)
- Commingling of human remains (two counts) (misdemeanor)
- Failure to inter human remains within a reasonable time (misdemeanor)

Dismissed:
- Conspiracy to commit murder of Elie Estephan
- Conspiracy to remove body parts
- Removal of body parts (nineteen counts)
- Mutilation of human remains
- Conspiracy to bribe a witness
- Falsifying death certificates (four counts)

Pending (with a promise of no additional jail time provided he pleaded guilty):
- Solicitation of murder of Lawrence/Lucille Lamb (one count each)
- Solicitation of murder of Walter Lewis
- Solicitation of perjury
- Bribery of a witness (two counts)
- Offering to bribe a witness (two counts)

Laurieanne

Dismissed:
- Conspiracy to remove body parts
- Removal of body parts (twenty-one counts)
- Mutilation of human remains
- Conspiracy to bribe a witness and solicitation of perjury
- Falsifying death certificates (four counts)
- Offering to bribe a witness
- Bribery of a witness

Pending:
- Removal of body parts (five counts)
- Conspiracy to mutilate human remains
- Multiple cremation of human remains (two counts)
- Commingling of human remains (two counts)
- Failure to inter human remains within a reasonable time
- Misappropriation of income from preneed trust accounts
- Embezzlement
- Failure to include required language in trust accounts
- Failure to deposit trust funds within thirty days (two counts)
- Forgery (three counts)

Jerry

Dismissed:
- Conspiracy to mutilate human remains
- Removal of body parts (twenty-six counts)
- Mutilation of human remains

- Conspiracy to bribe a witness and solicitation of perjury
- Falsifying a death certificate
- Embezzlement

Pending:
- Conspiracy to mutilate human remains
- Multiple cremation of human remains (two counts)
- Commingling of human remains (two counts)
- Failure to inter human remains within a reasonable time
- Misappropriation of income from preneed trust accounts
- Failure to include required language in trust accounts

To say that prosecutors were displeased with Smerling's disposition of the case would be a vast understatement. But they could kick wastebaskets until their toes were nubs; there was nothing they could do immediately to rectify what they considered a gross injustice. They could appeal, of course, which they did. As soon as they could get the papers together, they asked a higher court to make Smerling reinstate the charges that he had thrown out, except the embezzlement charge against Jerry and two falsification of death certificate charges which the prosecution conceded it could not prove. But that amounted to little more than an automatic reaction. Even if the higher court decided that Smerling erred in tossing out the accusations, the most it could do was order Smerling to reconsider; the appeals court not tell Smerling what kind of sentence to impose.

The fact was, there was nothing the prosecutors could do about the lenient five-year term David had drawn, or about Smerling's offer to grant probation on the remaining counts. The severity of a sentence—except where it is otherwise mandated, such as in the conspiracy-to-murder charge—was entirely within a judge's discretion.

There was, however, one other action they could take which would make them feel better: They could step up the investigation of Tim Waters's death. As circumstantial as the case was shaping up be, it was better than nothing. They felt it was important not to let David think he had skated away.

PART FIVE

Accused of Murder

28

In actuality, the decision to steam ahead with plans to prosecute David for Tim's murder was a relatively easy one for the district attorney's office to make. Translating the decision from move to motion, however, proved more than a little troublesome; there was a lot of red tape that had to be waded through before the determination could become reality.

For one thing, if David were to be tried for Tim's poisoning, it would have to be in Ventura County rather than Los Angeles County. Under state law, jurisdiction rests with the county where the crime was committed. But since there was no evidence in this case to show where Tim was administered the poison, jurisdiction would be determined by where he died. That was in Ventura County. But it was the L.A. D.A. who was determined to prosecute, not the Ventura D.A.

In the end, the two offices worked out a compromise. The Ventura D.A. would bring the charges, and the prosecution ultimately would be shared by the two counties.

At the time, those obstacles were viewed as surmountable, and in the end they were, although the process of sending an L.A. DDA to try a case in Ventura precipitated a significant threat to David's timely prosecution. But that problem would not surface for another year and a half. The immediate difficulties were deciding if murder charges were to be filed against David, and who—the person or persons, as opposed to which county—would prosecute the case. But first there had to be a case to prosecute.

On February 9, 1990, seven months after he had dared Hopkins to charge him, David was formally accused of poisoning Tim Waters. Two months later, on April 16, five years and eight days after Tim's death, David pleaded not guilty to the charge.

If nothing else, the filing of the charge ruined any hope that David would be free any time soon, not even when he finished serving Smerling's sentence in eight months time. It was unlikely that a court, knowing that David was accused of murder, was going to let him go until the accusation had been disposed of.

In preparation for his expected trial, David was transferred from a state-run prison to the Ventura jail, which was run by the county, to await his expected trial. He had no sooner been transferred to Ventura than the warden called the prosecutor and asked if he had any idea about David's occupational capabilities, that is, if he had any suggestions about where David might be put to work. Ever anxious for the opportunity to make a quip, the prosecutor fired back: "Just don't put him in the kitchen."

The filing of the charge also propelled David into a fresh round of legal activity. To begin with, he had to find a lawyer. Although he was offered help from the public defender's office, David insisted that he be allowed to hire Roger Diamond, who had represented him at the Pasadena preliminary hearing. In a complicated series of court proceedings that bounced through five courts, including the court of appeal, Diamond, whose motto is "I never give up," finally won.

Diamond had not been reappointed as David's lawyer when the Pasadena proceedings moved from municipal court to superior court, because he also represented Randy Welty—and that set the stage for a possible conflict of interest. In Ventura, however, the issue was different. The Ventura courts took the position that state law mandated that an appointed attorney come from either the public defender's office or from one of the backup attorneys on contract to work as public defenders. Diamond successfully argued that the law did not apply in Ventura because it was not within the population boundaries set out by the state law. Furthermore, because of his prior history in the case, he was more qualified to represent David than a public defender, who might take months just to sift through the huge stack of documents and transcripts from Pasadena.

Diamond began fighting the battle to represent David in February 1990, almost as soon as the murder charge was filed. He won the final round when he was appointed on August 20, six months down the road.

A determined workaholic, Diamond was filing motions in the case within four days of his appointment and was ready to appear in court in October when a preliminary hearing was set on the murder charge. Throughout his twenty-three-year career as a lawyer, many of his clients, like Welty, had been persons connected with the adult entertainment business. Even while he was trying to win the right to represent David, he was fighting on behalf of the owners of five adult video arcades who were refused permits to operate in the town of Garden Grove, in Orange County. Simultaneously, he also was waging a losing battle in Glendale, near Pasadena, on behalf of the owner of a similar business. Both of those cases, as well as David's, had received a lot of local media attention, so Diamond's name was not exactly unknown.

An unimposing man with brown, curly hair going gray

around the temples and deep crow's-feet around his eyes,
Diamond looked more like a high school physics teacher,
right down to his usually rumpled suits, than a champion
of porn brokers. But rather than being the quiet retiring
type, it seemed he often attached himself to high-profile
causes. In fact, though sex shop owners took up a lot of
Diamond's time, he also has been active over the years in
other well-publicized efforts. As president of a group
called No Oil Inc., he helped lead a long, successful,
headline-grabbing fight to keep the Occidental Petroleum
Corp. from drilling beneath Pacific Palisades, an exclusive
Los Angeles beachside community where Diamond had
his office at the time. Later, after the Sconce case was
well under way, he moved to unostentatious quarters on
Main Street in Santa Monica, only a block off the beach.
Before becoming involved in the Occidental Petroleum
fight, he was an attorney for the American Nonsmokers
Rights Foundation and the Los Angeles branch of the
American Lung Association. In that capacity, he became
committed to supporting a controversial 1987 ordinance
banning smoking in restaurants, stores, and public meeting areas in Beverly Hills. It was a case that garnered
considerable national attention. However, except for
David's case in Pasadena and the porn cases in Garden
Grove and Glendale, Diamond had no recent record of
participation in controversial criminal trials. This particular lack of experience was expected to put him at a disadvantage when he went up against the team the district
attorney's office had chosen to prosecute the Tim Waters
case.

Making up half of the prosecuting duo was Jim Rogan,
who had taken over from Walt Lewis in Pasadena and
who later inherited the Jerry and Laurieanne file after
David copped his plea. It was Rogan who had become so
outraged with Smerling over the way the judge had han-

dled David's case. Rogan had grown up on the streets of San Francisco's rough Mission District, the son of an unwed mother who also was a convicted felon. He dropped out of high school in the ninth grade to help support his younger brothers and a sister, and never returned. Instead, he wrangled his way into a community college where he earned enough credits to get into the University of California at Berkeley. Working all the while at a series of low-paying jobs, he applied for admission—and was accepted—to the UCLA Law School, where he became a member of the Law Review. After graduating in 1983, he took a job as a litigator with a prestigious civil law firm, only to find that he was obsessively attracted to the criminal law side of the profession. Following his instincts, he quit his cushy post in 1985 to be a DDA. A slim, pale man with thinning light brown hair and a tentative smile, Rogan appeared mild and quiet until he got in the courtroom. As a DDA he was especially aggressive in prosecuting members of the L.A. street gangs, perhaps extracting a bit of punishment against the types who had made his childhood and adolescence miserable when he was struggling to keep his fragmented family together.

Forming the other half of the team—the lead prosecutor in the case—was Harvey Giss, who was as brash as Rogan was reserved. A hyperactive, sharp-tongued lawyer who keeps in trim by running four miles a day through the Malibu hills, Giss also graduated from the UCLA law school, but in 1964, nineteen years before Rogan.

After graduation he worked as a clerk for the chief justice of the Arizona Supreme Court for two years before deciding to go into private practice. Although he was making good money as an independent, he discovered his job was not giving him much of an adrenaline rush. In 1972, about the time Rogan dropped out of high school, Giss put his shingle in a trunk and signed on as a DDA. Between then and the time he took over David's file seventeen years later, Giss had prosecuted more than a hundred felonies, including twenty-two murder cases. Only one of the murder defendants was acquitted. Four times Giss had sought the death penalty, and twice the jury went along.

He prosecuted the Bob's Big Boy Killers—Franklin Freeman and Ricky Sanders—and the highly publicized case involving four men accused of kidnapping, robbing, and murdering UCLA sweethearts Michelle Boyd and Brian Harris. Each of those cases stretched over four years. The Freeman and Sanders case, which got its nickname because the defendants were accused of herding a group of restaurant employees and customers into a freezer and opening fire, killing four, was tried several times. In the end, both were convicted. Freeman was sentenced to life without parole, and Sanders got a death sentence. In the UCLA sweetheart case, Damon Redmond, Donald Bennett, and DeAndre Brown got life sentences, and the fourth man, Stanley Davis, was sentenced to death. In 1990, only a few weeks after murder charges were filed against David, Giss was named California's Prosecutor of the Year.

If Diamond was intimidated by the records of the two prosecutors, however, he did not show it on October 1, 1990, when the three of them took their places in Courtroom 20 in the Ventura County Hall of Justice. The occasion was the opening of a preliminary hearing to determine if David should be brought to trial for Tim Waters's death.

On the bench was Municipal Court Judge John Hunter, a blond, hulking man who had played basketball at Brigham Young University during his undergraduate days in the late fifties. After graduating from the University of Southern California Law School in 1963, he decided that he did not want to practice in Los Angeles. So he and two friends got into a car and started driving west, stopping wherever they could find a USC Law School grad who might encourage them to stay. When they got to Ventura, they popped in on District Attorney Woody Deem, who offered all three of them jobs. Hunter accepted on the spot; his two friends did not. Hunter worked as a prosecutor for four years before taking a job as a civil litigator. But when Governor Ronald Reagan offered him a judgeship in 1970, Hunter jumped at it.

As far as the philosophies of the judges involved in David's case went, they seemed to flip from one extreme to the other. Where Smerling made no bones about his reluctance to sentence defendants to jail, Hunter was just as outspoken about his eagerness to put violators away. It was his belief, he told one reporter, that a jail sentence was the best way to get a criminal's undivided attention. But as a municipal court judge, like Person in Pasadena, Hunter had no authority to rule on David's guilt or innocence. His job, as Person's had been, was to hear the prosecution's evidence and determine if it was sufficient to make David accountable in superior court.

Hunter's domain, being a corner room, was laid out differently from most courtrooms. Instead of being centered along the far wall, the judge's bench stretched diagonally across the corner opposite the entrance. Opposing attorneys were assigned separate tables on the bench side of the barrier—the bar—that separated the court proper from the spectator section. Looking down from his raised perch, Hunter saw Diamond on his right, looking disheveled, and David, clad in prison blues. On the judge's left, separated from the defense table by only a few feet, was the prosecution's table. Giss, as if anxious to get into punching range, took the chair closest to Diamond.

In one important respect—the length of the proceeding—the Ventura preliminary hearing was definitely *not* going to be a repeat of the Pasadena performance. Testimony took only one week, compared to thirteen weeks in Pasadena. The main reason for this was there would not be nearly as many prosecution witnesses. Also, in Pasadena there had been three defendants involved and a multitude of charges. In Ventura, David was the only defendant and there was only one charge. Giss called only those witnesses who could help him convince Hunter that David should be tried for Tim Waters's murder. Plus, in Pasadena, there had been the bail reduction hearing which was held concurrently with the preliminary hearing. In Ventura, David's request for bail—his Smerling-imposed sentence had just expired—was denied outright.

The Ventura hearing also would be made shorter because of a decision by Giss soon after he accepted the case. Early on he had announced that he did not intend to call any of the inmate witnesses who had testified for Walt Lewis. In one way, this seemed to put the prosecutor at a disadvantage. Instead of eight witnesses who could testify to David's boasting about his involvement with Tim's death, there would be only two: Dan Galambos and Dave Edwards.

But there had been several developments in the three-year span between the two hearings that made inmate-informant testimony an incredibly risky proposition. Since the Pasadena hearing, such testimony had been roundly criticized for its inaccuracy and unreliability. Ironically, the inmate most responsible for bringing informant testimony into ill-repute—a thief named Leslie White—had been a star witness for Diamond during the Pasadena hearing. Summoned by the defense lawyer as an expert on jailhouse informants, White had contended even then that inmates could not be believed, that they frequently collaborated against another prisoner, using a number of devious methods to gather enough facts to make their stories sound credible. To prove he knew what he was talking about, White later demonstrated for sheriff's deputies how, via an accessible jail telephone, he could call law enforcement agencies and, by posing as a brother law enforcement officer, relatively easily secure confidential information about another inmates's case. With that information in hand, he said, it was easy to manipulate the details to damage a targeted inmate. If it were done right, he added, the trumped-up case could lead to the target-inmate being convicted of a crime he did not commit.

Knowing that Diamond would be waiting to pounce on Steve Warren, David Gerhardt, and the others, Giss decided he would rather go without their testimony than risk getting bogged down in a long fight about the veracity of their information. He would, instead, rely heavily on the word of a handful of David's former employees; friends and family members of Tim Waters; the man who confirmed that Tim had been killed by oleander poisoning; and detectives Diaz and Hopkins. None of them let him down.

29

To a large degree Giss's witnesses repeated what they had already testified to at the Pasadena hearing. But it was not so much *what* they said as *how* they said it that made an impression.

Without the testimony of Gerhardt *et al*, Giss relied heavily on Galambos and Edwards to show David's intent to harm Tim Waters, so it was important that they appear credible. First up was Galambos.

Clad in jeans and an open-necked sport shirt with the sleeves rolled up to better display his massive arms, Galambos sauntered arrogantly to the front of the courtroom and plopped into the witness chair, not so much taking it as commandeering it. At six-foot-three and 220 pounds, with upper arms as big around as the trunk of a Joshua tree, he easily was the most intimidating physical figure in the courtroom, almost twice the size of defense attorney Diamond. David, who had pumped no little amount of iron in his time, looked puny next to his one-time friend.

Leaning forward, cupping his chin in a fist that seemed the size of Giss's head, Galambos stared fixedly at the chief prosecutor. In response to most of the questions, Galambos answered tersely: "Yes" . . . "No" . . .

"That's what I was told" . . . "No, I didn't" . . . "Yes, I did" . . . "That's right."

When he was infrequently called upon to give longer answers, he furrowed his brow in concentration and his heavy eyebrows pouched outward, making his forehead look like it was layered with Play-Doh. By reputation, he was mean and tough, and there was nothing in his demeanor during his brief appearance in Courtroom 20 to contradict that assessment.

A little later in the hearing, with Galambos absent from the room, Diamond expounded at length on the muscleman's personality faults. In an attempt to denigrate the weightlifter, he characterized him as a violent, volatile man, and an insufferable one to boot. Giss interrupted the defense attorney in mid-sentence. "I'll *stipulate*," the prosecutor said loudly, emphasizing the commonly used legal term meaning he would agree without argument, "that Galambos is obnoxious."

Everyone in the courtroom burst into laughter. But no one laughed when Galambos was physically present, certainly not when he described, in short, abrupt sentences, how he helped beat up three men without thinking twice about it.

As he told how David had paid him to carry out the attacks and urged him to be as violent as he wanted, David glared at him from his chair behind the defense table. Galambos glared back. Clearly, there was no bond of affection between the two; each had taken his shots at the other, Galambos from the witness stand, David in interviews with Diaz and Hopkins.

Whatever David said about Galambos, however, did not change the fact that Galambos had admitted beating Hast, Nimz, and Waters, even though by doing so he was confessing to breaking the law himself. Nor did it change the fact that David had admitted hiring Galambos to do it. No matter how much David and Diamond tried to denounce Galambos before Judge Hunter, it remained a fact that Galambos and David agreed on one thing: Galambos had assaulted three people because David had paid him to do it. The reality was that one of those people later may have been murdered, and that David allegedly had bragged to his stooge about his involvement in the death. That could not help but influence the court, no matter how badly Diamond tried to trash the witness's reputation.

While Galambos had been an intimidating presence in the courtroom, Dave Edwards, despite his bulk, did not appear threatening at all.

Dressed neatly in a shirt and tie, his hair cut short and well-groomed, Edwards appeared shy rather than belligerent, as his reputation seemed to indicate. When asked to describe his relationship with David, Edwards appeared reluctant to admit how he once had worked closely with an accused killer. Even when he described in detail how he, Galambos, and Andre Augustine had jumped on Hast and Nimz, it seemed as if he were talking about a movie he had seen, rather than a scene from his own not-too-distant past. When he finished his story about David allegedly telling him that he had poisoned Tim Waters, he adjusted his horn-rimmed glasses and turned to Diamond, waiting for the cross-examination.

Edwards was such a credible witness, however, that the best the defense attorney could do was try to get him to admit that when he first told police about that conversation, Edwards had said David told him that *someone,* as opposed to David himself, had slipped a potion into Tim's drink.

Edwards considered the question for several seconds, then conceded that what Diamond had suggested may have been at least partially true. "It may have been both," he said, meaning he may have said "someone" at one point and "David" at another.

However, when Rogan questioned him on re-direct, Edwards was very specific about his recollection of hearing David use the word "I" when suggesting that Tim had been poisoned.

Although Edwards and Galambos formed the foundation of the prosecution's case, they had both told their stories before, and what they said in Judge Hunter's courtroom was no different from what they had said in Judge Person's. But there was one witness called by Giss who the defense had not yet heard: Dr. Frederic Rieders. And he turned out to be quite a star for the prosecution.

An avuncular man in late middle age, Rieders proved to be very sure of himself, very articulate, and a very savvy witness.

After detailing his background for the record, Rieders related how he came to be regarded as an oleander expert, then launched into a description of the tests he had performed on the Waters samples sent to him by Dr. Lovell.

As soon as he saw the results, he said, he was almost positive that oleandrin was present. But just to be sure, he ran the same series of tests again. The results were identical.

"By then," he testified, "I was reasonably certain of the presence of oleandrin in significant amounts." Making a symbol of a gun by lifting his right hand to his head with the forefinger extended, he added: "Without another more obvious cause, such as a bullet hole in the head, I would say that this was the cause of death."

Giss wanted to make sure that Rieders's findings were sufficiently emphasized. Was he certain—within the bounds of expert opinion, of course—that Waters was killed with oleander?

Rieders shrugged; experts dislike being pushed into "certainty" boxes.

"Once you rule out the other possible causes, you have to look at what you're left with," he said; meaning that, in his opinion, if nothing else killed Tim Waters, than the oleandrin must have.

Diamond, however, was not convinced. When Giss turned the toxicologist over for cross-examination a few minutes later, Diamond tried to establish that the oleandrin found in Waters's specimens may have been the *result* of what killed him rather than the *cause*.

Flipping through Dr. Holloway's autopsy report, Diamond opened a series of questions relating to Holloway's notation about Waters's enlarged liver.

Could his liver have produced a substance that reacted like oleandrin? Diamond asked.

Rieders shook his head. "I seriously doubt it," he answered.

Well, then, Diamond pressed, just what substances *are* produced by an enlarged liver?

Rieders answered rather sharply. An enlarged liver produces the same substances as a normal liver, he said, only in increased amounts. "The size of the liver doesn't make it produce substances it wouldn't produce otherwise."

Unfazed, Diamond pressed on. Could the medication that Waters was taking for high blood pressure have killed him and made it look as though he had died from oleander poisoning?

"No," replied Rieders. The oleander plant produces other materials besides oleandrin, but the different substances react differently during testing. In the Waters case, everything pointed toward oleandrin, not any other substance. "It extracted, migrated, and reacted all in the same way," he said.

Diamond inserted disbelief into his voice. Did Rieders

mean that of all the possible substances that could have showed up in Waters's specimens, oleandrin was the only one? Did the toxicologist run tests eliminating everything else?

Rieders looked sad, as though he were trying to explain how a litmus test worked to a dull chemistry student. "There are eight million substances registered by the American Chemical Society, and we can't test for every one of them," he explained. "But I wasn't working in a vacuum. I had a history of the case before I began my tests. You don't give a scientist a substance and ask him to tell you what it is. That's what you do to a student, not a scientist. A scientist gathers all the facts he can beforehand. A scientist puts together a puzzle; he never works in a vacuum. The purpose of my tests was to rule in or rule out oleandrin."

In the Waters case, Rieders added, he had adopted what is called the "null hypothesis approach." Using that method, none of his tests ruled *out* the presence of oleandrin, and neither did they rule *in* any other substance. However, since scientists by nature are careful people, Rieders hedged his statements. "I do not *deny* the possibility that it could have been anything else." He added, with only the lightest hint of a smile: "I do not bet my life on science."

But Rieders's caveat was too weak to give Diamond anything to hang a hope on; the toxicologist was being as positive as he could, considering that science is not always exact.

Turning from substance to method, Diamond wanted to know if Rieders's tests had been designed specifically to examine for oleandrin.

Again Rieders shook his head. "My method of testing was not unique to oleandrin," he said, explaining that he relied primarily on three tests to show his results: Thin-layer chromatography, fluorescence spectrophotometry, and radio immunoassay, essentially the same tests he had used to pinpoint oleandrin in a situation in which he knew in advance what he was looking for, a case involving members of the Haitian community in Miami.

Diamond feigned amazement. No mass spectrometry? he asked, referring to a specialized test common in making other types of analysis.

Rieders answered patiently. As far as he knew, he said, no one had ever detected the presence of oleandrin with a mass spectrometer. "You would need at least three pounds of tissue to even get it ready for such a test, and even then I don't know what the results would be," he said.

Could something in asthma medication have shown up as oleandrin? Diamond queried, seemingly grasping at straws.

Rieders looked thoughtful, waiting a number of seconds to reply. "There is a remote possibility," he said slowly, "that something like that would have shown up on the radio immunoassay test, but not on the other two."

"You don't believe that humans naturally carry substances that would give these same results?" Diamond asked.

"Probably, but not in the concentrations in which I found them," Rieders replied.

To his evident frustration, Diamond had little better luck in cross-examining the other prosecution witnesses than he did with Rieders.

When he questioned Richard Gray, Diamond tried to get him to say that Tim Waters had been a homosexual who frequently picked up men on Santa Monica Boulevard and took them to his room at the Holiday Inn. By taking this tack, Diamond apparently was trying to offer a theory that Tim may have been killed by one of his short-term lovers.

Judge Hunter, however, refused to allow Diamond to question Gray directly about either his own or Tim's sexual preferences. He did, however, allow the defense lawyer to explore Tim's unusual living conditions. Under Diamond's questioning, Gray admitted that Tim moved frequently from one room to another at the Holiday Inn, but it was because he was worried about someone trying to rob him, not because he was hiding from anyone. He had been robbed once, Gray said, and he didn't want it to happen again.

Diamond looked down at David, who was seated at his elbow, and shook his head, signaling that he was running up a dead-end street. A few minutes later, however, he tried again. While questioning Gray about Tim's second business, a limousine rental service he operated in partnership with another mortuary owner, he asked: "Did Tim and his partner have female companions?"

"Objection," yelled Rogan.

Judge Hunter looked coolly at Diamond. "I agree," he said, "unless you're going to argue that they all killed him."

Diamond let the matter drop.

And when George Bristol was on the stand, Diamond tried to get him to implicate himself in some of David's more devious schemes, hinting that Bristol had good reason to cooperate with the prosecutors so he could shift all the blame to David, thereby diverting attention from himself. But Judge Hunter slammed that door as soon as he saw what Diamond was trying to do.

"You have a fertile mind, Mr. Diamond," he said, "but what you are implying is beyond the realm of reason."

A few minutes later, though, Diamond scored a significant point.

While questioning Bristol about his recollections of David's demands for a poison to kill his grandparents,

Diamond asked Bristol if he thought David had been serious when he brought the subject up.

"There was a part of me that couldn't take it seriously," Bristol said, explaining how David had led him on about so many other things, such as being a former deputy sheriff and about having once played for the Seattle Seahawks, that he wasn't sure when David was speaking truthfully.

Diamond jumped at the opening. "He would take credit for things he did not actually do?" he asked. "Sort of bragging and joking and boasting?"

"Yes," Bristol replied.

Diamond look satisfied. He had successfully implanted the idea that if David *had* actually bragged or joked about murdering Tim Waters, it would be consistent with his personality and did not necessarily have any connection to reality.

But the law is a give and take profession; lawyers may win a point here, but they almost invariably lose a point there. A few minutes later Diamond lost a point.

While still questioning Bristol, Diamond was particularly insistent on getting the witness to admit that at one time he, Bristol, had suggested poisoning Randy Welty.

Bristol denied it. And he kept denying it although Diamond persisted in asking the same question several times in slightly different form.

Giss finally lost patience. "Objection!" he screamed, jumping up. "Obviously the defense attorney does not understand the word no."

"You know what they say," Diamond shot back, "never take no for an answer."

Giss smiled, assuming the role of a comedian who had just been fed a juicy line. "You're not on a date, Roger," he quipped, breaking up the judge and the spectators.

On re-direct, Rogan moved quickly to try to rectify the damage done by Diamond.

"Was David joking when he grabbed you by the throat?" he asked.

"No," Bristol said decisively.

"Was he joking when Lisa Karlan kept calling and he said he would kill anyone who threatened his family?"

"No."

"Was he joking when he *kept* asking for a poison?"

"No."

Diamond seemed not only to be having trouble with the witnesses, but with his client as well. A take-control type person to begin with, David could hardly be expected to sit placidly throughout the hearing. When both he and Diamond were seated, David kept up an active patter, whispering almost constantly in his lawyer's good ear. When Diamond stood to question a witness, David tugged at his sleeve or poked his arm to demand his attention. Diamond was particularly forgiving of this insistency, never showing irritation at having his questioning interrupted, or giving any indication that he was aggravated at being told by his client how to conduct his case.

Diamond also was getting direction from another source: Jerry and Laurieanne. The two were present every day, situating themselves precisely in the center of the first row of seats in the almost-empty spectator section, he in a jacket and tie, she in a stylish dress.

A heavyset, husky man with close cropped, age-thinned hair rapidly turning to gray, Jerry habitually appeared optimistic and chatted animatedly with Diamond whenever the court was in recess.

Laurieanne, her makeup meticulous, wore her salt and pepper hair swept upward in a fashionable coif and usually had a scarf tied loosely at her throat.

They both took copious notes, and at first tried to exchange pleasantries with their son. That was forbidden by courtroom rules, but rather than publicly rebuke them for it, Judge Hunter came up with a more tactful solution: He simply ordered the bailiff to seal off the first row of seats with silver duct tape, which effectively put the Sconces, parents and son, out of whispering range.

The separation, however, did not dampen their spirits. Each day they appeared outwardly confident, aloof from the others—particularly Tim Waters's mother and sister, who also were there every day, sitting almost within touching distance in the small room—but always acutely aware. When they were not writing in their separate notebooks, they kept their eyes riveted on their son. Whenever he turned around and their eyes met, all three smiled brightly, as if the proceeding were a high school graduation rather than a preamble to a murder trial.

Despite the horrible things the witnesses were saying about his client, Diamond treated only one of them roughly. That was Jim Dame, the former employee who had opened up the entire case by contacting authorities soon after the incident at Oscar's Ceramics.

Actually, Dame had been a thorn in David's side for several years. While he was still working for David at the crematorium, Dame claimed, he had loaned his boss $25,000, money from his father's inheritance that he had borrowed from his mother, to help David buy his house. The loan was never fully repaid, Dame said, so he had filed a civil suit against his employer in an attempt to get the rest. The court later ruled in Dame's favor, but he never got the cash.

A short, slightly pudgy man with a heavy, dark mustache and a receding hairline, Dame had worked for David for more than two years and had ample opportunity to observe the Sconces' operations.

For the most part, Dame's testimony added little to what had already been said about David earlier by other witnesses. Except for one thing. Of all the people who had worked for David and who later came forward to testify against him, Dame was the only one who claimed to have heard his former employer specifically mention oleander as a possible poison.

It had happened, Dame said, one day when he was riding with David to pick up a vehicle at the garage. As they were driving down the freeway, Dame said he picked up a book that was lying on the floor of David's car. "What's this?" he had asked curiously, noting the title was *The Poor Man's James Bond*.

Dame said that David told him it was a book about ways to kill people, especially through the use of poisons.

"Like what?" Dame had asked.

"Like oleander," David replied.

"Oleander?" Dame had asked, puzzled.

"Yeah," David said. "Oleander." Pointing out the car window at the shrubs decorating the highway median: "That stuff growing there."

It was damaging testimony, making Dame the first witness to directly link David both with the book Dave Edwards said he had loaned to him and with oleander.

The accusation did not sit well with Diamond. When the defense lawyer's turn came to question Dame, he was so belligerent that he had to be ordered twice by Judge Hunter not to yell at the witness. However, despite his efforts, the defense attorney was not able to shake Dame's testimony. Finally, when he saw that he was making little progress, Diamond dismissed Dame with a wave.

Notwithstanding the solemnity of the occasion, the hearing was not infrequently spiked with humor. Since there was no jury and it was not a trial, a certain looseness prevailed that would not have been present under more formal circumstances.

One witness, in response to a question from Diamond,

mentioned that Galambos had been described to him before he actually saw him.

"And how was that?" Diamond wanted to know.

He was depicted, the witness said, as a Neanderthal-looking man with heavy eyebrows that met in the middle.

"That sounds like a pretty good description to me," Judge Hunter interjected.

When Rieders was called to the stand, he appeared wearing a dark suit and white shirt, but no tie. If the court did not object, he said in his faintly Germanic accent, he would prefer to testify with an open collar because he had a bad cold, and if he closed the top button, his breathing would be restricted. "But I have a tie," he blurted out, digging into his jacket pocket, extracting a bow tie and waving it for the judge to see. "This is my instant respectability." The judge chuckled, apparently feeling that some amount of levity was permissible in the proceeding, which was not a formal trial.

Sometimes, however, the humor was unintentional.

With Scott Sorrentino, the boyhood friend who had spent Good Friday evening with Tim, on the stand, Diamond again tried to elicit testimony to show that Tim may have been gay.

"Was Tim Waters a homosexual?" Diamond asked.

Sorrentino looked shocked. "Absolutely not!" he answered.

"Are you?" Diamond countered.

Again Sorrentino seemed taken aback. "No!" he answered resoundingly.

In response to further questioning from the defense attorney, Sorrentino explained that Tim did not drink alcohol so it was unlikely that he ingested the oleander via a spiked cocktail.

"Did you ever use amyl nitrate?" Diamond asked, referring to a compound used to dilate a person's blood vessels. Available in a commercial form, it is popular in some circles as an orgasm enhancer.

Sorrentino looked puzzled. "What is that?" he asked. "It sounds like something you embalm a body with."

During his cross examination of Richard Gray, Diamond worked hard at trying to give the impression that Waters may have been given the fatal dose of oleander by practically anyone other than his client.

When he turned the witness back over to the prosecution for re-direct, Rogan could not resist an attempt to show the absurdity of the defense's assertions, forgetting that Gray had not been present when Rieders testified about an herbal doctor in Florida who had prescribed a rectal administration of oleander to help a patient gain weight.

Rogan was solemn. "Did Tim Waters, as far as you know, ever receive an oleander enema from a Haitian witch doctor?"

Gray did not have the faintest idea what Rogan was talking about. He looked totally blank for a moment, then stammered, "N-Nooo."

And sometimes the humor was black.

The day after Rieders testified at length about oleander poisoning, a cut-glass vase filled with creamy-white oleander blooms appeared on a desk in the courtroom. No one admitted to knowing how it got there, but at the first recess, it disappeared.

30

When it came time for Diamond to call his witnesses, he had three, but only one was really pertinent to the defense: Dr. Holloway.

By calling the pathologist and asking him to go over in detail his autopsy of Tim Waters, Diamond hoped to convince Judge Hunter that the late cremation service owner had died a natural death, and that attempts by the prosecution to point to murder were indicative of a vendetta against his client. Holloway fell into this plan in that he continued to insist he had no reason to believe that Tim's death was anything but spontaneous.

Diamond opened the questions by asking Holloway if he remembered Tim Waters out of the some 13,000 persons he had autopsied during his career.

A tall, heavyset man with thinning gray hair, Holloway said he had no trouble recalling Tim because he had been so obese. "He was a grossly overweight individual," he said in a soft, kindly voice, the kind of voice that seemed more suited to a bedside physician than a pathologist, "and that finding influenced my other findings."

Far from apologizing for filing a report saying that Tim had died a natural death, Holloway said the signs all showed that Tim had been a very sick man when he died.

"His heart had come to the point where it could no longer function," Holloway maintained. "His lungs filled up with fluid because his blood circulation had ceased. He was suffering from a metabolic overload. The displacement of his diaphragm had reduced his breathing capacity, and obesity added to the problems. As a result, his heart was working at its limit." All of this, Holloway said, was obvious to him as soon as he took a firsthand look at Tim's heart. His opinion was only strengthened, he added, when he examined slides of Tim's heart tissue under the microscope.

But he had clues even before he cut Tim's chest open that he was going to find problems. First of all, the pathologist explained, when he studied Tim's hands, he had noticed that the base of his fingernails had been blue. Called cyanosis, that was an indicator that his blood was not carrying enough oxygen throughout his body. Then when Holloway slit open Tim's chest, his suspicions were confirmed. Tim's heart was enlarged and the left ventricle had thickened, which were other danger signs. When he examined the slides under the microscope, Holloway also discovered that Tim's heart tissue had begun to fragment, which was another indicator that Tim's heart was not getting sufficient oxygen.

There were other beacons to Tim's ill-health besides the heart, Holloway added. Tim's lungs were congested and his liver was blown up twice the size of a normal organ. When he examined the spleen, Holloway discovered that also was enlarged. "It did not cause his death," Holloway said, "but it was another point showing an impeded flow of blood to the heart."

Finally, the pathologist said, he also found congestion in Tim's kidneys. Although the condition was minor, it was another hint that blood was not circulating as it should have been.

When the doctor finished, Diamond looked satisfied,

smiling perhaps for the first time during the hearing. Even David seemed contented; he remained silent.

Under cross-examination by Giss, Holloway defended his conclusions, claiming that he had no reason to be suspicious about Tim's death. "There was nothing to indicate that a detailed toxicological test should be done," he said, adding that in any case, Ventura County did not have the equipment to perform the sophisticated examination carried out by Dr. Rieders. "I felt, and I still find, that an adequate cause of death had been found in my autopsy."

When Giss pressed him about the possibility of oleander poisoning, Holloway said from what he had read about the plant, it was fatal within a few hours if it was going to be fatal at all.

"Here we have something that took much longer than would be expected for oleander," Holloway said, "especially considering his [Tim's] condition."

Giss took his time, phrasing his next question carefully.

"Take as a given," he said slowly, "that oleander was in Tim's system. Are you saying that regardless of those findings, he would have died anyway at that time?"

Holloway did not hesitate. "Yes!" he replied emphatically.

Giss's heart sank. Holloway was a credible witness and his opinion would carry a lot of weight. If he was willing to go on the record as saying that in his expert view Tim would have died when he did with or without the oleander, it could present major problems for the prosecution.

What was especially troubling was Holloway's insistence that oleander was a fast-acting poison. The fact that Tim had lived so long after allegedly ingesting the oleander could cause doubt that Tim had taken a fatal dose. But before Giss could try to pick Holloway's assertions to pieces, the pathologist blurted out: "Tim Waters was so hugely overweight, I think the toxin found its way into his fat. Otherwise he may have died sooner."

Giss sighed in relief. Holloway, an M.D., had offered a detail that had not been alluded to by Rieders. But Rieders was a Ph.D. and a toxicologist, not an M.D., and therefore not as well-versed in pathology. Holloway, however, had volunteered that oleandrin was a fat-soluble substance, that is, that the poison could be stored in a person's body fat, and the degree of obesity could directly effect the speed with which the poison acted.

Up to that point the prosecution had been unable to explain why Tim had not gotten sick earlier if he had been poisoned, as they contended, on Good Friday evening. Holloway inadvertently had provided an explanation. In the future the defense would still be able to argue that Tim's death occurred too long after the time he could possibly have been poisoned by David, but the prosecution would have a ready answer: The oleander had not killed immediately, as oleander usually does, because the poison had been absorbed into Tim's layer of fat and the deadly substance was released slowly. It was the difference between a person taking a Contac that emits medication over a period of time and taking an Excedrin that kicks in immediately at full strength.

Feeling more confident, Giss resumed his questioning. It wasn't exactly a major victory for the prosecution, but it gave the DDA a considerable wedge that he could use to help weaken Holloway's tenacious stand that it was Tim's bad heart that killed him, not oleander.

"Would you say Tim Waters's heart was grossly over-sized?" he asked.

"No," said Holloway.

"His liver? For a man his size?"

"Yes."

Since Tim did not drink alcohol, what could have

caused his liver to be in such poor condition? the prosecutor wanted to know.

Holloway shrugged. "Malfunction," he replied, more question than answer.

Without preliminary, Giss switched back to oleander. "Are you saying that Dr. Rieders's findings are inconsequential?" he asked.

"Not at all," Holloway answered forcefully. "Other findings would have to be considered." He added, however, that he would view the presence of oleander in Tim's system as a contributing cause of death rather than the primary one. "The myocardial insufficiency *was* acute," he said. "It *did* cause pulmonary edema."

Was Tim's severe diarrhea consistent with his findings? Giss asked.

"It might have been," Holloway replied. "There is an overlap of symptomatology to be considered."

"Had you been familiar with Dr. Rieders's findings, would your report have read *exactly* like it does?" the prosecutor persisted.

"I would have added as a contributing cause oleandrin toxicity," Holloway conceded. Then he added: "It is a matter of interpretation. How much oleandrin does it take to disable the heart? Dr. Rieders says oleander was the main cause of death. I would not necessarily agree."

Giss was unwilling to let it go. "Dr. Rieders says that regardless of what you found, oleander would have killed Tim Waters."

Holloway shook his head. Tim, he said, could possibly have survived the poisoning in the level in which oleander was found in his system. He would have been very sick, the pathologist said, but he could possibly have survived.

But then it was Holloway who was unwilling to let it go. He added a caveat. "Oleander is fat soluble and it could have gotten into Tim's fat tissue. In other words, it could have been cumulative as a contributory factor."

Giss, anxious to get Holloway off the stand and salvage what he could, asked if it would be a fair statement of the pathologist's position to say that, in his opinion, the concentration of oleandrin found in Tim's system was the contributing if not the independent cause of Tim's death.

Holloway nodded. "I can't deny that," he said.

"But you can't say that, but for the oleander, you couldn't say *when* Tim Waters would have died?" Giss asked, pushing his luck.

In his opinion, Holloway said, even without the oleander, Tim probably would have died within a matter of hours. But to Giss's delight, he softened the statement. "He was alive before the oleander was ingested. I don't know when he might have expired absent the oleander."

31

In his closing argument before Judge Hunter, Giss made accommodation for Holloway's contention that Tim was doomed with or without the oleander. "It is still a homicide," the prosecutor asserted.

Without making an issue of his belief that it was oleander that had killed Tim and not the illness outlined by the coroner, Giss argued that what was important—and which Holloway did not figure into his testimony—was that David *intended* to kill Tim, whether it was the oleander that actually killed him or not. Under California law a death is regarded as a murder even if the victim was already weakened by disease, or would have died soon from another cause. Giss's reasoning was similar to Walt Lewis's contention about the money that had been skimmed from the preneed accounts: Just because the money was returned did not mean that a crime had not been committed when it was initially taken. But in this case, even if he conceded the accuracy of Holloway's diagnosis, Giss said, and even if Tim *was* fatally ill, and even if he died from another cause first, David was still guilty of murder if he gave Tim something intending to cause his death and he subsequently died.

To back up his argument about David's intentions, Giss

pointed out that, according to Galambos and Edwards, David had bragged that he had poisoned Tim. And even if David had been indulging in his customary braggadocio, his statements could not be rejected out of hand. Galambos and Edwards were so closely allied with David that it was not unreasonable to assume that he would be candid with them.

David's motive, the prosecutor continued, was the simplest of all: greed. David was making a lot of money in his various operations, particularly by selling the dental gold, a practice that brought in some $6000 tax-free every month. If someone were to try to put an end to his various enterprises, it would hurt David badly in the pocketbook. And that was a situation that David could not tolerate. "Anyone who interfered with his business was marked for extinction," Giss argued, paraphrasing statements allegedly made by David himself to others.

During the speech by the prosecutor, David sat rigidly at the defense table, rocking agitatedly back and forth. A deep scowl creased his brow; he looked as though he could hardly keep from charging across the courtroom and grabbing Giss by the throat. But the moment passed quickly. A few minutes later, when Diamond rose to present his argument, David visibly relaxed.

The defense attorney implored Hunter not to take too seriously everything the prosecutor had said, especially the part about testimony from Galambos and Edwards. "They are both convicted felons," he reminded the judge, "and they have reason to blame someone else."

As for others against whom David allegedly made threats, they are all alive and healthy. That in itself, Diamond maintained, should be enough to demolish the prosecution's contention that David regularly indulged in violence against his perceived enemies.

But the most incomplete part of the prosecution's case,

he claimed, the biggest flaw of all, was in the fact that there had not been a single witness who could place David and Tim together, particularly not on Good Friday afternoon when the poison apparently would have had to be administered, if it had been administered at all. That, he said, was a "gigantic hole" in the case against David. To Diamond, the fact that the prosecution had not provided testimony linking the two was a significant gap, one so broad that the lack of such proof virtually demanded that David be released. "Justice requires that he be discharged now," Diamond insisted.

However, the defense attorney seemed only to be going through the motions; in his heart he must have known that Judge Hunter was going to do no such thing. Even without the inmate testimony that Lewis had used with such effectiveness during the preliminary hearing in Pasadena, Giss and Rogan had made the only point that was required of them in such a proceeding: They had provided probable cause for David being tried for Tim Waters's murder.

Seemingly certain that Judge Hunter was not going to allow David to walk out of the courtroom, Diamond had an alternative suggestion ready, one that would bypass completely the entire question of David's possibly having murdered Tim Waters: Diamond suggested that Hunter simply declare that he did not have jurisdiction in the case, thereby bringing a speedy end to the proceedings.

"There is no evidence that David Sconce ever came to this county," Diamond argued. "Tim Waters became ill in Malibu or, arguably, Burbank," both of which are in Los Angeles County. What he was asking Hunter to do was send the case to Los Angeles County, where the whole process would have to be repeated provided the prosecution had the will to continue the fight. If Hunter were to accept Diamond's argument, he could free David on jurisdictional grounds without having to consider whether the evidence was strong enough to justify David's being bound over for trial.

But Hunter was not looking for an easy out; Diamond's proposal, in fact, visibly irritated him. "Where *was* [the poison] administered?" the judge asked Diamond, speaking sharply. "You tell me!"

"The poison would have had to be administered in Malibu," Diamond responded, not even slightly repentant. If that were true, the preliminary hearing should have been held in the Malibu municipal court. On the other hand, he continued, if the timetable were moved back a couple of hours, the poison could have been administered in Burbank, and it should have gone to a court there. Diamond argued that the doubt about where the oleander was slipped to Tim should be sufficient to make the judge pause. "The law favors the place where the injury takes place," he asserted.

Hunter shook his head. Giss was on his feet, waiting his chance to rebut Diamond's allegations, but Hunter waved him back into his chair. He did not need to hear the prosecution's arguments, he said. He had made up his mind; he was going to order David bound over for trial.

"I feel that Tim Waters, who was a dying man, was poisoned by oleander," Hunter said, speaking clearly and deliberately, "and that was the cause of his death. I feel that his death was a homicide. The fact that oleander is fat-soluble is why it took him longer than normal to die."

Also, he added, demolishing Diamond's alternate proposal, the fact that Tim *died* in Ventura County while the place where the poison was administered was unknown was sufficient to bring David to trial there. End of discussion.

As David was led from the courtroom in handcuffs and ankle chains, Diamond told Hunter that he planned to file a series of motions to try to block a trial in Ventura.

Hunter smiled indulgently. Go ahead and file your motions, he told Diamond. But in the meantime he was sending the case record to superior court so it could be set for trial as soon as possible.

But it was not as simple as that. True to his word, Diamond filed a flurry of motions, one of which, particularly, almost succeeded.

While waiting for a trial date to be set, Diamond's research uncovered an obscure state law that prohibited a district attorney from delegating his authority to anyone else. The defense attorney hoped to use this little-known statute as a wedge to stop David's trial.

Pouncing on the regulation, Diamond filed a motion before Superior Court Judge Frederick A. Jones, who had been assigned to the case and would, unless something unforeseen occurred, preside over future proceedings, including the trial. Diamond's document insisted that the illegal delegation of authority was precisely what happened when Ventura D.A. Michael D. Bradbury agreed to swear Giss and Rogan as special prosecutors to try David's case. Additionally, Diamond contended, it had been the Los Angeles district attorney's office that had been calling the shots from the beginning. It was the L.A. D.A.'s office that decided to prosecute, not Bradbury, he said, and it was the L.A. D.A.'s office that announced that Giss and Rogan would be seeking the death penalty against David.

Judge Jones, a former prosecutor and FBI agent who had been elected to the bench in the late seventies on a law and order platform, let it be known in late November that he was inclined to go along with the defense lawyer on that issue. To the surprise of most of those who had been following the case, Jones said he was seriously considering Diamond's arguments and might dismiss the murder charge against David.

The announcement hit the district attorney's office like

a bomb. If the judge acted as he indicated he might, it could just about wreck the prosecution, which already was wounded from one blow. About the time Diamond filed his motion, it was announced that Giss's trial assistant, Jim Rogan, had been appointed a municipal court judge in Glendale by Governor George Deukmejian, so he would be lost as far as any other work on the case was concerned. Rogan had proved himself adept in the courtroom and—since he had been in charge of the prosecution in Jerry's and Laurieanne's case—he knew the details of the case as well as anyone, including Giss and Walt Lewis. He would be missed.

Rogan's departure, however, was a reality, something the district attorney's office was going to have to live with. A Jones decision in favor of the defense, on the other hand, was anything but a foregone conclusion. Giss would fight Diamond's motion as hard as he could for a very basic reason: If granted, it could bring an abrupt halt to plans for a trial. If, upon examining the evidence that would be presented by Giss and Diamond, Jones did indeed dismiss the charge as Diamond had requested, the prosecution would either have to refile it—and go through another preliminary hearing—or forget about it.

Both sides had a lot to win or lose; Jones's ruling would be crucial. And neither Giss nor Diamond had any feeling for which way the judge would come down.

In his first few years on the bench, Jones was regarded as an extreme conservative, handing down such stiff sentences that even prosecutors were often surprised. But over the years, he had mellowed, and by the time David's case came before him, his reputation was that of a man equally balanced between the prosecution and defense. He was known as a tough judge, but a fair one, a man who could examine the issues with intelligence rather than bias. To help him make his decision, Jones ordered a hearing to give Giss and Diamond the chance to argue their points in person, and reserved a formal ruling until he had listened to the debate. The hearing began early in December.

Giss, realizing that months of work and one of the most important cases of his career were on the line, called Bradbury as his main witness, hoping testimony from the Ventura district attorney would put to rest the defense contention that he had allowed another district attorney to make his decisions for him.

On the stand Bradbury swore that it had been his call, not that of Los Angeles D.A. Ira Reiner, to charge David with the death of Tim Waters. But before Giss could breathe too large a sigh of relief, Bradbury added that he had left to Giss and Reiner the decision on whether the prosecution would ask for the death penalty against David. That, Bradbury confessed, had been a mistake.

Asked how *he* felt about seeking the death penalty against David, Bradbury said he was not sure; he would have to give it considerable thought.

Eventually, after a DDA from Ventura named Kevin De Noce was named by Bradbury to help Giss at trial, replacing Rogan, the Ventura district attorney said he felt that the nature of David's crime justified asking for David's execution.

Bradbury's decision was far from arbitrary; there are several factors that have to be considered before announcing an intention to seek the death penalty. Under California law, a death sentence can be sought only in cases in which "special circumstances" prevail. Poisoning is considered a special circumstance.

However, at the time Bradbury testified in Jones's court —before he made the death penalty decision—it was far from certain that there would *be* a trial. But after listening to Bradbury, Judge Jones said he felt the prosecution had acted correctly and that the trial would go ahead as planned, which was exactly what Giss wanted to hear.

° ° °

The relief over the judge's recommendation to the opposing lawyers to start pointing toward a trial was so great, in fact, that Giss was unworried about another of Diamond's requests: permission to exhume Tim's body. The defense attorney wanted to run another series of tests on Tim's tissue so he could have some documentation to refute Rieders's powerful testimony. Giss offered no opposition. He was confident in his expert's reputation, and he figured that additional tests would only confirm the Pennsylvania toxicologist's findings. In a way, Giss seemed almost to welcome the opportunity since it would give added strength to his argument. Besides, it was something his new assistant, De Noce, had been quietly pushing for anyway.

Although he was only three years out of law school at Pepperdine University, De Noce exhibited a marked bent toward science that went a long way toward compensating for his comparative lack of courtroom experience. He had a real knack for scientific subjects, and Giss respected this. In fact, Giss's loosely formed trial plan was to let De Noce handle the scientific arguments while he concentrated on the aspects that would allow him to use his expertise with witnesses. De Noce's job, in other words, would be to prove that Tim Waters was murdered, while Giss's would be to convince the jury that David was either the actual murderer or that he paid someone to have it done.

Unknown to the prosecution team, Diamond had by this time half decided on a trial strategy as well. Rather than go into court and slug it out with Giss to try to prove David not guilty, Diamond had tentatively determined to concentrate on proving that Tim *had not even been murdered.* But he had to be careful; he could not afford to tip his hand by pointing too strongly in that direction. Instead, he continued with tactics that would make it appear to Giss that he was striking blindly in an effort to find something, virtually *anything*, to keep the case from ever coming to trial. In an attempt to camouflage the importance he was placing on the proposed new scientific tests —which he hoped would show that Tim had died a natural death—Diamond also asked Jones to toss out the charges. If Jones granted Diamond's request, it would effectively prohibit David from being tried for Tim's murder not only in Ventura County, but possibly in Los Angeles County as well.

Giss shook his head in frustration, regarding the motion as simply another delaying tactic. In a way he was right; it ultimately would prove ineffectual. But in another way he was wrong. While Giss was busy fighting the defense motion, Diamond was sneaking up behind him with a raised club.

32

The defense attorney's argument went like this: When San Bernardino County officials entered Oscar's Ceramics on January 20, 1987, they did so illegally because they did not have a warrant. As a result of that allegedly illegal search and the publicity that followed it, Jim Dame was prompted to come forward with information that eventually led to David being charged with, among other things, Tim's murder. If—and this was the crucial part—it had not been for that so-called illegal search, David would be a free man.

In legal terminology, a source of material or evidence is called a "tree." If the source is questionable—for example, if the origin of the material is a prohibited process such as an illegal search—the "tree" is referred to as "poisoned," and any evidence that flows therefrom is known colorfully as "the fruit of the poisoned tree." If a judge determines that a prosecutor, for example, has relied on "fruit from the poisoned tree," the law compels that the tainted evidence be declared invalid. That was precisely what Diamond was trying to do: convince Judge Jones that Giss and De Noce's entire case was built on "fruit of the poisoned tree" and therefore was nonviable.

But that was not all of Diamond's multipronged argument. He also asserted that David's interviews with Detective Diaz on July 15, 1987, and with Detective Hopkins on July 6, 1988, as well as his taped telephone conversation with David Edwards on June 5, 1987, had violated his client's rights because David did not have an attorney present at the time the incidents occurred. In his view, since those acts also were improper, they formed additional grounds for having the charge dismissed.

Despite the fact that it looked like a stalling tactic by the defense, Jones ordered another hearing. It began in mid-January, 1991, and lasted for four days.

While the prosecution was willing to acknowledge that Wentworth and others entered Oscar's Ceramics without a search warrant, Giss and De Noce argued it was irrelevant because David had given his consent, not just to Wentworth, but also to his employee, John Pollerana. With consent, a warrant is not necessary. Therefore, the prosecutors continued, if the search was not illegal, then the progression of the case, including Dame's statements to police and everything that stemmed from them, could not be considered contaminated.

Summing up the prosecution's position on the issue, De Noce put it picturesquely: "Law enforcement didn't shake the tree of Oscar's Ceramics to cause Dame, the fruit, to fall. Dame comes from another tree," he argued, "and that tree grows out of Lamb Funeral Home. It is not even the same tree. There's no indication that anybody, in shaking the tree of Oscar's Ceramics, would ever have brought about the fruit of Dame."

In his response, Diamond picked up on De Noce's reference and carried it a step further. "As far as Dame being found out of a different tree than Oscar's, who is in a better position to Oscar's and Lamb's than Dame? Dame knew the connection; Dame knew that the search of Oscar's was intimately involved with the Lamb Funeral

Home. So it's not accurate to say that the trees were different, that Dame fell out of the Lamb Funeral Home tree when it was only the Oscar's tree that was shaken."

Judge Jones shook his head. It really didn't matter which tree Dame fell out of, he said, because it was Dame's decision to go to the police; the police did not go looking for Dame. Since Dame instigated the contact, the fruit—his information—was not poisoned, that is, obtained illegally. It did not matter either, Jones added, what prompted Dame to come forward. "While it is uncertain whether Dame first became aware of the investigation at Oscar's through his attorney or on his own, his decision to contact law enforcement turned upon his acceptance of his lawyer's advice and was prompted by his concern for his own future welfare," Jones said, effectively demolishing Diamond's contention.

Even if one assumed, Jones continued, that the entry into Oscar's was illegal—and *he* as the judge did not think that it was—that did not in itself establish a link between what happened and Dame's decision to talk to investigators. David had twice given his consent for Wentworth and the others to enter Oscar's, Jones reminded Diamond. "Therefore," Jones explained, "this court concludes the several consents were not obtained by coercion, nor were they products of duress or results of submission to assertions of authority. Instead, they were freely and voluntarily given."

Although that seemed to settle the issue, Jones was just getting warmed up. While the fruit of the poisoned tree concept is a valid legal principle, Jones expounded, the Dame case was an exception, one of only three such cases he had seen in his twelve years on the bench.

"I doubt that I could script a factual setting more compelling than the application of this well-recognized yet unique exception than that which has been proved here," he commented. "[David] had put in operation this unper-

mitted body-burning operation in complete violation . . . .
of virtually every regulation which might control or regu-
late the enterprise. These repeated complaints caused fire
and air quality enforcement officers to react just as . . .
anyone would have reasonably expected of them."

In addition, Jones said, the Cemetery Board's investigator, Westall, was not "idly casting about," blindly searching for violations. "He was on the trail of Mr. Sconce and
for good reason, apparently." David's persistence in continuing to operate the illegal crematorium, Jones continued, would eventually have led to a search of Oscar's
under almost any circumstances. "I conclude from all
these circumstances," Jones declared, "that the illegal operation at Oscar's Ceramics would have been inevitably
discovered in the normal course of those investigations."

Jones also made quick work of Diamond's claims that
David's rights had been violated in his conversations with
Edwards and Diaz. At the time he talked over the phone
to Edwards, which was three days before he went into
Judge Mitchell's court expecting to be released almost
immediately on $5000 bond, David had not been charged
with any of the crimes alluded to by either man during the
telephone discussion, therefore his right to counsel "had
not yet attached." In other words, at that time and in
those circumstances he *had* no right to a lawyer. And as
far as his jailhouse interview with Diaz, Jones pointed out
that it was David, not the detective, who had asked for the
meeting. "This communication occurred upon the instiga-
tion and request of the defendant and was not in any
manner the product of law enforcement suggestion,"
Jones said.

There was, however, one point the judge failed to rule
upon immediately. And that was the assertion involving
David's interview with Detective Hopkins. In Jones's
mind, the defense's claim in that regard was of little value

anyway. "I feel no sense of immediacy . . . in making a decision as to that conversation," Jones said dryly, "particularly in light of my impression that there's very little within that conversation that will ultimately be considered profitable . . . by the [prosecution] and, more importantly, because I don't feel that a delayed ruling on this issue is going to affect the ability of either party to prepare for trial." Translation: Enough's enough. See you in court!

Giss's spirits soared. He had, he assumed, cleared the last major hurdle leading to David's long-awaited trial on charges that he murdered Tim Waters. With Diamond's latest obstacle removed from the scene, Giss felt that he and De Noce could then concentrate on finally getting into court and working for David's conviction.

Not that he didn't have problems with his case, he admitted to himself. During the trial there would still be two major issues that he considered weak spots in the case.

Foremost—and this was a situation he readily conceded was a problem, a condition he called the prosecution's Achilles heel—was the fact that investigators had never been able to prove that David or anyone hired by him had met with Tim Waters the evening of Friday, April 5. For jurors to be convinced that the two had indeed gotten together at a restaurant where David (or one of his hired guns) would have been able to slip the oleander extract into something that Tim would have consumed—a drink, a salad, whatever—prosecution witnesses, especially Galambos and Edwards, would have to be especially persuasive. Their persuasiveness, in turn, would depend largely on how well the prosecution had presented its case up to that point. Giss would have to lay such a well-documented foundation for a Tim/David meeting that jurors would have to conclude that it probably occurred even if could not be substantiated by witnesses.

Working in the prosecution's favor, while not nearly as incriminating as testimony of a single witness, was the fact that three-plus hours are apparently missing out of Tim's life late in the afternoon and evening of Good Friday. One of his employees, Dawn Stickler, testified that she and Tim closed up the Alpha Society office at about five P.M. that day. Investigators were not able to find *anyone* who saw Tim again after that until he met his friend, Scott Sorrentino, at a freeway off-ramp sometime after eight P.M.

However, Giss was confident that he did not necessarily *have* to physically link Tim and David on that fateful Good Friday to convince a jury that David was a murderer. David had already pleaded guilty to paying his stooges to beat up Tim, so whether David was actually the one who slipped something into Tim's food or drink, or whether he paid some as yet unidentified person to do it, was immaterial. Paying someone else to commit a murder would not reduce David's culpability.

The second major obstacle facing the prosecution, which had been addressed publicly by no one up to that point, was more subtle. During the Pasadena preliminary hearing as well as the one at Ventura, a number of prosecution witnesses told how David had been anxious to kill his grandparents. George Bristol had been particularly vocal on that point, explaining in detail how David had been pressuring him to come up with a poison that he could use. But no one, neither prosecution nor defense, had publicly asked why David felt he needed *another* poison if he had already used oleander successfully against Tim Waters.

There also was a possibility, albeit an unlikely one, that Giss had a ready answer to that but had not revealed it for any of a number of reasons. A trial is not just a matter of opposing sides presenting everything they know and leaving the jury to sort it out. There is a great deal of strategy involved, not only concerning what evidence will be presented, but how, by whom, and under what circumstances. Cross-examination, for example, also is a vital part of a trial, and if one side can destroy another's witnesses, that sometimes can be as effective as having a well-positioned witness of your own.

Another important factor, one that old hands like Giss and Diamond were well aware of, is that a case seldom is won entirely in the courtroom. There is a lot of psychology involved in preparing a case for trial, not the least of which revolves around the media. In this case, at various stages of its development, both the prosecution and the defense had been relatively accessible to reporters.

But of all the stories written about the case, one of the more interesting ones appeared in the San Diego *Union* on November 25, 1990. The story, by reporter Norma Meyer, was published after the preliminary hearing in Judge Hunter's court but it predated the two motion hearings before Judge Jones. The article provided a comprehensive summary of the case up to that point, but what it did best of all was afford a sounding board for Giss and Laurieanne to exchange insults, which all was part of the psychological battle that was raging backstage.

Giss bitingly referred to Laurieanne, fully aware of how sensitive David was to any comments about his mother, as "Tammy Faye Sconce," ridiculing her penchant for makeup. He also labeled her a "fraud," and claimed that she was the one who ultimately was responsible for the way David had turned out. "The son is like the parents— an incredible con," Giss said. "That apple fell real close to the tree."

By making these comments, Giss was playing a mind game with the defendant, perhaps hoping he could goad him into making a fatal mistake, or at the very least, putting him even more on the defensive.

But Laurieanne proved she had teeth as well. Not to be

Ken Englade

outdone in the slur swap, Laurieanne accused Giss of being a publicity hound "who wanted to have himself another Charlie Manson case." Manson also had been prosecuted by the L.A. district attorney's office, and the man who convicted him, Vincent Bugliosi, went on to literary fame with *Helter Skelter*, his book about the case. As her final word, Laurieanne told Meyer that even the name of her son's prosecutor was abhorrent. "Giss rhymes with hiss," she spat, "like a snake."

If the prosecution seemed to have its problems on the eve of trial, so did the defense. The most important one from Diamond's point of view was that both Galambos and Edwards—especially Edwards—were strong witnesses, each capable of convincing a jury that David had indeed claimed he had murdered Tim, and that his statements were not idle boasts.

Backing up the statements from the two was the taped conversation David had with Edwards while the former was in Arizona and the latter in investigator Loeb's office. The most incriminating part was when Edwards had mentioned Tim's death and how he and Galambos were afraid police might try to tie them in to the mysterious demise. When Edwards said that, David had responded: "Well, you weren't around with that." As obscure as it was, Diamond was certain the prosecution would make a big deal out of it at trial, claiming it was, in essence, a confession of his knowledge of what happened that was firmly on the record. Also, there was the testimony from Dame, which directly linked David to oleander and, more importantly, seemed to corroborate Edwards's claims about David's familiarity with *The Poor Man's James Bond.* Plus, there had been Dr. Rieders's testimony before Judge Hunter about the oleander derivative he claimed to have found in Tim's system.

From what David had said to Diaz and Hopkins during

their interviews, and by the types of questions Diamond asked some of the prosecution's witnesses during the Ventura preliminary hearing, David's defense seemed to be pointed toward a contention that a "mystery man" murdered Tim, maybe a homosexual lover, if Diamond could introduce the possibility (as he had not been able to do during the preliminary hearing) that Tim Waters had been gay. But that would be a difficult position to maintain at trial, particularly without witnesses of Edwards's quality to offer substantiation.

One of the big unanswered questions was whether David would take the stand. Up to that point, Diamond had exerted a surprising amount of control over his client, successfully persuading him that it was in his best interest not to submit himself to a prosecutor's cross-examination. Whether he would be able to continue to do so if David thought his life hung in the balance was something else. Also, David's personal animosity toward Giss, spurred no doubt by Giss's comments about his parents, particularly his mother, might provoke David enough to *demand* that he be allowed to testify.

That, of course, would please Giss immensely. Deep in his heart, the prosecutor did not think Diamond would be able to stop his client from taking the stand. For one thing, Giss felt that David was too secure in his belief that he could talk his way out of any situation to agree to be muzzled yet again. In addition, there was the fact that David had a quick temper, and Giss was sure he had gotten to him with his remarks about Jerry and Laurieanne. David would come into the courtroom steaming and spoiling for a fight. At least Giss hoped that would be the case. If there was anything he wanted from the trial more than a conviction, it was the opportunity to go head to head with David.

But these scenarios, carefully worked out and refined by the opposing lawyers, would prove to be worthless.

Ken Englade

Virtually on the eve of trial a series of events occurred that sent Giss and De Noce reeling. Diamond, who had never quit even when it looked as though he were facing impossible odds, came up with a masterful piece of evidence that effectively demolished the prosecution's arguments. Ironically, it came from Giss's blindside, a direction from which he thought he was invulnerable: the scientific foundation for his entire case. On March 20, 1991—to the surprise of everyone who had been following the saga, even Giss himself—the prosecution's immediate plan to try David for murdering Tim totally collapsed.

The basis for the prosecutions' defeat and the defense's victory was a technical report written in scientific gobbledygook. Translated, what it said was that Tim almost certainly had *not* been poisoned with oleander, which is what Diamond had contended all along. But this time the contention had legs. Strong ones. Marathon-winning ones.

· 310 ·

33

A lot of people think the law is dull and predictable, that surprises in a courtroom occur only during episodes of Perry Mason. They are wrong. A criminal trial or a proceeding leading up to a trial is a touch-and-go process in which anything can, and frequently does, happen. David's case was a prime example.

Virtually until the day that jury selection was scheduled to begin, Giss was secure in the strength of the prosecution's case. He knew that Dan Galambos, Dave Edwards, George Bristol, and Jim Dame, among others, would deliver powerful testimony against the former crematorium operator, testimony that would be rounded out by equally damning words from people like Detective Diaz, Richard Gray, Steve Strunk, and John Pollerana.

The only area in which he had a growing reservation was in the solidity of his medical evidence. Although Dr. Frederic Rieders was a widely acknowledged expert in the field of toxicology, and an adept witness as well—that is, someone not likely to become rattled under cross-examination or fall into a defense trap—the prosecution team of Giss and De Noce had become worried. While Giss had even wrung a concession from the pathologist who performed the autopsy on Tim Waters—the man who had initially ruled the death a natural one—that poisoning likely was a contributing factor in the victim's demise, there was a cloud on the horizon.

One of the first things De Noce had done after being named to the case was to go over Rieders's report with a critical and scientifically knowledgeable eye. When he had been on the stand in October 1990 describing his findings, the toxicologist had been careful to say that his determination was based largely on the fact that he had not been able to discount oleander as the poison that possibly killed Tim. This was subtly different from saying that oleander had actually killed Tim. At the same time, Rieders's testing process divulged nothing else as a possible poison. Therefore, it had been Rieders's *opinion* that oleander in some form had been administered to Tim and that was what had caused his death.

Looking at the situation objectively, De Noce felt that was not quite good enough. As he shuffled through Rieders's report, which described in enigmatic scientific jargon the procedures he had followed and the results he had obtained, De Noce became worried that, despite the Pennsylvania scientist's expertise, his findings lacked "substance-specificity." That is, Rieders did not find with unwavering certainty—and with the data to back it up— that it was oleander that had killed Tim.

After Rieders's testimony, too, Giss found an obscure medical report that said persons with liver ailments for some as yet unknown reason also registered an unusually high reading for digoxin in their systems, a situation generally referred to as a "false positive." This was particularly troubling to the prosecution because the pathologist who had autopsied Tim had very specifically pointed out that Tim had a liver that was twice as large as that of the normal adult male. It was, in fact, in the pathologist's opinion, a major contributing cause in Tim's death.

De Noce felt that what the prosecution really needed

for an airtight case was testimony that said unequivocally that oleander had been the poison. If he and Giss did not have that, he feared the defense might come up with an expert at trial who would make mincemeat of Rieders's report.

Shortly before Christmas 1990, De Noce went to Giss and confessed his fears. If they went to trial with Rieders as the prosecution's only expert, he said, they might be asking for trouble. Rieders would be able to testify that his tests showed such-and-such, which *led him to believe* that oleander had been the source of the poison. But, and this was the crucial part, Rieders's methodology had not *proved* that it was oleander that had killed Tim Waters.

Rieders's testimony, De Noce pointed out, was subjective, based on his experience in another case in which oleander was the known agent. But what if the defense found another scientist who used a different method of testing which would be able to pinpoint with uncontestable accuracy that it was *not* oleander that killed Tim? As long as the defense was going to be running new tests, De Noce suggested, it might not be a bad idea if the prosecution did the same thing. What they should look for, he proposed, was a scientist who used a testing method different from the one employed by Rieders. If those tests were positive as well, they would confirm Rieders's findings, and the prosecution would have two experts in its camp. If the results were different, it was something the prosecution needed to know before the trial began.

Giss, whose confidence in Rieders's findings was waning as far as stand-alone testimony was concerned, recognized the practicality of De Noce's suggestion. "Find somebody," he told De Noce.

De Noce's search for an expert led him to a man named Dr. Jack Henion. Like Rieders, Henion was a Ph.D. rather than a medical doctor. But while Rieders was also a businessman who operated his own toxicological testing firm, Henion was an academic, an associate professor of toxicology at Cornell University in Ithaca, New York. However, what really interested the prosecutor was the fact that Henion also worked for the New York State Racing and Wagering Board and the Equine Drug Testing and Research Program. In that capacity, he examined specimens from race horses, testing to see if their performance had been affected by chemical substances.

Over the years, Henion had built a high-tech lab whose centerpiece was a machine that by itself had cost $2 million. Using that equipment, Henion had developed a method for testing for the presence of a foreign item in tissue or fluid that was extremely sophisticated. More important, it was substance specific. His tests could determine with near irrefutable accuracy if a specific substance was or was not present in a particular sample. While there was a world of difference between a long-dead cremation service operator in California and a live race horse in New York, the testing principle was the same.

At the same time that De Noce was looking for a new expert, Roger Diamond was talking to Dr. Bryan Finkle, who was with the Center for Human Toxicology at the University of Utah. Finkle had come to California at Diamond's request and had been on hand to take tissue samples when Tim's body was exhumed. But later, when it came time to do the analysis, Finkle suggested to Diamond that there was another toxicologist who could probably run a more definitive series of tests than he could. That man's name, Finkle said, was Dr. Jack Henion. It was one of those coincidences that people would look at later and exclaim, "What a small world," which in those circles, in fact, it is. Both De Noce and Diamond—operating from totally opposite directions—ended up in exactly the same place: with Henion.

De Noce was the first to discover the coincidence. As soon as he found out that the defense also planned to use

Henion as its expert, he telephoned Diamond to tell him about the prosecution's plans.

"You can't do that," Diamond had exploded in indignation. "You can't contact our expert."

Almost as soon as he said it, Diamond reconsidered. "On second thought," he said, thinking quickly, "that won't be any problem." What had made him rethink his original position was his rock-solid personal belief that Henion was not going to find oleander in Tim's tissue samples. If that were the case, if the prosecution were using Henion as well, Giss and De Noce would not be able to attack the Cornell toxicologist's findings, not if he was their expert as well.

As it turned out, Diamond's decision was amazingly accurate, and his decision to reverse himself and not contest the prosecution's choice proved to be the smartest move he would make in the case.

Even as Henion was bending over his test tubes, David was moving inexorably closer toward trial on the charge of murdering Tim. Only a few noncritical issues had to be settled before Judge Jones called the first panel of prospective jurors, thereby formally beginning the laborious *voir dire* process that Giss estimated might take as long as eight weeks.

When the court convened on March 19 after a one-day postponement, Diamond, as expected, submitted a flurry of last-minute paperwork. Among the documents was his copy of Henion's preliminary report.

It was five pages long and most of it dealt with details of the procedures Henion had followed in testing the samples removed from Tim's long-buried body, details so technical that they were all but unintelligible to a nonscientist.

Take a 50 ml. polypropylene centrifuge tube (Becton-Dickinson, Blue Max) on an electronic balance and using

*a clean scalpel remove and weigh out a 1-gram piece of
tissue . . .* the report began. And from there it got *really*
complicated. *These experiments all used the precursor ion
at m/z 577 for oleandrin plus m/z 517, 373, and 145 product ions at the heart-cut time window of 2.8 min.,* it continued. *The corresponding ions for oleandrigenin were
m/z 433 for the precursor ion with m/z 373, 355, and 377
as characteristic product ions from the heart-cut time
window at 2.7 min for oleandrigenin . . .*

Giss, who had received his own copy of the report only
shortly before, felt like punching the wall. As soon as he
had received Henion's document, he skimmed through it,
looking for something recognizable among the unfamiliar
scientific words. "Oleandrin" and "oleandrigenin" jumped
out at him, but not in the context that he had expected.
He had been hoping for confirmation of Rieders's findings. Instead he got refutation. The closer he read the
document, the tighter he clenched his jaws. He didn't
have to be a scientist to interpret Henion's one-paragraph
conclusion. He stared at the paper and gulped. Summing
up his findings, the toxicologist had written: *Neither oleandrin nor oleandrigenin were detected in any of the
heart, kidney, and liver tissues, or the fixing solution provided from Mr. T. Waters.*

In other words, according to the findings of this hand-
picked expert extraordinaire, Tim had *not* been killed
with an extract from the oleander plant.

The testing procedure that Henion had used, called
liquid chromatography/tandem mass spectrometry, or LC/
MS/MS, was so new that it probably had never been introduced in a courtroom. Still, that did not reflect unfa-
vorably upon its accuracy. The tests, in layman's terms
subsequently articulated by De Noce, were performed
like this:

First Henion bombarded a sample of known oleandrin
with electrons in order to split the oleandrin molecule.

Then he weighed the fragments in a magnetic field to determine oleandrin's molecular weight. Finally, he studied a tissue sample from Tim to see if he could find a molecule with a weight identical to that of the known oleandrin molecule. If there had been a positive match, that would have definitively shown the presence of oleandrin. But there was no match, and that just as definitively ruled out oleander as the source of a poison that may have killed Tim.

In a way that frightened as well as startled the prosecution, Henion's process was basically very simple. It also was entirely scientific, not a mixture of science and opinion, as Rieders's had been. Rather, the Pennsylvania toxicologist had based his report on his *interpretation* of the results of the tests he had used: radio immunoassay, thin-layer chromatography and fluorometry. But they could not compare for accuracy with the methodology used by Henion. Rieders had been required to interpret his results, but with Henion's method, there was very little to interpret. Either oleandrin or its derivatives were there or they were not. Henion's tests had shown they were not.

Henion's words had rippled through the prosecutor like an electric shock. The Cornell University toxicologist, for all practical purposes, had wrecked the prosecution's case. The argument that Giss had planned to use at trial was a carefully constructed vehicle that led progressively from one segment to another. The prosecutor wanted to demonstrate to a jury, in essence, that David had both the motive and the means to murder Tim Waters; that David was well-aware of the properties of poisons, especially oleander, and that he had, in fact, used an extract from the common garden plant to kill the Burbank businessman. But the whole thing hinged on two facts: (1) Tim had been murdered, and (2) he had been killed with oleander. Henion's test results had destroyed fact number two, and

Ken Englade

without that it would be extremely difficult to prove fact number one. To get a murder conviction against David, Giss first had to prove that Tim was murdered. Henion's test results would make that extremely difficult if not impossible.

Diamond, on the other hand, felt like cheering. His major claim, at trial, would be that there was no murder and no oleander. Henion had confirmed the latter and, by implication, the former, which obviated Diamond's need to fall back on alternative theories for Tim's demise—namely, that someone other than David had murdered him; that he committed suicide, or that he had died as a result of medication he was taking that produced readings indicating the presence of oleander. It was the best possible position for Diamond to be in. And the worst for Giss and De Noce.

Because of Henion's report, Giss knew that if he went into court and tried to pit Rieders against Henion or, more accurately, Rieders's testing procedure against Henion's, Rieders's methodology would come out on the short end. Besides, Henion was the prosecution's expert as well as the defense's. Giss and De Noce had sought him out just as eagerly as had Diamond. The prosecution had, in fact, paid half of the $38,000 it had cost to run the tests—normally they cost $20,000, but the request to expedite the results fairly doubled the cost. Just because Henion's findings did not fit into the prosecution's trial plan, Giss could hardly go into court and attack the findings of his own expert. Not if he expected to win.

Jumping on the only ray of sunlight he could find in the report, Giss focused on the fact that Henion had *not* said that Tim had not been murdered, only that he had not been murdered with oleander. Henion's findings had done nothing to make Giss change his mind about David. The prosecutor was as convinced as he had ever been that David had poisoned Tim Waters. He just did not know with what. Before the Cornell scientist submitted his report, Giss felt sure that David had used oleander. But after reading the report, Giss had to admit to himself, however reluctantly, that oleander had not been the weapon. The only way he could recoup, he felt, was to order up another series of tests to try to find out what the poison actually was.

But this brought up another problem. Henion's report had arrived literally on the eve of the beginning of jury selection. There was no time for Giss to order up new tests unless Judge Jones agreed to give the prosecution a postponement.

Giss felt sick. For more than a year he had been working on David's case exclusively. He knew the details inside and out, backward and forward. He had fought off Diamond's successive and well-thought-out attempts to block a trial. He had mapped out his trial strategy, and he had his courtroom offensive planned in detail. But Henion's report was devastating.

Giss had been ready and eager to go to trial, to take the offensive against David, a person whom Giss found personally repugnant. But there was one thing the prosecutor had learned in his experience, and that was when to retreat. Giss had not been chosen the top prosecutor in the state by exhibiting tendencies to commit courtroom suicide or by demonstrating certifiable stupidity. He *knew* when he had a case and he *knew* when he did not. As things stood in the light of Henion's report, he did not need anyone to tell him that overnight his plans had self-destructed, that his case had dissolved before his eyes. Even his earlier contention that he could always claim degeneration of Tim's tissue would lead to inconclusive results, fell apart in the wake of the New York scientist's indisputable methodology.

In a vain attempt to postpone the inevitable, Giss asked Jones for a delay, hoping he might get lucky and win some

extra time, which he could use to have more tests performed and perhaps determine what the poison had been.

Diamond grinned to himself. He had been involved in
David's case in one way or another much longer than
Giss. He had first come in as a retained attorney by David
in 1986, even before DDA Walt Lewis had charged David
with paying for the assaults on Hast, Nimz, and Tim. He
slipped out of the case after the preliminary hearing in
Judge Person's court because he was not reappointed in
superior court, but he had reappeared as David's attorney
when the murder charge was filed in Ventura County.

He had even more time and effort invested in the case
than Giss, and he could not have been happier to see the
balance of power abruptly shift. Suddenly the defense was
on the offense; it was Diamond who had moved into position to call the shots. He knew that if he agreed to a delay,
it could only hurt his client. But if the trial were to begin
on schedule, before the prosecution could get another
opinion or order up more tests, he was all but positive he
could get David acquitted despite the testimony of Giss's
witnesses. Henion's report, Diamond knew, would out-
weigh any medical evidence the prosecution could present. With inward glee the defense attorney voiced
strenuous opposition to Giss's request for a five-week
postponement. Judge Jones held the key.

Jones agreed to a temporary delay to give himself time
to ponder the possibilities. Although the new information
had come at the last minute, and the prosecution had not
had time to formulate a response, the prosecution had
agreed beforehand to have Henion perform the tests. If
they were harmful to the prosecution's case, that was a
risk Giss and De Noce had been willing to take. They had
gambled and they had lost. Jones was disinclined to order
a lengthy postponement in a trial that already was long
overdue. Instead, he announced that he agreed with Diamond; the case would have to go to trial forthwith.

* * *

The judge's decision prompted a hurried meeting among members of the prosecution team. But in the end they knew they had no option. As distasteful as the action appeared to the prosecutors, the murder charge would have to be dismissed. There would be no trial. At least not immediately.

From a practical point of view, the decision to dismiss the charge made sense. Giss and De Noce figured that if they took the case to trial and David was acquitted, which would likely happen, he could never again be tried for murdering Tim Waters. To even attempt to do so would violate his rights against double jeopardy. But if they dismissed the charge, and evidence later surfaced to bolster their case, David could always be recharged. There is no statute of limitations on murder.

On April 4, just four days shy of the fifth anniversary of Tim's death, the district attorney's office told Judge Jones that it was abandoning the charge that David murdered Tim Waters. Separate documents affirming this position were filed by Ventura County District Attorney Michael Bradbury, Giss, and De Noce.

"The circumstantial evidence was and continues to be compelling in the sense that it implicates the defendant in the death of Timothy Waters," Bradbury noted in his formal notice of motion for dismissal.

"Certain facts remain indisputable despite the recent scientific findings," he added, citing statements from Galambos and Edwards, virtual concessions from David that he had a motive in wanting to retaliate against Tim [meaning that he paid to have him beaten up], and the unusual circumstances of Tim's death. But, he admitted, Henion's findings had dealt the prosecution a fatal blow. "Based on these results, I believe that there is a reasonable doubt as to whether the defendant poisoned Timothy

Waters by way of oleander, and therefore move that this case be dismissed."

But he appended a caveat, a warning, really, to David. "It should be noted," Bradbury said, "that Dr. Henion has not excluded the presence of all possible poisons, and thus this case will remain in an investigatory status until the prosecution's beliefs are confirmed or dispelled." In essence he was telling David he could be released but he had better check his closet and look under his bed every night.

However much it hurt them to do so, Giss and De Noce also filed statements supporting Bradbury's motion. The prosecution was in a very delicate position, Giss asserted. If he and De Noce were to proceed to trial, it would have to be based on the theory that the oleandrin that Rieders had determined was in Tim's system broke down to undetectable levels between August 1988, when the Pennsylvania toxicologist performed his tests, and March 1991, when Henion performed his. However, to try to argue that before a jury, Giss loathingly admitted, would be futile. "I do not think that the evidence is sufficient to prove this theory beyond a reasonable doubt," he concluded. The defense, on the other hand, also could have claimed that what Rieders had taken to be oleandrin was some other substance formed when the samples taken from Tim during the autopsy were fixed with preservative.

To Giss it was a no-win situation, although he meticulously listed eight reasons he had for believing that David had murdered Tim, ranging from David's boasts to Galambos and Edwards, to David's admission of having Tim beaten up. "Nevertheless," Giss said, "the confessions referred to are not admissible evidence without the ability to establish that the victim died by criminal means. Further, absent the ability to establish that the victim was poisoned, the original ascribed cause of death [metamorphosis of the liver] cannot be ignored and will prevail as the cause of death." He could not try David for Tim's murder if he could not prove that Tim had indeed been murdered.

At this point, with victory in his grasp, Diamond made a possible mistake. Holding his breath, Giss hoped that Diamond would not oppose the motion to dismiss, although it was entirely within the defense attorney's purview to do so. When Diamond let the moment pass, Giss sighed in relief. If the defense attorney had protested and Judge Jones had gone along, David could have been ordered to stand trial despite the prosecution's wish that it not happen. And that could have given the prosecution all kinds of problems.

The prosecution's main concern, the one that led to the decision to dismiss the charge, was that David would be acquitted at a trial. If that happened, he could never again be charged with Tim's murder, no matter what new evidence developed, because the law prevented him from being placed twice in jeopardy for the same crime. But if Diamond had opposed the dismissal motion and Jones had upheld the defense attorney, jury selection would have begun. And once a jury is picked and sworn in, jeopardy attaches. That is, from the point jurors take their oath, there is no turning back; the trial proceeds, almost always to be resolved by a verdict. However, the judge has the option, after listening to the prosecution's case, to dismiss the charge if he feels the district attorney has not made a strong enough case to warrant conviction. If David's trial had gone on and Jones dismissed the charge at the end of the prosecution's presentation, it would have been the same, legally speaking, as an acquittal: David could never be charged again with Tim's murder. Giss's nightmare was that Jones would listen to the prosecution's case and then decide that Rieders's testimony was not strong enough to refute Henion's and that the prosecution had failed to prove that Tim had been murdered, therefore a dismissal was mandatory.

But in the absence of opposition from Diamond, Jones approved the prosecution's request to dismiss the charge *before* jury selection began, thus leaving the way open for the district attorney's office to refile the murder charge at some future date.

Asked later why he did not oppose the motion to dismiss, Diamond said his main concern had been to get David released from jail. He had, after all, been behind bars since June 8, 1987—some forty-six months. If he had protested, Diamond reasoned, David would just have had to remain incarcerated for another indefinite period of time while the jury was selected and the prosecution built its case. Plus, going to trial, even with Henion's report in his pocket, still would have been a gamble for Diamond. Giss and De Noce may have been able to put on such a convincing case that a jury, always an unpredictable group, may have decided that David was guilty anyway. The risk, in Diamond's view, was not worth it. In any case, Diamond viewed the possibility of a murder charge being refiled as extremely slim.

PART SIX

Full Circle

34

In actuality, the dismissal of the murder charge against David was not the end of the Sconce saga at all; it simply represented a lull, a truce in the war, as it were. The murder charge had been only the most prominent boulder on the hillside.

That was the good news. The bad news was that what was left after the murder charge was dismissed was an unbelievably complicated legal mishmash, the likes of which few lawyers and judges, much less spectators, ever see.

To begin to understand the status of the case still pending against the Sconces in the summer of 1991, one had to go back to what had transpired in Judge Terry Smerling's court in Pasadena in the summer of 1989. Smerling, the former ACLU lawyer originally appointed to the bench by Governor Edmund "Jerry" Brown, had waded through the stack of sixty-eight charges that were then current against the Sconces, and decided they were excessive or irrelevant or both. So he started clearing the decks.

On June 30 he announced his decision to dismiss ten of the more serious charges against the Sconces, using a variety of excuses. In tossing out many of the counts of stealing body parts against David and his father, for example,

Smerling gave as his reason the fact that the words "to remove tissue," which were printed on the cremation consent forms used by the Sconces, provided justification in allowing them to remove and sell hearts, brains, lungs, and eyes. While admitting that he found the practice "despicable," Smerling said the form was in essence a contract, and it had been the responsibility of those who had signed it to challenge its validity.

Another of the charges Smerling dismissed was one accusing David of conspiring to murder Elie Estephan. As outlined during a separate preliminary hearing before Judge Judson Morris Jr. in January 1989, six months before Smerling began trimming the charges, David had hatched a very complicated plan to take over the business *and* help his brother-in-law, Brad Sallard. Once Estephan was murdered, David would get the business and Sallard would share in a $250,000 life insurance policy then held by Estephan's estranged wife, who at the time was living with Sallard.

According to preliminary hearing testimony, David committed at least six separate overt acts in helping to plan Estephan's death, including sitting in a restaurant with one of the hired hit men, Bob Garcia, and spying on Estephan through a pair of binoculars. Despite the powerful evidence pointing toward David's participation in the murder plot, Smerling dismissed the charge because testimony also showed that David had told Garcia to "forget about" the plan before it could be consummated. The judge reasoned that since the plan was never carried to fruition, the charge of conspiracy was not valid.

Outraged, the district attorney's office filed an immediate appeal, claiming Smerling had overstepped his authority, and the decision to dismiss the Estephan charge was illegal.

Less than a week later, on July 6, ignoring the prosecution's complaints about his handling of the cases,

Smerling dismissed twenty more charges against the Sconces, citing lack of evidence supporting the accusations. The records, he said, were too skimpy to justify bringing them to trial. Among the accusations dismissed in the second round of charge-trimming were additional counts of stealing and selling body parts, committing multiple cremations, forging organ-donor consent forms, embezzlement, and falsifying death certificates. By the end of that round, Smerling had reduced the number of charges against the Sconces by almost half. However, what was left was still an impressive list of accusations.

Still pending against David were some two dozen charges, excluding the murder of Tim Waters, which ranged from solicitation of the murders of three people—DDA Walt Lewis, and David's grandparents, Lawrence and Lucille Lamb—to three counts of assault with great bodily injury. Pending against Laurieanne were eighteen charges ranging from five counts of illegally removing body parts to three counts of forgery, while Jerry still faced eight charges ranging from two counts of performing multiple cremations to misappropriation of income from preneed trust accounts.

Smerling examined this list and decided it was still too cumbersome an agenda to bring to trial. Although he had earlier announced his decision to hold two separate trials, one on the cases involving violence and another on the no-violent accusations—essentially one for Jerry and Laurieanne and another for David—he figured that unless he took further action, he would be tied up in court for the better part of a year just hearing charges against the Sconces. In negotiations with David's attorney—talks from which Prosecutor Jim Rogan was for all practical purposes excluded ("I had to be physically present under the law," Rogan said, "but they treated me like a piece of the furniture")—Smerling devised an elaborate plea-bargain offer for David. If David would plead guilty to the charges still pending against him, the judge would guarantee him that he would serve minimal prison time.

Specifically, in return for pleading guilty, Smerling sentenced David to five years in prison, complete with credit for time served. In addition, the judge said, if David would plead guilty to the remainder of the charges, he would not levy any additional prison time. *Plus,* if his decision to dismiss the Estephan conspiracy charge was overturned by the appeals court and the case came back to him, he would promise not to levy any prison time on that charge either, simply giving David probation.

As if that were not enough, there was still one other carrot. David, Smerling said, did not have to give an immediate answer on the offer. He could go ahead and serve the five-year sentence—which would automatically be cut three years and four months when credit for good behavior was figured in—and he could respond to the remaining part of the offer at any time up until it looked as though he might actually have to be brought to trial.

At the end of the summer of 1989, the Sconce situation stood like this:

• David, who had been sentenced to five years after pleading guilty to twenty charges, still faced eight more felony charges ranging from accusations of soliciting three murders—including that of the deputy district attorney who was then prosecuting him —to two counts of bribery, all of which would result in a sentence of probation if David would only formally admit that he committed the crimes. (The charge against David of murdering Tim had not even been filed at that time, so it did not figure into the equation.)

• Laurieanne still faced eighteen charges.

• Jerry still faced eight charges.

After the murder charge against David was dismissed, the focus of attention on his case switched back to Pasadena since the charges David had not yet pleaded to were still active in Smerling's court. Theoretically, to clear the record, David would either have to plead guilty to the charges and accept the offer of probation offered by Smerling, or plead not guilty and go to trial. However, in the meantime, one other major development had occurred that muddied the water.

At roughly the same time the murder-charge prosecutors agreed to dismiss the accusation that David had killed Tim, the California Court of Appeal ruled on the district attorney's request to overturn Smerling's dismissal of the Estephan charge. By unanimous vote, the three-judge panel voted against Smerling, agreeing with the D.A. that the judge had erred. In an opinion written by Presiding Judge Joan Dempsey Klein, the appeals court found that "regardless of Sconce's motivation for withdrawing [from the conspiracy], it cannot insulate him from liability" because conspiracy "is complete upon the commission of an overt act." In other words, when David announced that he did not want to participate further in the murder plot, that did not remove his responsibility for having initiated the plot to begin with. And there seemed to be little question that he *had* participated. Even Smerling, the court pointed out, had conceded the existence of an intrigue when he commented: "No doubt about it, until the time of withdrawal . . . there was a conspiracy."

In the light of these facts, the appeals court concluded, "withdrawal from a conspiracy is not a valid defense to the completed crime of conspiracy itself." Translation: In the court's opinion, David should be called to account on the conspiracy charge, conviction of which carried a sentence of twenty-five-years-to-life.

Several weeks later the state supreme court effectively upheld the appeal court's opinion by refusing to review the case.

That, nevertheless, did little to clarify the situation still existing in Los Angeles County, that is, what to do about the charges still pending against all three Sconces.

Even though more than four years had passed since the charges were filed against Jerry and Laurieanne, Judge Smerling had never ordered them to stand trial. As best as could be determined from a very complicated record, their trial had been postponed twenty-six times for various reasons. In the meantime, they remained free.

Exactly why so much time had been allowed to elapse without a trial was puzzling. Their cases were not overly complicated. They faced a number of charges for which they presumably, eventually, would be called to answer. If that day ever occurred, they could either plead guilty and throw themselves upon the considerable mercy of Judge Smerling, or they could plead not guilty and go before a jury. When this book was written, reports were circulating in the courthouse that Smerling was considering another plea bargain under which Jerry and Laurieanne would plead guilty in return for little or no jail time despite the severity and the copiousness of the charges against them. He had already offered them a sentence of no more than one year in the county jail, but they were holding out for a better deal.

While the situation involving the charges against Jerry and Laurieanne was not unduly complex, the same could not be said for David's.

On the surface it seemed fairly clear-cut: He could either plead guilty to the charges still pending against him and accept Smerling's two-year-old offer of no prison time, or he could plead not guilty and face trial. If he pleaded not guilty and he were subsequently convicted, he could end up back in prison for a considerable period. That much was fairly explicit. But what *really* threw the situation into confusion was the reinstatement of the Estephan charge.

The district attorney's office was extremely, and understandably, reluctant to let David escape without being called accountable for the alleged crime. Still smarting from the defeat in Ventura County, and still convinced that David was a dangerous criminal—immediately after dismissing the murder charge, Bradbury told reporters that in his view David was "a cold-blooded murderer"—the prosecutors would have liked to see David back in prison. A conviction on conspiracy to murder and the resulting sentence of at least twenty-five years, while perhaps not as satisfying for the prosecutors as one for capital murder, would do nicely. If nothing else, David would be off the street and investigators would have as much time as they needed to try to redevelop the charge that he murdered Tim Waters. But getting him to trial on the conspiracy charge was no easy matter. In fact, it looked as though it might ultimately prove impossible.

Although the appeals court had overturned Smerling's decision to dismiss the charge, the case still went back to the Pasadena judge. The appeals court could rule that he had erred, but it could not order him to take any specific action. If Smerling wanted—indeed as he had *promised* David in the summer of 1989—he could simply sentence him to probation on the charge, thus avoiding ordering him to prison. However, probation was contingent upon David pleading guilty.

The district attorney's office definitely did not want that to happen, but they were limited in what action they might take to prevent it. On July 19, 1991, Prosecutor Harvey Giss filed a motion with Smerling demanding that the judge disqualify himself from the case, citing the judge's asserted unwillingness to apply the statutory prison term for the conspiracy charge, and questioning the legality of his decision regarding the conspiracy charge.

According to Giss, Smerling should not have promised David probation on the conspiracy charge because by the time he made that promise, the case had already been removed from his jurisdiction. When Smerling dismissed the charge and the district attorney's office immediately appealed, Giss contended, that automatically transferred the case from Smerling's court to the court of appeal. Furthermore, even if the case *had* been within Smerling's jurisdiction, he could not have promised probation on the charge because his offer was expressly prohibited by state law.

EPILOGUE

Early in June 1991, almost four years to the day from the time he surrendered to authorities in Pasadena, and some two months after the murder charge was dismissed, *David Sconce* filed a $1.25 million damage claim against Ventura County alleging that he suffered "extreme mental anguish, pain and suffering, anxiety and fear at being held in jail on a nonmeritorious death-penalty murder charge." In the one-page document, David said the invalid charge kept him behind bars 178 days longer than he should have been under the sentence handed down by Judge Smerling, and that he was entitled to $500 in damages for each of those days, plus additional damages totaling $1,161,000. Not surprisingly, the county board of supervisors rejected the claim, clearing the way for David to file suit against the county.

At the July 19, 1991, session, the one at which Harvey Giss filed his motion to have Judge Terry Smerling disqualified from hearing the most serious charge still pending against David, Smerling, as he had done so many times before, postponed setting a trial date for *Jerry* and *Laurieanne Sconce* on the charges still pending against them. A trial had been anticipated for more than four years, but every time it appeared imminent, Smerling delayed it, frequently because the two lawyers involved—three, if David's is figured in—had not been able to coordinate their schedules. It is an unfortunate fact of life in Los Angeles that the demand for top-notch criminal lawyers exceeds the supply. As a result, the high-profile attorneys have more work than they can handle and it is extremely difficult for a judge to find a time when two or more defense attorneys can set aside a large block of time for trial. In the meantime, David's parents remained free.

Further complicating the situation was the fact that the Los Angeles County District Attorney's Office appealed Smerling's decision to dismiss numerous charges against the Sconces. One result of this appeal was an additional entanglement of the case involving Jerry and Laurieanne. Apparently before they could be tried on the charges that were *not* dismissed by Smerling, the court of appeal, and presumably the supreme court, would have to decide if the dismissals were proper. If the appeals courts were to rule that Smerling acted inappropriately and reinstituted the charges, the two then could be tried on a considerably expanded list of accusations. Again, as it has been repeatedly throughout this saga, no speedy or simple resolution seemed forthcoming.

Although he also was free, David was prohibited by conditions of his three-year parole from leaving California, except with special permission. That meant that visits to the family at their home in Bullhead City, Arizona, could be made only with authorization.

Not surprisingly, *Judge Smerling* proved unwilling to admit to judicial misconduct in the David Sconce/Elie Estephan matter. Soon after Giss presented his motion to have him disqualified, the judge filed papers opposing the request with Superior Court Judge Robert T. Altman of Santa Monica, who had been chosen to hear the dispute by an agreement between Giss and Diamond, who had reemerged as David's attorney. Although his official connection with David ended when the murder charge was dropped in Ventura County, Diamond prevailed upon Smerling to appoint him to the Pasadena case. Smerling obligingly complied when he saw that David's court-appointed attorney, Guy O'Brien, had no objection. Diamond had been involved in the case from the very beginning, first as a retained attorney and then as an appointed one, and he welcomed the chance to jump back into the fray.

After reading Smerling's explanation of his actions as well as prosecution and defense briefs, Judge Altman surprised just about everyone who had been following the case by ruling in favor of the prosecution, agreeing that Smerling had displayed prejudice against the state to such a degree that he was incapable of being unbiased. It was believed to be the first time any California judge had found a brother judge biased since the law covering such situations was revised in 1984.

"The court finds," Altman wrote in his August 8 decision, "that . . . Judge Smerling, operating on the assumption that Mr. Sconce would be tried on a death penalty case in Ventura County, clearly acted in good faith in trying to save [Los Angeles] County the costs of protracted trials in both this case and [the other charges]." But, despite Smerling's "good faith," Altman continued, quoting from the prosecution's request, " 'a person aware of the facts might reasonably entertain a doubt that the judge would be able to be impartial' in this case."

As expected, Diamond appealed. However, both the court of appeal and the state supreme court rejected the defense requests, presumably setting the stage for David's trial on the conspiracy to murder charge before Superior Court Judge Paul Boland, who took Smerling's place as trial judge after Smerling was disqualified. There also was a possibility that the charges still outstanding against David (solicitation of the murders of his grandparents and Prosecutor Walt Lewis, as well as four counts dealing with alleged bribery of a witness) would be heard before Boland at the same time as the conspiracy to murder charge. A decision in that regard was expected late in 1991 or early in 1992.

These developments buoyed the prosecution, and for the first time in many months raised hopes that David might finally be brought to trial on at least one of the charges still pending against him. But there was still a wild card. No one seemed to know what would happen if David, before he could be tried, demanded that he be allowed to plead guilty to the outstanding charges, as he had been promised he could do by Smerling. Even with Smerling removed, the fact that he had given his word to David and David had accepted it in good faith (in fact, he had already served his sentence) could complicate the issue tremendously.

As they have virtually since the news of the situation broke, *Lawrence* and *Lucille Lamb* remained in seclusion but maintained ties with, and apparently continued to support, their grandson David and their daughter Laurieanne. On the afternoon after the last court hearing, a family reunion—the first since David was released—was held at Lawrence's and Lucille's home on Orange Grove Boulevard opposite the starting point for the annual Rose Bowl parade. Although Lawrence was confined to his bed, reportedly with a terminal illness, the gathering proceeded with Lucille, Jerry and Laurieanne, David and Barbara, and their two children all in attendance.

Conspicuous by their absence were Laurieanne's two brothers, Kirk and Bruce Lamb, who had long before agreed to repay the $100,000 that had been diverted from the mortuary's preneed accounts. At the same time, they took over the business and renamed it the Pasadena Funeral Home. While meeting what they considered to be their familial obligations, they apparently harbored a resentment for their sister and her husband for putting them in such a position. Although the brothers have not publicly commented on the case in recent months, it was clear from statements made earlier to reporters that both Kirk and Bruce were unhappy with what had happened. From all indications, the Sconces and the Lamb brothers remained estranged.

In December 1990, *Daniel Galambos* was sentenced to four years in prison after pleading guilty to a charge of possession of cocaine. However, only ninety days of the sentence required incarceration, and that was only part-time. Under the terms of the sentence, he spent ninety days as a sleep-over resident in a drug rehabilitation center, which meant that he was allowed to leave the facility during the day to work, but was required to report back every evening. During the period, he received daily drug tests to make sure he was clean. The remainder of the sentence was probated. Galambos had been arrested on the drug charge two years previously, not long after he had pleaded guilty to assaulting Hast, Nimz, and Waters. He had been given five years probation on those charges.

Not long after David pleaded guilty to the initial series of charges in Judge Smerling's court in August 1989, *David Edwards* pleaded guilty to charges of assaulting Hast and Nimz and was given a five-year probated sentence.

About the same time, *Andre Augustine* pleaded no contest to a misdemeanor charge of assault by means of force likely to produce great bodily injury and was sentenced to one year on probation.

o o o

John Pollerana, who worked for David from December 1982 until January 1987 and was charged along with David with offenses in San Bernardino County in connection with the operation of the illegal crematorium at Oscar's Ceramics, eventually pleaded guilty to a misdemeanor charge of performing cremations without a license and was sentenced to one year on probation. All San Bernardino charges against David, including the felony charge for discharging hazardous wastes, were dropped, a fact that did not sit very easy with Pollerana, who contended he was only doing what David had ordered him to do.

Ron Jordan's death in August 1985 remains classified as a suicide. His body was buried soon after his death, without toxicological tests being performed. Although specimens from his body were kept for a while, they had been routinely destroyed by the time prosecutors had charged David with Tim's murder and began wondering about Jordan's death as well. Giss said in the summer of 1991 that the prosecution was considering whether to ask for an exhumation order to take new samples from Jordan's body, but the problems there would be the same as in Tim's case: tests for possible poisons are time-consuming and exceedingly expensive.

As of the summer of 1991, *Mike Engwald* had yet to have his probable cause hearing on charges of receiving stolen property—that is, the gold taken from cadavers at Coastal Cremation, Pasadena Crematorium, and Lamb Funeral Home. He was reputed to be suffering from a terminal illness and it was unlikely that he would ever be tried. *Brad Sallard*, David's brother-in-law, was also awaiting a preliminary hearing on felony charges of trying to bribe a witness. It was uncertain as well if he would ever be brought to trial.

Tim's mother, *Mary Lou Waters,* died of cancer in the spring of 1991, not long after the dismissal of the charge that David had murdered her son.

Walt Lewis continued as a prosecutor in Pasadena, but David's threats continued to haunt him. He was so worried by the potential for retaliation against himself or his family that he encouraged his adult children to move to other states.

Not long after the incidents at Lamb Funeral Home/Pasadena Crematorium were made public, Walt Lewis received a telephone call from a state legislative leader. A relative of one of the legislator's staffers had been cremated by David, and his ashes were believed to have been among those that were mixed. The legislator asked Lewis if he could make some suggestions for keeping such incidents from occurring in the future. Lewis replied with several recommendations, some of which subsequently were submitted as proposed legislation, were approved, and eventually signed into law.

Beginning on January 1, 1989, Cemetery Board agents were allowed to inspect, upon demand and without prior notification, a crematorium's books or premises, including its retorts and cold room. Failure to submit to an inspection request could lead to suspension or revocation of the organization's license. If this or a similar law had been in effect in 1986, the Sconces' activity might have been discovered months earlier.

As of the same date it also became a felony in California to remove tissue or organs from a cadaver awaiting cremation or burial without specific written permission, and/or to remove or possess dental gold or silver that came from a cadaver.

A lingering mystery has been what happened to all of David's money. By conservative reckoning, at the time of the search of Oscar's Ceramics, David was bringing in at least $500,000 a year from cremations alone. Since his overhead was low and his lifestyle was not extravagant, it is uncertain what happened to those funds. His legal representation almost exclusively has been at state expense, and he has claimed that his family is living in virtual poverty. So where is the money? It could be squirreled away someplace. He could have spent it, since he was, in essence, supporting two families—his own and the Sallards. Or he could have given it away. But unless some powerful agency with the interest and the ability to conduct an extensive investigation, such as the Internal Revenue Service, gets involved, it is likely that the puzzle will remain unsolved.

If the situation involving the criminal charges against the Sconces seemed puzzling, it was a model of clarity compared to the hodgepodge that existed in the civil courts as a result of the incidents at the funeral home/crematorium. Four and a half years after Melvin Belli's San Francisco firm initiated litigation as a result of the Sconces' operation, the situation was even further from a resolution than was the criminal case. In fact, in the summer of 1991, California courts were still trying to determine who would be allowed to participate in the class-action claim, an issue that could easily take years longer to determine. And that would be only the beginning.

Looking at the situation realistically, there seems little chance that David will be back behind bars anytime soon, if ever.

It is true that there is no statute of limitations on murder. David could be recharged with Tim Waters's death next week, next month, or thirty years from now. Indeed, there was a case in California not long ago in which a man was tried and convicted of murdering a young girl twenty years previously. He was only brought to trial after his daughter came forward and said she had, as a child, witnessed the killing. She had not mentioned it before because the facts were brought out only after she began receiving psychiatric treatment for some unrecognizable event that had been haunting her dreams; she did not know what that something was until she began receiving professional help. Someone *could* come forward and say they saw David and Tim together that Good Friday evening in 1985 and that they saw David slip something into Tim's food or drink. That *might* happen, but it is not very likely. A more probable scenario would involve development of new evidence along scientific lines. If there is proof to be found that David dispatched Tim, or even that Tim actually was murdered, it probably will be uncovered in a laboratory rather than on a psychiatrist's couch. But how much time and money will prosecutors in Ventura and Los Angeles counties be willing to spend on toxicological tests? I doubt if David is staying awake nights worrying about it.

Still, the ramifications of the Sconce case—and I'm speaking of the Sconces plural, parents and son—have already proved to be extremely far-reaching:

• If it had not been for the Sconces, new and more efficient laws governing crematoriums in the state might never have been written.

• Testimony at the Pasadena preliminary hearing helped lead to an in-depth examination of jailhouse informant practices and attendant reforms.

• Precedent was set when Diamond won his fight to represent David against the murder charge in Ventura.

• The civil cases resulting from the revelations of what was occurring at Lamb Funeral Home/crematorium promise to lead to new guidelines regarding who can be considered an injured party in cases involving burial and cremation.

• And then there is Judge Robert Altman's ruling against Smerling. If nothing else, it may make judges more careful about letting their *personal* opinions influence their *professional* opinions. Considering that he was speaking about a brother judge and that his opinion was couched in legalese, Altman pulled few punches. Smerling had no authority to promise David probation on the conspiracy charge, Altman said, because the case was not even before him at the time he made the promise. By doing that—in essence grouping the conspiracy charge in with the other charges on which he was making a plea bargain offer—Smerling denied the state any opportunity to argue against the appropriateness of the sentence. Furthermore, Altman added, Smerling exhibited his bias when he said on the record that he did not agree with the law governing such situations. As Altman put it: "While it is appropriate to consider the seriousness of a crime in determining the appropriateness of probation . . . Judge Smerling's indicated sentence appears to be based on his personal disagreement (whether correct or not) with the severity of the penalty fixed by the legislature . . . and again gives the appearance that the People could not hope to convince him of the inappropriateness of probation." Translation: Smerling seemed to have his mind made up and refused to listen to any argument, no matter how valid.

When he was preparing his motion to disqualify Smerling, Giss spent an entire week trying to find an example of how another judge may have handled such a situation in the past. He was unable to find one. Not one.

Why do you think that was? I asked.

Giss, always ready with a quip, replied: "Because no judge has ever been stupid enough to do something like that before."

While Giss was trying to be funny, his remark apparently hit very close to home, as evidenced by the Altman ruling. The troubling questions are: Was Smerling's decision the result of stupidity? Was it failure of logic? Was it a lack of legal knowledge? Was Smerling testing the system and his authority? Or was he simply extremely sympathetic to a young defendant who he did not want to send to prison for any additional time? Altman seems to think it was the latter.

Regrettably, one thing the world may never know in this case is if Tim Waters was poisoned. Barring the discovery of new scientific evidence, there is only one real hope, and it is a slim one. The only probable thing other than new tests which could resurrect the prosecution's case would be for David to volunteer to tell what he knows, if anything.

In the July 15, 1987, interview with Detective Dennis Diaz, long before he was charged with murdering Tim, David tried to make a deal: his freedom for fingering Tim's murderer. Earlier in the interview David had hinted that Dan Galambos was involved.

"Basically," Diaz said, "I guess maybe the bottom line would be to say that if we would get you out, then obviously you would give up whoever the person is that actually hired Danny and them to kill Waters."

"Yeah," replied David. "And I'll prove it. And I'll give you two witnesses besides that heard him arrange it on the telephone. And then I'll sit there and I'll cooperate with you."

A few minutes later, when Diaz did not respond enthusiastically to his suggestion, David added: "Okay, here's what we could do. Just lower my bail to a hundred thousand dollars or something so that I can bail myself out, and then immediately upon bailing out I'll go with you and give you a deposition . . . And then I'll tell you about Waters."

Almost a year later, in an interview with Detective Robert Hopkins, also before he had been charged with Tim's murder, David claimed several times that Tim had died a natural death, that he had not been poisoned. But the persistent Hopkins kept coming back to the subject.

"Would you be willing to cooperate with us and give us information regarding that person [who knew about Waters's death]?" Hopkins asked.

"I could give you everything you want on Tim Waters," David replied, "and why this guy wanted to kill him, and why he talked about killing him, and how he talked about killing him."

Hopkins asked David why he would not divulge that information.

"Because then it will get right back to the cops," David responded. "This is very relevant to my defense. It's very important, and if I knew for a fact that you guys were not going to talk to the Pasadena police, I would tell you this right now. I'll give you the person who had the motive, why he had the motive, what he talked about, and four other people [the number had doubled since his interview with Diaz] who heard him talking about why he wanted to have Tim Waters whacked."

A few minutes later David again promised to reveal what he knew.

"I'll help you guys and you can pound the guy who had this done because I even went with this guy to the Holiday Inn to talk to Tim Waters but he wasn't there."

The more Hopkins pressed, the more David kept promising crucial revelations.

"You get me a workable bail, I'll give you the guy and the motive, and four other people who heard him talking about it with Tim Waters, and it ties Galambos into it too . . . I'll give you the guy. I'll even testify for you as to what the guy told me. I'll testify for you and put this guy away so fucking deep—and I want to put this guy away because this guy lied to me . . . I could have done this a long time ago, but I'll tell you this: he's my source of information on everything to do with Tim Waters."

Maybe David was playing a game with the investigators

in an attempt to get bail. Maybe he was serious. No one knows but David.

After the murder charge was dismissed, I asked Roger Diamond about David's statements. What did David know about Tim's death? Was Tim murdered? Would David go to investigators and disclose what he had promised to reveal years before?

Diamond did not answer the questions directly. "Our contention," he said, "is that Tim was not murdered." Presumably, that is David's position as well. If that is true, David was either lying then or he is lying now. Or maybe he was lying both times. With David there is no way of telling.

In the end, it seems as if Jerry and Laurieanne will get off with little more than slaps on the wrists. Many of the more serious charges against them were dismissed by Smerling; the rest remained only to be settled via a long-delayed negotiated sentence. Although the dismissals have been appealed, hardly anyone who has been watching the case feels there is much hope that they are ever going to be called to fully account for their actions, much less be required to do any serious jail time. At this writing, it appears that the very most they might have to do is a few weeks in a minimum-security county institution. And even that is very doubtful.

As far as David goes, the worst may already be behind him: the prison sentence mandated by Smerling, plus the additional six months he served while he was held pending trial on charges of murdering Tim. That is not exactly a stiff sentence considering the severity, the grotesqueness, and the number of crimes with which he was charged.

Giss bitterly took note of these peculiar developments in a document filed in support of his motion to have Smerling disqualified. The prosecutor was addressing the conspiracy charge against David specifically, but his comments could apply to the case as a whole. "Judge Smerling . . . handled the matter in such a manner as to deprive the state of its day in court," Giss wrote.

He is right. What Smerling did, in effect, was indefinitely delay, if not permanently negate, the possibility of a final resolution in the Sconce case, particularly as far as David is concerned.

Disregarding for the moment a debate about the judge's questionable judgment and his propensity toward lenient sentences, that still leaves in question one of the most important tenets of this country's judicial system, namely that every criminal charge be resolved in some fashion. It is important to the system that an accused be either convicted or acquitted, but in David's case this may never happen. Smerling, as Giss put it, "emasculated the adversarial aspect" of the system. In short, he may have made it impossible for David or his parents ever to be called totally accountable.

Despite the severity of the accusations against him, David to date has never been brought to trial; has never been required to explain his actions to a jury. Instead his punishment, or lack thereof, has been determined by a single, overly compassionate jurist. The possibility that he may one day be tried on the conspiracy to murder charge is enticing to prosecutors, but it may be more illusion than reality. Smerling may have botched things up so badly that a trial may indeed be impossible.

Considering that Jerry and Laurieanne may get the same generous treatment from Smerling as their son, there is not much left for prosecutors to cheer about. Dave Edwards, Danny Galambos, and Andre Augustine escaped without ever serving a day behind bars for their roles in accepting money to attack three people. Christopher Long, who allegedly helped Galambos beat Tim Waters, was never charged. Brad Sallard and Mike Engwald have never been called to account for the parts they played in the complicated series of developments. Odds are they never will. Does this depressing chronicle represent an aberration? Or is it a clear sign that the California criminal justice system is strangling on itself?

Even if the latter is true, there is no indication that California is alone in this regard. Similar situations, although maybe not of the same magnitude, could undoubtedly be found in every state. What makes the Sconce case so unusual is the nature and grotesqueness of the incidents and the broad impact they had upon a large number of innocent, trusting people.

What makes it so frustrating for those who have been involved in the proceedings is the seemingly inescapable conclusion that the punishment has not fit the crime. After closely watching the progress of this case for more than a year, I have to take that pessimistic view. I don't think the Los Angeles District Attorney's Office is ever going to get its day in court against David Sconce. And I think that is truly sad.

K. E.

An Abbreviated Chronology of Events

Mid 1970s

Laurieanne Sconce begins assuming control of Lamb Funeral Home as her father, Lawrence Lamb, moves closer to retirement. She gradually brings her husband Jerry into the operation.

1982

David Sconce, then twenty-six, begins managing, under his parents' supervision, Pasadena Crematorium, a branch of the Lamb Funeral Home.

1984

July 1—David formally leases Pasadena Crematorium from his mother, an act that gives him the independence to operate the business on his own.

August 23—David Edwards, Daniel Galambos, and Andre Augustine, hired by David, beat up Ron Hast, co-owner of a Los Angeles area mortuary, and his house-mate, Stephen Nimz, because Hast is perceived as a threat to David's business.

October 8—David applies to open a crematorium in the community of Shafter in the San Joaquin Valley. His request is refused by Kern County supervisors.

Autumn—David allegedly tells Andre Augustine that he plans to kill his grandfather, Lawrence Lamb, by poisoning him.

1985

February 12—Daniel Galambos and another ex-football player, hired by David for $1000, beat up Tim Waters, owner of a rival crematorium service. Soon afterward, David asks Galambos and Augustine to watch Frank Strunk, owner of another mortuary, the Cremation Society of California, preparatory to having him beaten up. At the time, David wanted Strunk to sell the business to him but Frank had refused.

April 8—The day after Easter. Tim Waters dies in Ventura County.

April 9—Waters is autopsied by Dr. John Holloway, deputy medical examiner. Cause of death listed as "pending."

May 20—Dr. Holloway signs an amended death certificate listing the principal cause of Waters's death as "acute myocardial insufficiency with pulmonary edema due to massive fatty metamorphis of [the] liver." Listed as a contributing cause was "exogenous obesity."

June—Joyji "George" Bristol is recruited by David to start an eye and tissue bank.

August 1—Ron Jordan, one of David's former employees, is found hanged in his apartment in Newport Beach a month after leaving Lamb Funeral Home. His death subsequently is ruled a suicide.

Late summer—With Bristol's help, David opens the Coastal International Eye and Tissue Bank.

September 30—Laurieanne Sconce formally purchases Lamb Funeral Home from her father.

October—Lisa Karlan joins the CIE&TB.

1986

January—Lisa Karlan, after a brief, stormy period as David's employee, quits the CIE&TB.

June 9—Bristol, operating on David's behalf, applies for permit to operate CIE&TB. On the same day, Leigh Dusatko, an examiner with the state Department of Health Services, wrote his boss, Roderick D. Hamblin, chief of laboratory field services, detailing an interview he had with Karlan in which she reported improper activities at Lamb Funeral Home, Pasadena Crematorium, and the CIE&TB. Dusatko's recommendation that the department get more information before issuing a permit to the CIE&TB is apparently lost in the bureaucratic shuffle.

June 17—The California Department of Health Services approves the application for a permit for the CIE&TB, certifying it as a nonprofit organization authorized to harvest human eyes and distribute tissue for transplants and research.

October—David begins cremating bodies in Hesperia at Oscar's Ceramics, telling officials that he is making tiles for the space shuttle.

November 23—Fire destroys the Pasadena Crematorium. That morning workers loaded thirty-eight bodies into the two furnaces, each of which is only three and a half feet high, four feet wide, and eight feet long. David shifts his entire crematorium operation to Oscar's Ceramics.

December—David stops Bristol in the carport behind Lamb Funeral Home and allegedly tells him he needs a poison to kill his grandparents.

1987

January 20—Fire department raids Oscar's Ceramics.

January 21—Authorities link operation to David. Soon afterward, David moves to Bullhead City, Arizona, and he takes a job at a gambling casino.

January 27—Six law firms file a class-action lawsuit against David and the Pasadena Crematorium, claiming they mishandled bodies.

January 29—David and his father Jerry are arrested in Pasadena by San Bernardino County deputies in connection with the removal of gold teeth from cadavers. They are soon released on $1500 bail each.

February 11—Thirty-three investigators from sheriff's offices in three different counties and two county coroner's offices pounce on the Lamb Funeral Home looking for evidence of illegal activity.

February 18—Auditors going through the books at Lamb Funeral Home discover that Laurieanne has apparently been skimming money out of the preneed accounts.

March 9—David is arraigned on the charges stemming from the January raid on Oscar's Ceramics. He pleads not guilty.

March 29—The state attorney general's office, in a civil action, sues Lamb Funeral Home for siphoning $100,000 from interest in prepaid funeral accounts.

April—The Pasadena Police Department and the Los Angeles County District Attorney's office begin investigating Lamb Funeral Home.

April 23—Felony charge against David in San Bernardino County for discharging hazardous waste is dismissed.

June 5—David's attorney learns that David and his parents are about to be charged in Pasadena with forty-one counts, most of them felonies. The charges against David and/or his parents include accusations of mutilation of bodies, theft of body parts, theft of dental gold, falsification of death certificates, forgery and embezzlement, multiple cremations and commingling of remains.

June 8—David, Laurieanne, and Jerry surrender to authorities in Pasadena. Municipal Court Judge Elvira Mitchell releases Jerry and Laurieanne on $5000 bond each, but, much to David's surprise, sets his bail at $500,000.

June—Dr. F. Warren Lovell, medical examiner and coroner in Ventura County, begins investigating Tim Waters's death. He discovers that toxicological examinations had not been done on Waters's fluids and tissues.

July 22—David pleads not guilty to a charge of soliciting the murder of his grandparents. Jerry and Laurieanne plead not guilty to charges that they stole body parts.

August 3—A preliminary hearing for Jerry, Laurieanne, and David begins in Pasadena. Its purpose is to determine if there is sufficient evidence to bring them to trial on the accusations.

August 13—On a related but separate matter, an auditor for the State Board of Funeral Directors and Embalmers begins auditing the preneed trust accounts at Lamb Funeral Home.

Throughout the summer and autumn a series of events allegedly occur relating mainly to David's case. According to later testimony, David promises to pay one prisoner $2500 for false testimony. David also allegedly brings his mother and his brother-in-law in on the plot and encourages them to take an active role. David also allegedly asks the prisoner to help draw up a plan for murdering the deputy district attorney who is prosecuting his case, Walter Lewis. At about the same time, David also allegedly asks another prisoner if he knew anyone who would be willing to kill for money, listing as potential victims his grandparents, his former friend, David Edwards, and Prosecutor Lewis.

November 4—The Ventura County coroner issues an

amended death certificate for Tim Waters listing the cause of death as "undetermined."

December 18—Testimony ends at the Pasadena preliminary hearing.

1988

January 20—David, Jerry, and Laurieanne are charged with conspiracy to bribe a witness. They plead not guilty.

April 20—A Pennsylvania toxicologist, Dr. Frederic Rieders, who had been asked to examine Waters's tissue, reports that he has found a fatal concentration of oleandrin in Waters's specimens, thereby clinching the prosecution belief that Waters was murdered.

May 9—Municipal Court Judge Victor H. Person, ending the longest preliminary hearing in Pasadena court history, rules that there is sufficient evidence to try David and his parents on the variety of charges then pending against them. David also is ordered to stand trial on charges of assaulting three morticians and soliciting the murders of his grandparents and Prosecutor Lewis. The case goes to superior court and is assigned to Judge Terry Smerling.

September 15—A preliminary hearing before Judge Judson Morris Jr. on a charge that David conspired to murder Elie Estephan, who bought a cremation service David was interested in owning. Morris rules that the prosecution has probable cause to make the charge.

1989

February 6—David pleads not guilty to charge of conspiring to murder Elie Estephan.

June 30—Judge Smerling dismisses accusations of stealing body parts against the Sconces. More importantly, he dismisses the charge against David that he conspired to murder Elie Estephan.

July 6—Following his action of less than a week earlier, Judge Smerling dismisses another twenty charges against the Sconces, including accusations that they mutilated human remains, conspired to obstruct justice, conspired to remove body parts, and conspired to bribe a witness. Charges of removing and selling organs also were deleted, as well as accusations that Jerry and Laurieanne falsified death certificates.

August 30—At Judge Smerling's urging, David pleads guilty to twenty charges. Smerling sentences him to a total of five years in prison. With time off for good behavior, David's effective sentence is two and a half years.

1990

February 9—David is charged in Ventura County with the murder of Tim Waters.

October 1—A preliminary hearing begins in Ventura to determine if there is enough evidence to bring David to trial for Waters's murder. David is nearing the end of his sentence from Los Angeles County.

October 10—The preliminary hearing ends. Judge Hunter orders David to stand trial for Waters's death. The defense asks for permission to exhume Waters's body to run additional toxicological tests, and the prosecution does not object. The case moves to superior court to be set for trial and is assigned to Judge Frederick Jones.

December 6—Judge Jones sets a trial date for February 6.

1991

January 14—Judge Jones opens a hearing on a defense motion to declare illegal the search warrant used in the raid on Oscar's Ceramics. David's lawyer contends that if it can be proved the warrant was illegally issued, everything that followed it would have to be dismissed under the legal thesis called fruit of the poisoned tree. After four days of testimony and argument, Jones ruled against the defense.

March—David's lawyer files bombshell documents with Judge Jones showing that the additional toxicological tests—more sophisticated ones than those done by Dr. Rieders—show *no sign* of oleander in Tim Waters's tissue. The prosecution asks for more time to conduct still another series of tests, but the defense presses for an immediate trial.

April 4—Faced with the prospect of having to go to trial without benefit of new tests, the prosecution dismisses the murder charge against David, clearing the way for his release from jail. David is free for the first time since he surrendered to authorities on June 8, 1987. He leaves California for Arizona.

Remaining convinced that David murdered Tim Waters, Prosecutor Harvey Giss vows to conduct additional tests and says he will refile murder charges if those tests provide evidence of poisoning.

At roughly this same time, a California appeals court rules that Judge Smerling acted incorrectly in dismissing the conspiracy to murder charges involving Elie Estephan.

June 5—David files a claim for $1.25 million in damages with Ventura County, claiming he was incarcerated for 178 days beyond his normal release time because of a "nonmeritorious" charge accusing him of murdering Tim Waters. The county had forty-five days to act on the request before David could file suit.

August 8—Superior Court Judge Robert T. Altman of Los Angeles County disqualifies Judge Smerling from acting in the case involving the conspiracy to murder charge.

Altman's decision subsequently was upheld by the court of appeal and the state supreme court, seemingly clearing the way for a future trial on the accusation that David conspired to murder Elie Estephan.

October 28—As of this writing, neither David nor his parents have been tried on any of the charges still pending against them.

HERE IS AN EXCERPT FROM *UNANSWERED CRIES* BY THOMAS FRENCH—A TRUE CRIME SHOCKER COMING IN MARCH FROM ST. MARTIN'S PAPERBACKS:

David Mackey was still at the conference in Rhode Island, and when he finished with the day's work he called Karen at home. There was no answer. He called again later, several times. Still no answer.

By midnight David was growing worried, so he called Anita Kilpatrick, Karen's roommate from the apartment on the beach. Anita said she hadn't seen Karen and suggested that maybe she'd gone to see her sister Kim, who lived in Dunedin, about twenty miles northwest of St. Petersburg. David called Kim's house, but Karen wasn't there, either.

The next morning—Thursday—David picked up the phone in his hotel room and tried again to reach Karen at the house. He called early, around 7:30, so he wouldn't miss her before she left for work. No answer. He tried again. No answer. Next he called Datacom. But Karen's boss said no one had seen or heard from her, either that day or the day before. He did not know where she was.

David called Anita Kilpatrick again. Both he and Anita were upset now. Clearly, something was wrong. Karen was not the type to skip work, especially a new job.

Anita started checking with police departments and hospitals to find out if there'd been an accident. But no one seemed to know anything about a Karen Gregory. Anita waited for David to call back. She was sitting on her couch when suddenly these pictures entered her mind. She saw Karen struggling with a man, shoving and fighting with a man who was taller than Karen. Then she saw Karen lying on the floor. Anita pushed the pictures out of her mind and told herself she was dreaming. She tried to read the paper but couldn't concentrate. She kept reading the same sentence over and over. She got up from the couch and started pacing.

Meanwhile, David was calling Amy Bressler, a neighbor who lived just up the street from his house. He asked Bressler to look out her living room window and see if Karen's Rabbit was parked in the driveway. Bressler looked over. Yes, she told him. Karen's car was there, along with David's.

Now David was sure something was wrong. He asked Bressler to go over and check on the house, saying he would stay on the line until she came back.

Bressler put down the phone. She walked over to the house and knocked on the nearest door, a side door. No answer. She walked around to the front door. It was closed, but she noticed that several of the jalousie window panes had been broken and that glass was scattered along the walkway. She knocked on the door. No answer. She walked around toward the back and saw that a bedroom window was open, the curtains moving in the breeze. She called out.

"Karen?"

No answer. With the curtains drawn, Bressler could not see inside the bedroom. But there was a slit, four or five inches wide, in the screen of the window—it had been there as long as David had owned the house—and so she put her hand through the opening and pushed back the curtains. An unmade bed was directly in front of her. She looked to the right, toward the bedroom door leading into the hallway, and saw a woman lying on the floor. The angle allowed her to see only the lower half of the body, but it was surrounded by blood.

"Karen?"

Bressler ran back to her house, where David was still waiting on the other end of the line. She was crying now. She was hysterical. She said she had to get the police.

"Something really horrible has happened," she told him. "I don't know what it is."

At 8:39 A.M., slightly more than thirty-one hours after the neighbors had heard the scream, Bressler called the Gulfport Police Department. Unsure whether the woman she'd seen on the floor was alive or dead, she reported what officially was recorded as a "nonresponsive person."

She was waiting in the street a few minutes later when Officer Cheryl Falkenstein drove up in a cruiser. Falkenstein got out, walked past the broken glass on the sidewalk, and tried the front jalousie door. It was locked. She walked around the house to the back bedroom window, pushed aside the curtains, and saw the woman on the floor.

"Can you hear me?" the officer said. "Are you OK?"

No answer. By now a team of paramedics had arrived and joined Falkenstein at the side of the house. They needed to get inside quickly—for all they knew, the woman might still be alive—yet the doors to the house were locked. So they decided someone would have to go through the window. They removed the screen and Falkenstein crawled inside head-first. She walked toward the woman, saw that she was not breathing, then quickly walked past her toward the front porch, where she unlocked and opened the jalousie door for the others.

Falkenstein, a twenty-one-year-old rookie, was badly shaken. She had been with the police department for only five months, and in that time she'd never seen anything like what she was seeing now.

All of the lights in the house were off. Inside the back bedroom, the one into which Falkenstein had crawled, a fan was sitting on the floor, still blowing. On top of the bed, stained with blood, was a blue flowered Hawaiian shirt. Next to the bed were the faded green shorts Karen had worn to Neverne Covington's house two nights before. Karen's tennis shoes were there too, with the laces still tied. Not far from the shoes was a black umbrella and a stack of magazines. One top of the magazines was a phone, and as Falkenstein and the others looked around, the phone began to ring. It kept ringing, even as the minutes passed and no one answered. It would stop for a second and then start again. It just kept going.

A few feet away, on the carpet just past the bedroom door, lay Karen. In the darkness of the hall, the paramedics had to use their pen lights to see her. Even so, it was obvious that there was no need to check her pulse. She was on her left side, almost in a fetal position, with her face turned toward the wall. She was still wearing the jewelry she'd had on that night at Neverne's, and the same white T-shirt, too, but it had been pulled up to just below her breasts. A black teddy was bunched around her waist. She wore no other clothing.

It was difficult, there in the hall, to be sure exactly what had happened to her. Her neck and head were covered with dried blood, covered with so much of it that it was impossible to see the exact nature and number of all of her wounds. But it was clear that she had been stabbed repeatedly. On her lower back and one of her legs, marked in blood, were several handprints, placed at such an angle that they could not have been made by Karen. Scattered around her along the stretch of hallway carpet was a series of bloody bare footprints. Not far away, on the tile floor of the bathroom, was another bloody footprint—a partial one, about the size of a silver dollar.

Blood had been left all through the house. There was some on the sill and curtains of the window where Officer Falkenstein had crawled inside. There was more on the bed. Outside the bedroom, across the walls and floor of the hallway where Karen's body was still lying, there were large stains and smears. Out on the front porch, three drops had dried on the floor. On the door that led from the porch into the rest of the house—the door on which the visitor had knocked the evening before—there were smears below the doorknob. In the window panes of the front jalousie door there was a hole, and around the hole were some hairs that were the same shade of brown as Karen's. The broken glass from the door was strewn along the front walkway, all the way to the curb and out into the street. In the driveway, on the windshield of David Mackey's car, the visitor's note was waiting to be read.

Inside the house the phone was still ringing.

It was David, calling from his hotel room. He'd been pacing, staring at the walls, trying to imagine what could have happened. He'd waited several minutes, waited as long as his patience would let him, then repeatedly dialed the number at his house, letting it ring and ring until finally someone answered. It was a woman whose voice David did not recognize. An Officer Falkenstein.

"Is Karen there?"

"Yes."

"What's happened?"

The officer hesitated a moment.

"She's dead, sir."

UNANSWERED CRIES—COMING IN MARCH FROM ST. MARTIN'S PAPERBACKS

Newlyweds Pam and Gregg Smart seemed like the perfect American couple. He was an up-and-coming young insurance executive, she the beautiful former cheerleader who now worked in the administration of the local school.

But on May 1, 1990, their idyllic life was shattered when Gregg was murdered in the couple's upscale Derry, New Hampshire townhouse—a single shot to his head. Three months later, the grieving widow was arrested and charged with the brutal crime.

In the dramatic trial that followed, a dark portrait of Pam Smart emerged—one of a cold manipulator who seduced a high school student with a striptease and then had a wild affair with him—until he was so involved with her that he was willing to do anything for her...even murder...

DEADLY LESSONS

BY EDGAR AWARD NOMINEE
KEN ENGLADE

DEADLY LESSONS
Ken Englade
_____ 92761-4 $4.99 U.S./$5.99 Can.

Publishers Book and Audio Mailing Service
P.O. Box 120159, Staten Island, NY 10312-0004
Please send me the book(s) I have checked above. I am enclosing $ _____ (please add $1.50 for the first book, and $.50 for each additional book to cover postage and handling. Send check or money order only—no CODs) or charge my VISA, MASTERCARD or AMERICAN EXPRESS card.

Card number _____

Expiration date _____ Signature _____

Name _____

Address _____

City _____ State/Zip _____
Please allow six weeks for delivery. Prices subject to change without notice. Payment in U.S. funds only. New York residents add applicable sales tax.

Bob Evans. Legendary producer of megahit movies like *Chinatown* and *The Godfather*, he was now on the verge of his biggest blockbuster ever. All he needed was one more investor...

Roy Radin. A flashy New York entrepreneur, he tried to make it big in Hollywood—until his bullet-riddled body turned up in a dry desert creek...

Laney Jacobs. Beautiful, glamorous, seductive, she clawed her way to the top of Miami's fast-living super-rich. Now, she wanted a piece of Hollywood—and it seemed as if no price would be too high to pay for it...

From the sprawling mansions of Long Island to the tantalizing glitz of the Sunset Strip, this is the startling truth behind the sensational "Cotton Club" murder—a story more shocking than any Hollywood script!

BAD COMPANY
by Pulitzer Prize-Winning Author
STEVE WICK

"A mean tale of unspeakable deeds."
—Dominick Dunne, author of *People Like Us*

When the sheriff of East Chatham, N.Y. first described the bloody scene—"Worse than anything I ever saw in Korea"—he was reduced to tears. Four people—a popular local businessman, his live-in girlfriend, his nineteen-year-old son, and his three-year-old orphaned nephew—had been brutally murdered in an isolated country cabin.

By the next day, a stunned community learned that the dead man's seventeen-year-old son, Wyley Gates—vice-president of his class and voted "most likely to succeed"—had allegedly confessed to the murders. What could possibly be the motive for such a grisly crime—and how could such an upright teenage boy explode with such lethal fury?

MOST LIKELY TO SUCCEED

ALAN GELB